WordSmith

A Memoir

For Sally and Charles

WordSmith

A Memoir

A.C.H. SMITH

Ever, Anthony

v '12

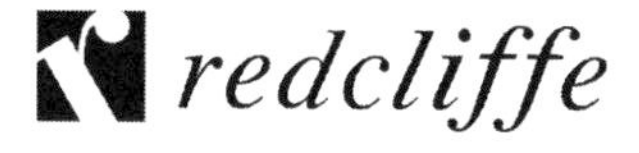

First published in 2012 by Redcliffe Press Ltd.
81g Pembroke Road, Bristol BS8 3EA

www.redcliffepress.co.uk
info@redcliffepress.co.uk

ISBN 978-1-908326-20-1

British Library Cataloguing-in-Publication Data
A catalogue record for this book is available from the British Library

Design and layout Stephen Morris www.stephen-morris.co.uk
Garamond 12/12
Printed in the Czech Republic via Akcent Media

Contents

For the Smithereens:

Inni

Lois

Nick

Marnie

Eva

Bruno

Cleo

Freddie

Foreword

How's your memoir coming on? Can't you remember?
Oliver Smith, December 2010

I started writing with a subtitle in mind, *How I have spent my life as a writer and yet managed to pay the gas bills*. But you find out what you are writing when you have written it, and a deeper theme has emerged: friendship is the greatest good, including the loving friendship between parents and their children. To explain where I came from, I have added two opening chapters which are more autobiography than memoir, written with my grandchildren in mind, and theirs, in case they are of genealogical or social-historical interest. Another thread is the fifty-year-long love affair I have had with Bristol. And there is cricket. I found that I could not keep it out. Because some readers might find cricket boring, I was inclined to suggest to my publisher John Sansom (who has a stylish cover-drive) that he use a different font for the cricket stuff, to assist them in skipping, but I never did expect him to comply.

The salient friendships are those I have enjoyed with four writers, my contemporaries. Janet Burroway was born in Arizona, Zulfikar Ghose in pre-partition Pakistan, B.S. Johnson in London, and Tom Stoppard in Czechoslovakia. Between the five of us we have produced around fifty books of fiction, one hundred plays and screenplays, nine collections of poetry, twenty works of non-fiction, and acres of journalism, both critical and sporting. In no sense at all have we ever been a group, and only incidentally have we influenced each other. It is just that they have been my friends, we all started out in the late 1950s, and some conclusions about standards in public discourse and literary taste might be drawn from the confluence of our early aspirations and what was actually in store for us. Ghose's manuscripts and correspondence and mine all sleep in the same archive, in Texas, along with many of Stoppard's letters and manuscripts. Not far away in Tallahassee, are Burroway's papers. Johnson's are mostly in the British Library, but there is plenty of him in Texas too, among the correspondence they bought from Ghose and me. For their permission to quote from letters, I thank the friends mentioned, and Johnson's widow, Virginia. For critical reading and encouragement I am grateful to Ghose and Stoppard, Andrew Kelly, Peter Montgomery, Jeremy Mulford, Alison Smith, Oliver Smith and John Hudson.

1

Licking Honeysuckle

MY FATHER, CHARLES THOMAS SMITH, WAS BORN IN 1898 IN BRIXTON to a mother from Mortlake, father from Derbyshire. When you look through what my cousin Colin Winger has pieced together of the Smith family tree, the list of occupations is a line to the horizon of domestic service or manual labour, and my Smith grandparents were no different. They met when both were working for the Duchess of Teck at the White Lodge in Richmond Park. One day my grandfather was up a ladder trimming a hedge, probably not a footman's job, but he liked to keep himself busy. He fell off and broke a leg. The bone was badly set, so the Duchess sacked him: 'I cannot have a footman who limps.'

As he left his employ he assuaged his grievance by snatching a malacca cane with a silver pommel which the Duchess's daughter May, who would become Queen Mary, had carried when she went out walking. I have it now. If the royal family would like it back, they should let me know, but here it does keep amusing company, propped next to Oscar Wilde's deathbed cane, the provenance of which I'll explain later. I'm not a collector of anything in particular; I just happen to have come by two canes with form. Later, grandfather Smith was one of the earliest motor-cab drivers in London, before going back into service in Bredon, at the southern edge of Worcestershire, which left Dad with a slight Cotswold burr. He was a brewery clurrk, and took me to Epsom to watch the Durrby. His father lived long enough to see me, but not for me to remember seeing him. Grandmother Smith had died before him.

My mother, born Kathleen Mary Godfrey to a family of Kentish (Crockham Hill) origin in Long Ditton, Surrey, in 1899, was a typist at the British Oil and Cake Mills on the Embankment – a very good typist, I've been told. Her father was the longest-lived of my grandparents. During the war I was several times taken to stay with him and his second wife at Pitsea, near Southend, where they lived in a wooden house which stood on spindly legs, like the fearsome witch

Baba Yaga in Russian folklore. The journey to Fenchurch Street Station entailed riding in a tram with quarter-light panes of mauve and green. In the back garden at Pitsea were adders, and a stinking hut for a loo with newspaper scraps on a string and a pit beneath. My grandfather made me a bow and found some sticks for arrows. The first time I bent it, it snapped. In a nearby field Mr Pinnock kept cows. One day he told me to look after them while he went on an errand. I wanted to know how a cow would react when I poked it with a stick. Wiser and kinder than a six-year-old boy, it put its head down and warned me with a stopped-short charge. Grandfather Godfrey was not twinkly. Aged six, playing a family game of solo whist, I found his gnarled index finger in my face. 'When I prop, boy, you don't cop unless you've got three tricks in yer hand,' he growled. Nowadays I might reply, oh come on, grandad, all it took was a diamond finesse and a criss-cross squeeze. At that time I was quiet. I was often quiet. I got it from my Dad. I don't know what he did before, but I do know that grandfather Godfrey's last job before retirement was to supervise a rubbish tip at Leytonstone Gas Works. Why a rubbish tip would need supervision is a question I was not old enough to ask him.

Dad was a checking clerk at Mann, Crossman and Paulin's brewery in Putney. He once introduced me there to F.G. Mann, who had captained England at cricket, and whose son, decades later, did time for a botched coup in Equatorial Guinea. Dad proposed to my mother in Richmond Park, by Pen Ponds, a stretch of grass away from the White Lodge. He had little chance to express it, but he was a romantic. I got that from him, too. They had been married thirteen years when I, their only child, was born on Hallowe'en in 1935 in Sheen, parish of Kew. They expected me to be a girl, and were going to call me Arabella.

Of his married life with my mother, Dad told me they played tennis in a little two-court club hidden away behind Kneller Hall, Twickenham – that, and only one other story that I remember. They had held a party to celebrate something. When the guests were starting to worry about getting the last bus or train home, my Dad told them not to. Taxis had been booked for everyone, and paid for. He told me the story because he was justly proud of the gesture, on a brewery clerk's wages.

On June 17th, 1938 my mother died of breast cancer, aged thirty-nine. I've heard there is a correlation between the disease and middle-aged pregnancy. My poor Dad had to engage a nursemaid, called Mabel, to look after me while he was at work. After a year the war started. I was on a family holiday on the north Kent coast at Birchington, which had to be cut short. The rush to pack and get home is the earliest memory I have. Dad had gone back into the RAF, now Corporal Smith, *Sir! 217068,* one of the narrow generation who served in both world wars. He was still in France three weeks after Dunkirk, and got out through Brest. He spent most of the war driving a lorry in M Balloon Unit, a secret outfit which Churchill set up to deliver propaganda leaflets in German-held territory. *Give up, Fritz, You've Had It, Get Back Home, Your Wife's Cheating on You,* that kind of thing, in German. The leaflets, attached in bundles to a hot-air balloon, were held together by a timed fuse. When it burned through, they scattered down through the air. The trick, Dad said, was to gauge the wind strength and direction, and make sure the fuse was the right length to last until the balloon was over occupied territory.

When he knew he was going to be called up, Dad asked around the family: who would look after me for the duration? It must have been a question for any single parent who might be called up. Maybe he could have claimed an exemption. If he could and didn't, it was probably for patriotic reasons, but perhaps also because it was an escape from the lonely sadness he found himself in.

In 1939 my Aunt Lucy and Uncle Bub took me in to live with them at 192 Kingston Road, Ilford. Bub – real name Roland – was one of my mother's four brothers. They had two children of their own, Joyce, a little older than I was, and Bob, 15 years older. Bob Godfrey grew up to make animated films, and won an Oscar in 1973 for *Great,* a patriotic spoof of I.K. Brunel. He had got his art college training because my mother, seeing his talent, had persuaded his parents to apply. They were reluctant, needing the wages he might have been earning, but I'm told my mother had a warm way about her. Bob never forgot that, and has a soft spot for me still. In Ilford, where I was four and he was nineteen, he was like my big brother. In the morning I'd get into his bed and he'd do the noises of the farmyard awakening. Best was the farmer's boy arriving on his motorbike.

Dad had had less luck. He always did. He was a bright boy at Richmond Grammar School, and his grandmother wanted him trained as a teacher, but his parents couldn't afford to have him staying at school. At 14 he was apprenticed as an engineer. Two years into his apprenticeship World War One broke out, and soon he joined up in the Royal Naval Air Service, No.17068. When that war finished, he was told he had forfeited his apprenticeship. Homes fit for heroes. He met my mother soon after, but they couldn't afford to marry, so he joined the RAF as a regular. They sent him to Mesopotamia, the Iraq Protectorate, where he was the driver for General Sir John Glubb ('Glubb Pasha'). I have his album of photographs of the tour, in which he is posed proprietorially beside the gleaming bonnet of what might be a Hispano-Suiza or something flashy like that. Many years later, when I was to visit Iran, he advised me to bang my shoes out on the floor every morning, lest a scorpion had crept inside during the night. I did.

By 1926 he was in civilian life again, still without a regular job. He drove a bus during the General Strike. We took the *Daily Herald*, and I grew up believing in Attlee and Bevan. Had Dad held different views twenty years earlier or, newly married, had he just been desperate enough to blackleg? My guess is that he probably had few views of any colour in 1926, but was politicised in 1939-45, as many servicemen were. The estimate is that the Forces vote in 1945 was 90 per cent Labour. I never dared ask him, not because I had any fear of him – he had as mild a temper as any man I've known – but because I feared hurting him with the question.

For the same reason, more profoundly, I never asked him anything about my mother. I do regret that. After he died, in June 1986 (he'd always had a dread of June, the month in which she had died), I realised that I knew next to nothing about her, and went round the few remaining people who might be able to share their memory of her with me, but found out nothing beyond platitudes with fifty years of dust on them. Kind, always helpful, sense of fun. Not enough dots to join up. I got further by imagining the state of mind of a woman who on her deathbed had handed Dad a penny and said it was 'for Tony'. He had told me that story though had not kept the coin for me, which was perhaps wise of him.

I had never even visited her grave. Dad might have taken me, but couldn't face the pain of it. He had mentioned she was buried in Streatham. There are several cemeteries there, so I wrote to Lambeth Borough Council with such details as I knew, and they replied by return, bless them. She had not been buried but cremated. They told me in which cemetery her ashes had been scattered, and gave me a grid reference of whereabouts on the lawn. I went there on a January afternoon, stood in driving rain by the spot indicated, and spoke aloud, like Lear in the storm. I began by telling her that I don't believe in an afterlife, so I was probably wasting my breath, but just on the off-chance that I was wrong, and because you can get a nice return on a 1,000-1 shot, I was visiting her shade, at last. Dad never brought me, because he still missed you so much. I do wish I'd asked him to tell me about you, but you know how he was. I've got pretty well no idea about you. I've got a few photos of you, of course, and you look like the kind of girl I'd fall for, if I met you. I hope I'm not offending you. We talk pretty freely about such things nowadays, and maybe you were brought up to be more demure. I don't know. That's the trouble, I don't know. So look, I'm going to go on talking to you like this, and if it's shocking to you, I'm sorry, but I am your son, so I expect you can find a tenderness and pardon me.

I went on for about fifteen minutes, telling her how I'd turned out, wondering who she had been, how I grieve at thinking what she must have felt, dying with a two-and-a-half-year-old son still to be brought up, and what difference had it made to my life? I'll never know. Perhaps it was easier on me to lose her before I had any memory of what I had lost than it was on men I've known who lost their mothers in their teenage years. The rain storm was providential, because nobody else wanted to be out in it, so my Mad Lear act did not attract any wide eyes. I'll go again, and talk to her again, but will have to be quieter in fine weather.

Within six months of my being taken in at Ilford, it was plain that the east side of London was at more risk from bombs, and we all moved across to my Dad's vacant semi-detached house at 367 Whitton Dene, Isleworth, near Twickenham Rugby Ground. Bombs did fall around there, from time to time. One day the talk in the school playground was that John Goodgame had been killed last night and – get this – his father had gone mad with what he'd seen. John had been in my class. Three minutes later we were kicking a ball around, or flicking milk bottle tops against a wall, or playing fivestones. I walked home by a route that would take me past John's house, and saw, yes, it was a smoking bombsite, draped with tarpaulins. So soon after the event it was secured by wardens, but at times other bombsites were good adventure playgrounds.

I felt safe walking to and from school in my khaki tin hat, sixpence from Woolworth's. At home we had, first, an Anderson air-raid shelter in the back garden, corrugated iron walls dug in by my Uncle Bub, and roofed with earth. A few times I remember being taken along the road to a communal underground shelter, of which I am always reminded by the smell of turned earth. Later, we were supplied with a Morrison indoor shelter with a sprung floor, where we all slept, and a thick steel ceiling bolted on to corner pillars, serving as a large table top. Bob had joined up, in the Marines, so there might have been four of us sleeping there. Actually, I suspect that my uncle was elsewhere most of the time, perhaps working nights at one of the string of odd jobs he found.

Dad was home on leave one night when there was an air raid. After the all-clear siren he stood outside the front door, enjoying the summer night, and a German plane, stray from its formation, got rid of a stick of incendiary bombs across the field facing our house, where Land Girls worked in the daytime. The next morning, on my way to school, I saw a round hole punched in the pavement. Another night, after Dad had gone back from leave, a piece of jagged shrapnel weighing more than three pounds came through the roof and landed in the middle of the bed where he had slept the previous night. I've got it here; it's about six inches by four, nearly an inch thick and with edges like Satan's chisel. I had to take care carrying it to the scales. After the war finished there was a house-high crack in the bricks of our side wall, but the War Damage Commission denied that it could have been caused by a bomb.

Every day in the summer of 1944 there was a map on the front page of the paper with black arrows tracing our advance on Caen. The following year, Dad was home for VE Day. He took me to Green Park to see the victory parade and bought me a Seebackroscope, a little gadget that allowed you to watch what was happening behind you. There was a street party in Murray Park, where I won an erasable pad by ducking for apples.

As an only child I talked to myself, still do. First sign of madness, my Aunt Lucy said when she heard me, first sprouts of dialogue, say I. My alter ego was called Bill Jones, and together we flew in a Defiant against Jerry fighters. The first real friend I had, when we were aged about four, was also called Jones, Howard Jones. His Mum did wartime hairdressing upstairs in her corner house along the road. He told me he wanted to be a doctor, 'so that I can look at people's bottoms'. He wound up as governor of Belmarsh Prison, I've been told, but perhaps that was another Howard Jones. He had more self-knowledge than I had at that age, though soon afterwards I did ask six-year-old Brenda next door if I could kiss her bottom, and she pulled her knickers down and let me, the minx. It's a ten per cent world, so it's always worth asking. The next girl was Pat, when we were ten. I would walk her home from school (diametrically opposite to my route home), and on her doorstep we would engage in surprisingly heavy petting before she went in for her tea. After that, going to an all-boys' school, I didn't get near another girl till I was about eighteen.

I was warned off having anything to do with two adults who lived along the road. One was a spiritualist woman with straggly hair, who liked to tell me that my mother had been leaving messages with her for me. The other was a man who invited me in to eat cake and be given my first ballpoint pen and sit on his lap; I later learned that he was a distinguished scientist at the National Physics Laboratory in Teddington.

I never heard any talk about being evacuated and am glad of that, after hearing years later from B. S. Johnson what it had been like for him. The first time I did go away from my family, after the war, was for a holiday with my school friend Philip Newman at his aunt's house in Attleborough, Norfolk. I wet my pants, which was not a thing I remember ever doing elsewhere. Also, I fell off a bike and added to the bouquet of scars on my knees. Philip's aunt had to clean me up both times, and did it with ill grace.

Philip was one of the boys in a Subbuteo table soccer league seven of us formed. We played home and away in each others' houses. At Don Milton's house we once had to have the lights on at noon. It was like night outside because of what was to be called the Great London Smog of '52. I was at many fixtures, whether I was playing or not, because, without my recognising what it was, I already had a journalistic itch. I was bringing out *Subbuteo News*, my handwritten bulletin on the latest matches, with league tables and action photographs I took myself, having started to develop another itch, for photography. With money I earned from a paper round – what was left from 6s 6d weekly, after I had bought myself a fourpenny choc ice from the paper shop most mornings after my round, no discount offered for employees, the mean sod – I bought gear for developing, printing and enlarging, and took a photographic periodical. I earned more from a collect-and-deliver round on my bike for a commercial photographer who said he'd teach me to photograph properly, but he never did. It might have been a waste of time, because I have no visual gift.

What money I could spare from that I spent on building my model railway, with rails, sleepers and shoes I bought at Hamley's in Regent Street, again egging myself on by subscribing to a magazine. That, likewise, never came to much. It might have done if Dad, with his engineering knowledge, had advised me, but he took no interest in it. I think that odd, now. He bought me a junior engineering kit called Juneero, but again left me to get on with it alone, and I got nowhere, having no gift for that, either. Possibly he was just tired out after ten hours a day at the brewery, cycling eight miles to Putney and back; but I think the truth is that he was shy of me. I was a fairly introverted kid – semi-detached, my wife would later say – and although I knew he loved me, as I loved him, we were not close with each other. I suspect that was normal in his generation of parents. The shadow of my absent mother perhaps came between us.

> My father taught me how to fold a shirt;
> to pedal heel-and-toe; to scramble eggs;
> to close a penknife; read maps; share a bed;
> to answer mildly (too much so). He'd skirt
> the question that the truthful answer begs:
> Where's my mother? What have I got instead?

He kept her shoes in the wardrobe, and some jewellery in a little velvet-lined case, scented by lavender bags. A sepia photo of her, formally posed in a smart frock, was in a frame with no glass, and once, when I was little, I took a pin and carefully scratched around the ovals of her eyelids. I was told off, of course, but I bet it had Dad worried. The shrinks would get a chapter out of it. If the psychoanalyst John Bowlby was right, I must be damaged, and he would have made short work of a dream I had, that I was a solemn boy sitting on Dad's shoulders as he swam me away from a sinking ship. Alternatively, the scratching might have been no more than toddler mischief. *Who knoweth the interpretation of a thing?* – Ecc. 8.i

Before Subbuteo there had been many sports played out with buttons and counters on the carpet. Once Subbuteo arrived, there were not only games in the seven-boy league but entire league and cup tournaments played out on my own, or with my best friend Geoff Paddle, who lived along the road. Geoff was good at real sports, especially football. When he scored a goal in a match he expressed his jubilation by brushing his fingers through his quiff. I think of that gesture when I watch today's footballers gang-rape each other after a goal. With him, and others when available, I would bike to Old Deer Park for football and cricket, or the municipal parks for tennis, bowls even. Now and then we would hack our way around a public golf course, there was swimming, badminton, ping-pong.

Geoff's parents got him and me going on bridge. Facing his house there was a great tree to climb, known as The Flat-Top, on account of its having been pollarded. You had to make it to the top, maybe 40 feet up, even though there were the spikes of railings waiting below. Years later a kid did fall down on to the railings and died. I thought of him when I heard of a small boy's question: 'If I were a runner bean, who would be me?'

The way we lived, Dad and I, was weird, but typical of a strain in English social life. My aunt and uncle and their daughter were still in the house – they'd disposed of theirs, in Ilford – and after Dad came back from the war he and my uncle started not to get on. I have no idea why, and I wonder if they had. Dad, mindful that they had looked after me, did not ask them to move out. Instead, we all ate together, never mentioning money, sex or religion, because nobody had any of those. My aunt's cooking was short of ordinary, but that was normal in working-class homes. Dad and I spent the rest of our time in one room upstairs, sharing a double bed and a gas fire. He built a work bench in one corner of the room, and at first used it to make Perspex cigarette boxes with roundelled fighter planes as handles on the lids. The Perspex came from old aeroplane cockpits. He never sold one, and he gave up, and spent his evenings smoking his pipe, reading the paper and listening to the wireless. For some years our household was augmented by Nunky, an elderly relative of my aunt. His real name was Harry Butler, and he had been a butler, prefiguring Pinter. Years later I published a poem about him, 'Verses for Uncle Harry'. That set-up went on for years, until my cousin Bob Godfrey, now making money, bought his parents a similar house along the road, and we had the place to ourselves.

A few more significant details of everyday 1940s life, which might be of interest to a social historian, or my grandchildren. As well as milk and newspapers, bread was delivered daily, and a lorry came round regularly selling fizzy pop (Corona). A man with a horse and cart used to call out for rags. I was sent out with a bucket and shovel to scoop up horse dung as manure for the vegetable patch at the bottom of the back garden, which we had been encouraged to cultivate during wartime; we had also kept four ducks there. Another man sharpened knives on a wheel which he operated by turning the pedals of his bike. My aunt did the laundry in the kitchen. With a fat stick she swirled and blued the steaming clothes in a copper, put them through a mangle and dried them on a rack you pulled up towards the ceiling with pulleys and strings. Watching her do that, aged about six, I had a moment of pure self-consciousness: aware that I was aware. It felt as though I had made a psychic breakthrough for humankind, but I expect many can recall a similar moment.

In 1946 I dared to eat a peach, my first, which Dad had bought from a stall in Villiers Street, by Charing Cross, for half a crown, so that his son could start to taste the pleasures of peacetime. I calculate that half a crown, 2s 6d, represented his wage for half an hour's work at the brewery. He also took me out, occasionally, for a mixed grill. All through the war he had promised me that after it I would enjoy whipped cream walnuts. In my mind they became totemic of a war won, but I never had one. In the early 1950s sweets came off ration, the doors of heaven were open, and the nation went so wild for them that they were put back on ration, and the doors slammed in our face again. It was an early warning not to trust what politicians tell you. In Belgium, where Dad had made good friends in the war and took me for my first holidays abroad, there was no rationing, and in the village shop where patisserie and sweets were sold the perfume of sugar was heady for a post-war British boy.

I did the things kids do: conkers, marbles, daisy-chains, the buttercup test, shooting plantain heads, suffocating a grasshopper in mud, riding my trike along the pavement when I was little (the trike bought for me because it was thought to be a cure for knock-knees, a defect I had only mildly, if at all), knock-down-ginger, catapulting stones over back garden fences until a shout stopped me, snaking a whole tube of toothpaste into the wash-basin, stamping out lettered metal strips in the penny machines you found on railway platforms, blowing soapy-water bubbles from a white clay pipe, snapping a snapdragon, kazooing a grass stalk between my thumbs, twirling sycamore seeds, blowing dandelion seeds, growing stock seeds, licking honeysuckle nectar, sucking herbal cough sweets and lemon squash crystals and chewing liquorice root in the rationed absence of confectionery, hop-scotch, kneel-down cricket on the back garden lawn with a clothes peg bat and bottle-top fielders, making fire with a magnifying glass, capturing a stag beetle in a matchbox, jamjar fishing, transfers on the back of my hand, hanky parachutes, paper gliders, cap-guns, Dinky cars, a toy bus, a toy crane, a battery-operated model searchlight, tanks with guns that sparked from a flint, tanks I constructed out of cotton reels, pencils and rubber bands, metal puzzles, a gyroscope bought at the Schoolboys' Own Exhibition, a kaleidoscope, shooting an air-pistol, a craft I've forgotten of folding paper so that it gives out a crack when you whip it forward, stealing a complete set of Regimental Badges cigarette cards from a dealer (I was dared to), making an ice slide on the pavement, the sputtering pink or orange flare from sticks like chunky matches we'd buy in boxes in November, sticking up paper chains with flour paste, not telling my Aunt Lucy I'd seen her slip the silver threepenny bit into my portion of Christmas pudding, as well as all the board games and card games, and perfunctory stamp collecting, and a wooden fort with a drawbridge defended by a few soldiers, and some stone building bricks. I grew tired of the purpleness of potassium permanganate and tipped the entire contents of my chemistry set into a blue sugar bag and from the medicine cabinet added glycerine (I am not sure why – had I heard of nitro-glycerine?), put it on the dining table, and nobody had cleared it away when we sat down to eat and the bag quietly combusted. Dad grabbed the extinguisher he had always kept and never used till now, and we had to spend half an hour in the cold night garden until the fumes had cleared.

I read four comics every week: *Hotspur, Rover, Wizard* and *Adventure*, all of them long on dense type and short on comic illustrations. Then there were books of popular science, mythology, RAF plane recognition (my favourite was the Defiant), *The Water-Babies, The Swiss Family Robinson, Eric, The Adventures of a Penny, Coral Island* (twice – I can still smell its yellowing pages), read *Claudius The Bee* about five times, Biggles, the whole of Arthur Ransome, every P.G. Wodehouse in the public library. I didn't get into Dickens then, though Dad had the complete set, with the Phiz illustrations, acquired as an incredible bribe to order the *Daily Herald* for three months. Also passed down to me is the complete H.G. Wells from Odhams Press (another three months, would that have been?), and an eleven-volume series of classic novels from Daily Express Publications – Dad playing fast and loose in the mad circulation wars of the 1930s; not to mention a seven-volume series of *The World's Great Books in Outline*, provenance not apparent.

What the newspapers knew was that millions of people who had not had much education were aware that out there was something called literature which was worth getting hold of if you could, like the Beethoven and Schubert and Puccini 78s we had. Perhaps Beaverbrook and Southwood were cynical enough to expect no more of their readers than the vanity of putting such books on display in their glass-fronted bookcases, but readers of Richard Hoggart's *The Uses of Literacy* will know that plenty were like my Dad, with a genuine aspiration. How much of it all he actually did have time to read I have no idea, or what he might have made of it. He had the ambition to write stories himself, and must have felt very proud when one was published in the *Daily Express*, in the days when the popular press did wacky stuff like printing fiction. In a notebook, he professionally kept track of what he had spent on writing materials, postage, etc. In the Income column is just the one entry, *Daily Express: £2 2s 0d.* Two guineas. Somewhere back in the family tree is a side-branch named Gardner. It includes Goldie Gardner, who once held the world land speed record, achieved in a car I had on a cigarette card, and a woman who wrote a couple of books under the pseudonym Rengard. It would be pushing it to speculate on a gene.

Friday night was going-to-the-pictures night: to the Odeon in Whitton, the Dominion in Hounslow or the Regal in Richmond. Each meant waiting in a long queue for all but the most expensive seats, in the circle. The projector's beam lanced through clouds of fragrant tobacco smoke. Even during the war, when he was home on leave, Dad would have a bar of chocolate for me that he had brought home, from the Naafi I suppose. In the postwar, rationed years a Kunzle cake after the film in the Black and White Café was an acceptable alternative. There were two films, with the newsreel in-between them, and occasionally a brief, boring documentary about the natural world. In 1945 we went to see something at the Odeon. Without warning, the newsreel showed us what the soldiers had found at Belsen, mounds of emaciated corpses being bulldozed into a pit. Dad answered questions I put to him on the way home, and said nothing more. He must have been deeply shocked that such pictures could be shown to an unprepared audience. He refused to take me to *Snow White* because he'd read in the paper that some kids had been scared by the Witch. I've yet to catch it. I've caught Belsen again often enough, and Auschwitz and the rest, and still have the same questions as I had when I was nine.

It was eightpence day return for a kid from Whitton to London. Walking through waste land from Waterloo towards Hungerford Bridge, past the now-gone shot tower which became a landmark at the Festival of Britain in 1951, we were confronted by a gang, about the same age as we were. Geoff, the athlete, ran at and through them and I felt abandoned by him, then figured we had no other chance, did the same as he had and didn't feel a finger laid on me. I was not a fast runner, though once, to win house points, I surprised myself and the master with the stopwatch by getting the 1st standard in the 220-yards; my legs must have been on song. In the school's annual cross-country race through Bushy Park I was used to finishing among the stragglers. One year, though, I had heard about glucose tablets. I swallowed a couple as we started, and soon was gagging on the sweetness in my dry throat. Then they kicked in. I went past scores of runners, and in the finishing straight had the leaders in view as they sprinted through the tape. If I had had the nous to take the tablets an hour in advance of the race, who knows?

I swam backstroke for the school, though was always beaten by David Bligh, who took me to the Quaker meetings his family attended in Teddington. The Quaker precept of following your inner light was for me the bypass around Christianity I needed, but I would not have gone were it not for the fact that after the meetings the hall was cleared and we played badminton. I spent days at the Oval and Lord's, with squishy tomato sandwiches and Tizer, Saturday afternoons at Stamford Bridge and Craven Cottage, Highbury when I could get that far, and sometimes walked round with Dad to watch Harlequins or England but never did get keen on rugger. I kayaked on the Thames, collected train numbers at Waterloo and King's Cross and Southall (where you could put a halfpenny on the line for the train to embed in the rail), and best of all the marshalling yard at Nine Elms in Battersea, where Geoff and I once got in through a gap in the wooden fence and walked around, unchallenged, among the magnificent locos smelling of oil and soot, their wheels taller than we were, and spotted the legendary old tank engine *Hecate*, one of four mysterious Miscellaneous namers which we crossed off in Ian Allen's indispensable 1s 6d spotter book for the Southern Region.

Dad introduced me to horse racing and music. Both have lasted through my life. He took me sometimes to the Albert Hall. I remember the first visit: I was so bored by the *New World Symphony* that I spent the time scratching black paint off a rail in front of our seats, but at home I began to play the handful of 78s we had. When I had some money I bought myself some more, and later a baton to conduct them. Then Geoff's father bought them the first LP player I had ever seen, and we were off, playing Subbuteo to the sound of Sibelius. On summer afternoons, when I was playing in the back garden under the enormous flowering cherry tree, there was military band music from the nearby Kneller Hall, when they were rehearsing for their open-air concerts.

I was sent for violin lessons for a while. I would cycle to Miss Nell's house with the instrument's case on my back, held on by string. When I fell off, I opened the case and saw the violin in pieces. Dad had borrowed it from his friend Bill Hammond. Somehow we acquired another one, but Miss Nell left the district while I was still practising for Grade 1, and the violin stayed in the loft. When I set up home in Bristol, a dozen years later, I brought it back from London with the idea that it would look decorative on the wall, but I couldn't resist trying to get a tune on it and eventually found myself a teacher, Geoffrey Creese. The top floor of 11 The Polygon had a very low ceiling, which meant that Creese and I had to develop a special technique of ducking our left shoulders when we played on the E string. I still haven't done Grade 1.

The other gift Dad passed on to me was cycling. On Saturdays we often rode around the South Circular, across tricky tramlines, to the race track at Herne Hill, where I admired the likes of Reg Harris, Alan Bannister, Lew Pond and Dave Ricketts. Before the war my cousin Ted Sales had been national junior sprint champion and, while years as a Desert Rat had punctured his career, he still had quads that overlapped his kneecaps. Most Sundays Dad and I rode together up to a hundred miles, in the North Downs or the Chilterns, stopping at a British Restaurant for lunch at a government-controlled price of maybe half a crown a time. He started me at the age of ten on the back of a tandem; I wasn't strong enough to manage the front handlebars. Once, climbing out of the Medway Valley on our way to stay with friends in Birchington – a place with such happy associations for me that I thought it perfectly apt that Margate, near by, should have an amusement park called Dreamland – he found it very hard going, glanced around, and caught me with my feet up. After that I had my own bike, an old gate of a thing to start with; then he bought us two utterly beautiful orange Rudge Aeros, with toeclips, drinking bottles, Sturmey-Archer gears, narrow saddles, and on mine a mileage counter, clicked by a spoke. We joined the Cyclists' Touring Club and I wore its little badge with a spoked wheel on it.

We used to cycle to the races at Hurst Park, Sandown Park, Epsom and Windsor. Kempton had been commandeered by the Army, and was not back in operation yet. Dad acted as my bookie, allowing me a penny bet with him on each race. My system was to go for jockeys wearing red and green, a dazzling combination. Sometimes it paid off. Ah, Blarney Castle... At Windsor I asked the exotic tipster Prince Monolulu for his autograph; perplexed, he fobbed me off with a slip of paper with a tip on it for a horse that came in third. When I was out with Dad he would occasionally tell me to wait while he went into a telephone box. On occasions I waited right next to the box, and heard him start 'Sinbad here'. He was embarrassed when I asked him about it, wouldn't explain, but years later I realised it must be his betting account code name, in those days when the only way to bet off-course was to have an account or know a little man round the corner. He couldn't afford to bet much and no doubt had no more luck than most, but he told me he had once found the 40-1 winner of the Hunt Cup and tipped it to a friend, a risk to friendship I try to avoid.

As a teenager I went off for weeks on my own, around the Isle of Wight and Snowdonia, staying at youth hostels. They all smelled the same as each other, and like nowhere else I've known. Floor polish and boiled cabbage, I think. I walked up Snowdon along the marked track. The summit was not a Wordsworthian climax: workmen were knocking up some kind of snack bar, with a radio playing. On the way back down I decided to cut a corner and wound up slithering down 45-degree scree. When I saw a goat I thought of the Alps, remembered delivering papers with stories of mountain accidents, and made my way back to the track. On Easter Sunday, 1953, I finished a tour by riding to the top of Bredon Hill, in memory of Dad's childhood there, listened to the Cotswold bells, with Housman in my head, and then had to cycle more than a hundred miles home with no money left, bar whatever a packet of stoned dates cost me. I kept a diary of that tour, on exercise paper I used to steal in quantities from the school cupboard, but threw it away, because I could find no literary merit in it. What an idiotic thing to have done, precocious little self-critic that I was.

I often rode to Cambridge. My 'aunt' Val Green, who had been my mother's best friend at work, lived in Cherry Hinton, and I had a crush on her daughter Margaret. Margaret found me amusing in a family-friend sort of way, but anything steamy was never in question. She would have ridiculed any advance. We had a kind of Arthur Ransome hygiene in our relationship, jolly sensible friends. It wasn't unusual in the post-war period, at least not among the lower-middles of southern England. What I heard from Geordies in my billet when I joined the RAF was news from another country. They did things differently there.

It was on the road to Cambridge that I bought my first packet of fags, Craven A, and stopped to smoke one behind a hedge. The memory of how the first cigarettes tasted is every ex-smoker's *petite madeleine.* Once I cycled to Felixstowe, because the Greens were on a summer holiday there and had invited me to join them for a few days. On the way back Dad was to meet me on the Chelmsford bypass. I had lingered with Margaret, and was running late. To get from Felixstowe to Harwich you took a ferry. Then I pedalled as far as Witham, where, spotting a railway station, I took my bike on the train to make up time. When I got off – at Brentwood, was it? – it was getting dark. I didn't see Dad, but plugged on. I stopped for a cup of tea at a café, and found it full of a coach party from Hounslow. They let me put my bike on the coach, and ride nearly home with them. Intrigued that I'd used five forms of transport – walking, ferry, train, coach and bike – I arrived home with a merry little song I'd made up. I stopped it when I saw Dad's dark mood. He had endured hours of anxiety about what could have happened to me.

We had no telephone then. When we got one it was POPesgrove 7869. We never had a car until after I'd left home, even though Dad had spent much of his life driving for a job. I don't remember more than one or two cars in the whole of that mile-long road. I don't cycle a lot now only because Bristol, the most car-congested city in the UK, and one of the hilliest, is no fun on a bike. I imitated Dad by buying two beautiful bikes, Black Diamonds, for my son and me when he was a teenager, and we rode them around Normandy for a week. In the hills above Bayeux we heard the sound of a Scottish reel on bagpipes, from down in the valley. We went to investigate and found eight Scottish soldiers in kilts playing to the villagers, who then played their Breton bagpipes in return. It turned out to be the fortieth anniversary of the Scots regiment's liberation of the village.

Sometimes Dad took me to the theatre. My enjoyment of pantomime has remained with me. In 2005, in a play called *The Redcliffe Hermit*, I tried to integrate a number of themes by the use of pantomime elements, including a talking rat and a talking cat. We went to musicals, too. *Oklahoma!* in the West End cannot have been a cheap night out. Dad earned £14 a week. He would not have had any thought that I might myself work in the theatre. Indeed, when the time came for me to choose whether I was going to be a little arts student or a scientist/mathematician, we discussed it under the cherry tree; though he left the choice to me, he would have preferred me to go for the scientific side. He could see how one might get a decent job there. He was right. I used to listen to drama on the radio, also. In my early teens, turning the tuning knob, I found a play probably by someone like Strindberg and decided that this I really needed to listen to: not understanding a word of it, but nevertheless being impressed that such things could exist, a level of seriousness betokening a world I wanted to explore. By 1955 I was ready for *Waiting for Godot.* I can't pretend I wasn't very puzzled by it, but I knew I'd so enjoyed it that puzzlement was something I was prepared to put up with as part of the price to pay for how much I'd enjoyed the evening, been entertained by its pantomime.

* * *

From my junior school, Chatsworth, I remember disgusting school lunches, which you could smell from the playground, the stink of empty milk bottles crated in hot sunshine, the cool aroma of inkwells and the scratching of a nib in a wooden holder. At eight I was cast in the school play. I had the opening lines:

> I am the King of Strand-on-the-Green,
> The fairest kingdom you ever have seen.

My queen was a pretty girl called Jill Ireland, who could do the splits. Some time after me she found other consorts in David McCallum and Charles Bronson. What I cannot remember at all is that I had any of the self-possession you'd think the teacher would have looked for in her leading actor. Maybe my memory is traducing me. After that performance, she told me I was to produce and direct the next play, *The Silver Sword.* (This would have been about 1943, so it was not Ian Serraillier's later story of the same title.) I am baffled why she thought me up to it, handed me the book, and just left me to it. When the day of the performance came, I had not dared tell her that no rehearsal had taken place, no parts had been cast or lines learned. I had done no more than get a few of my friends to agree to be in it. While the school audience was gathering in the hall, I told my cast that we were going to improvise a story we all knew, Robin Hood in disguise at the archery tournament. I would be Robin. I did come up with one line for the boy who was playing the Sheriff: 'That man can shoot well.' The rest of the text and action was ad-libbed. The play ran for about three minutes, perhaps less. It haunts me still, comes to mind when I have some script to write or revise under pressure of time: what if I can't do it? I have sometimes had the actor's dream, that I am on stage and everyone else there is waiting for me to say my first line but I have no idea what it is, or what play we are doing. My Robin Hood production was the real thing, no dream. But I was eight years old, what did she expect?

At Chatsworth I experienced my first sense of true injustice. My Dad had brought an RAF friend home on leave with him, Taffy Evans. They were driving a lorry with a very long trailer, which stretched from next door to next door when they parked it in the street. Taffy tipped me half a crown, which seemed to me like a tenner would seem now. I wanted to keep it secret from my aunt, because she would have made me do something boring with it, like Post Office Savings. I idiotically decided the safest thing was to ask a friend at school to look after it for me. His mother found it in his pocket, heard how he'd come by it and took it to school, where our class teacher, Miss Booth, was in no doubt that I must have stolen it. Why, otherwise, would I have been secretive? So my half-crown was confiscated. I'd like to think she might still be alive, Miss Booth, and might read this, and understand what a rage of injustice her stupidity and arrogant insensitivity aroused in me. Why do people like that choose to teach children? It was my blacking-factory moment, and probably played a part in my political formation. I was never made a prefect, either at that school or later at Hampton Grammar School, and I think it was because the selectors detected a quiet bolshiness in me, a scepticism of people in authority.

There was a comparable moment at Hampton. In a Spanish class with our master George Calvert, who liked me as I liked him, we, the ten or so boys doing Spanish A-level, were larking around one day, and George fingered me as the ringleader. He told me to stand in the corner, which I figure was a neat, dry joke: if we were going to fool around like second-formers, then a second-form-type punishment was fit. The deputy headmaster, prim Mr James, happened to come in to see George about something. Why was I in the corner? George mumbled something in humorous exoneration, but Mr James knew a sinner when he saw one, and how to deal with him. He took me to his study and caned me, lightly. It didn't hurt, and my pride was only jostled. What did sting was how bad George must be feeling about it. I was a fast-track pupil, and it had all been no more than a shared joke, really, but it had come to this. About 30 years later George turned up in Bristol as the new headmaster of Fairfield, the school my daughters attended. I didn't remind him of that incident.

When we took the 11-plus, Geoff was going to Isleworth Grammar School and I'd have chosen to go with him, but Dad had heard that Hampton was a good one, and I didn't argue. We never did argue. He was right. Hampton, one of the old Tudor foundations, now in its umpteenth premises, built in the 1930s, suited me. In my first week I was appointed form captain because I'd come top in a mental arithmetic test, but I hadn't got the knack of popularity and after a term or two 1D rebelled against me. I had two supporters, Terry Stewart and Philip Stringer, both socialists, like me. The rest, all of them Tories I'll bet, persuaded our form master to depose me. I reckoned that he set a bad example by giving in to them. It wasn't as though it was a position for Coriolanus. All it entailed was failing to keep the rest quiet when the master was called away. I salved my wound thereafter by volunteering every year to be form gardener, which gave me a letter, G, against my name in the annual school list. Not as vainglorious as FC, but better than no distinction at all, and I never did a moment's work in the little plot that was our form garden, and neither did anyone ever ask me if I might think about it, even though food was still short in the postwar years. I do remember considering that I might build a racetrack there, cambering the mud after rain, and racing the little Jetex model cars you could buy; but I didn't do it, and neither did I buy any Jetexes, too practical for me, like Juneero. Dad made me a model sailing boat, and the only time we put it on water, in Kensington Gardens, it blew over at once, and we had to wait an hour for it to drift within reach. I had a model plane, which was powered by winding up an elastic band, but when I released the propeller the elastic band whirred around and tore the tissue paper out of the fuselage. Just so that you don't think I'm making all this up to create a comedy of fecklessness, I did learn enough to maintain my bike. But I loved my orange-and-chrome Rudge Aero, and I loved cycling, and I dare say it was good fitness, as the kids now say, for the rest of my life. That, and the sound diet that rationing imposed during the war.

After the first year the four forms were mixed up. I found myself removed from the teeny Tories who had brought their putsch against me, and made new friends. In my third year I was invited to take up one of two free places on offer to switch schools and go to Harrow. It was a class-levelling government scheme. I was willing to give it a go, curious to find out about life in the upper echelons – was it anything like the Bunter books, and other stuff I'd read? Dad was deeply unsure, and his doubt made me decide not to go through with it. I forget how he expressed it, but I see now that his anxiety was social, and perhaps influenced by *The Guinea Pig*, a recent Richard Attenborough film about a similar transition. How could his son survive at Churchill's old school? With my Middlesex vowels and habits, wouldn't I be wretched among the scoffing toffs? He was, of course, embodying the very division that the bursary scheme was addressing. His protective love for me was greater than his ambition for me. Perhaps he was right to be anxious, in which case the Boulting Brothers might have directed significantly the course of my life. Alternatively, did he fear that I might learn new tricks and that Harrow would steal me from him, play Henry Higgins to his Doolittle? That is what would happen a few years later, when I went to Cambridge, though by then it was simply the rite of passage that happens when any child has grown up and leaves home. My friend Eric Fiddy, a good mathematician, did take up the Harrow offer, and I never saw him again.

Eric came from the middle-class tranche in the Hampton catchment. I was lowlier. Class never made a breath of difference in school, after that initial shock of the putsch, which I now see clearly, and then saw darkly, as something to do with class. Class nuances were lost in the mix, once we had taken our place. Outside school it could be different. I sometimes visited the homes of friends, and saw shades of casual affluence that were unknown in Whitton Dene. Hampton was separated by wire fences from two other schools, Lady Eleanor Holles for fee-paying girls on one side, the Rectory for 11-plus failure boys on the other. With the LEH girls we had ballroom dancing classes. The Rectory might as well have been in Malawi. 'Rectory rats' is what the boys there were called by some of my contemporaries. No doubt the Rectory boys had names for us.

To judge by his accent, Brian Coshall was the most working-class boy of my age at Hampton. Entering the underground shelter which served Tiffin School as a cricket changing-room, he remarked, 'Cor, innit dank?' It is the only time I have heard that word used in conversation. He was the best batsman we had in the school XI, also played for the school at soccer and was exceptionally able at every subject he studied. I hope he wound up getting a starred First in something, but it would not have been easy for him, because at 16 he was taken out of school by his parents and sent to earn a wage, just as Dad had been forty years earlier.

The school's extensive playing fields were looked after by a grounds team headed by an Irishman, Pat Verth. He endeared himself to everyone with a trick he played in every annual school photograph. The camera had a clockwork mechanism that panned it slowly across the ranks, which gave Verth time to start at one side of the shot, judge when the camera had moved off him, and scuttle round behind to appear again, deadpan, at the other side. He was there, twinned, in every photograph that lined the corridors.

I played all the games on offer at school, but had fallen deeply in love with cricket. My first glimpse of the game had been in Valentine's Park, Ilford, when my eyes were bootlace-high to the cricketers. For about five Christmases I got Dad to pay for indoor coaching as a present. On Saturdays, for ten weeks from January each year, I rode to Chiswick, where there was an indoor school behind a pub. I carried my bat in clips you could buy, which held it between the handlebars and the front fork.

My first coach was Frank Lee, afterwards it was Harry Sharp, both of them Middlesex players. One look at me told them I was a kid without natural talent, so they taught me defence, forward and back. I suppose they reckoned that if they could teach me to stay in, runs would somehow accrue, and they were right. For years, what runs I made were mostly from cuts or glances. My defence was impregnable enough for me to wind up opening for the school 1st XI in my final year. On my last day of school we played against the Old Boys. By lunch, after two hours, I had made 24. My opening partner, Terry Lloyd, a fine, slender batsman, had nearly completed his century. I do wonder if my place in the team had something to do with an event two years earlier. I had come by a ticket for the FA Cup Final in which my team, Arsenal, were to play Newcastle United. (*Swindin, Scott, Barnes, Forbes, Compton L, Mercer, Milton, Logie, Lewis, Lishman, Compton D* is a mantra I can still recite, though I see it wasn't the Wembley line-up exactly.) They beat us by breaking Wally Barnes's leg; no substitutes then. A few days before it I was for the first time selected to play cricket for the school 3rd XI on Cup Final day. It took no time for me to make my choice. I sold my Wembley ticket to a friend. The story went around the school, especially because I had sold the ticket at face value, 7s 6d. After all, you don't look to make a profit from a friend, do you? Perhaps the master in charge of 1st XI cricket, Bill Collihole, heard that story, was impressed by my dedication to the game, and a couple of years later gave me preference. Or maybe he just liked to have an impregnable blocker at the top of his batting order. I did get to Wembley in 1953, to watch England lose 3-6 to Hungary (1-6 until two late goals). It wasn't fair, of course. The Hungarians had come up with the nasty little Magyar hoax of withdrawing their centre-forward, Hidegkuti, into what would nowadays be called the hole behind the strikers, and the England centre-half, Harry Johnston, spent ninety minutes looking for someone to mark.

I was batting indoors at Chiswick when an elderly, large black man in a brown three-piece suit crossed behind Harry Sharp on his way to the office of the man who ran the school. He looked at me down the net, picked up a ball and bowled it at me, gently. I blocked it. Harry told me: 'For the rest of your life you can tell people that you faced Learie Constantine.' I was perhaps the last Englishman to do so. I was also the last of hundreds to go *c.*Stephenson, *b.*Wellard a few decades later. I was playing at Weston-super-Mare for a team of media types which the Bristol journalist David Foot had got together to play against an Old Somerset XI in the county club's centenary year. He sent me in to open with Ted Drake, as famous a name to me as Stanley Matthews. He'd played in the legendary Arsenal side before the war, and had scored seven goals in a match against Aston Villa when I was a month old. At Weston he scored about seventy runs, and later told me he could have played first-class cricket for Hampshire, but didn't fancy being a double professional. Arthur Wellard was so far gone they nearly had to wheel him out to the square, but once he started I could hear his old bowling partner and rival, Bill Andrews, in the slips behind me, muttering: 'The old bugger's still bending it.' He was right. I snicked a little away-swinger and was out for two. By now my defence was not dogged. Playing club cricket for fifty seasons, I learned how to get it off the square, sometimes over the rope (four straight sixes at Hanham), and looked to play shots from the start. I was a decent club 2nd XI player, starting with Addison C.C. while I was still at school, and then the Old Hamptonians before joining Clifton when I moved to Bristol. At Cambridge I captained my college second XI for two years, and now and then filled in a gap in the first XI.

Harry gave me a pair of tickets for the pavilion at Lord's. Geoff came with me, to watch Middlesex play Glamorgan. We were close to the balcony outside the visitors' changing room, and could see the Glamorgan players there, watching. We took it into our decently brought-up, prattish little schoolkid heads to talk loudly about how one of the Glamorgan players must be struggling to keep his place in the side, because you could tell from his figures that he wasn't up to it. I have no idea why the chap didn't come and wrap a bat around our heads. I wish he had, I wouldn't still be feeling bad about it. I don't understand why either of us behaved like that. Blame the hormones, perhaps. We're all of us, in retrospect, sometimes a mystery to ourselves. Years later, when I was a cricket reporter, I wrote that Mervyn Kitchen might not keep his place in the Somerset side. He sought me out behind the pavilion at Bath, and told me I shouldn't have written that. In his position I might have done likewise. Confidence is crucial to a cricketer, and in Kitchen's case his professional living was in question.

And yet, and yet, what is a journalist to do? We are paid for, among other things, offering our judgments. It is the same when a theatre reviewer criticises an actor's performance. Or when I have read a bad review of some book or play of mine. You curse the idiot for his or her obtuseness, and the paper for employing fools like that, and you reflect that there is a cultural deficit, the old school of critics would have had more insight and sensibility, and enough disinterested learning to discern the true merit in what you have written, and all the time you know, first, that it is worth considering whether you can learn something from the bad review, and, second, that everyone who offers a performance to the public is inviting hard knocks. I see Kitchen now and then at Cheltenham races, where he clerks for a bookie, and we have a friendly chat. He's a nice man. Most cricketers are. It's a game that teaches you humble irony. The Americans should take it up again.

* * *

When I was little my Aunt Lucy sent me to Sunday school. A sanctimonious smell came off the books when they were opened. I was never a believer. No one, and no book, ever took hold of me and shook religion out of me. Simply, at no point, even when I was little, did I believe any of it, or need it. The closest I came was when Margaret Green disapproved of my not having been confirmed. Cycling back home from Cambridge, I decided that not even for her would I conform, and then went back to commentating aloud to myself about football (the upcoming Subbuteo fixtures) or singing some love song (for Margaret) that I'd have heard on the radio. *Strange dear, but true dear, when I'm close to you, dear...*

Soon afterwards, when I was around thirteen, the Scouts (1st Whitton Air Scouts, meeting in the same church hut where I had once gone to Sunday school, and later the Cubs) told me that if I went on missing the monthly church parade I would not be allowed to go to summer camp on Guernsey. I had already been on one camp, at Seaford. The first evening I felt so homesick that I rang Dad in tears. He came down the next day, riding his bike with one hand, and bringing mine with the other, a trip of seventy miles over the North and South Downs. When he found me I told him I was feeling much better, so he turned around and rode the bikes back home again. Just writing that story, I close my eyes. I told the Scouts that every Sunday I went cycling with my Dad, and surely that was a fine Scoutish thing to be doing instead? Skipper Kerswell, whom I loathed for his propensity to put an arm around us and squeeze, could not agree. So I quit. So did Skipper Kerswell, at about the same time. Our troop's farewell gift to him was a table lamp with a parchment shade, which each of us had to autograph for him. I had too much ink on my nib, and a dribble ran indelibly down the shade. I was embarrassed at my clumsiness, but quite pleased to have spoiled his souvenir of us.

At school at about the same time, K.M. Harrison had to take us one week for religious instruction because Mr Flood (great scriptural name) was off. I liked K.M. in his chemistry classes, and knew him to be a Marxist. I doubt if I could have got far in defining Marxism, but I was sure it embraced atheism, so had no qualms in standing up and declaring that 'Christianity is a double form of moral cowardice'. What I had in mind was fear of not understanding how the universe is, and fear of having no benign god to tell us not to worry about it. Fear of living with questions. My wordy phrase-making (those duplicated adjectives) might have won me a good beating-up in a tougher school, or a tougher age, but in 1950 it impressed some of my classmates. 'What was it?' they'd ask me. 'Double form of...'

'Moral cowardice,' I assured them.

Without recognising it I was drifting into a love affair, sometimes messy, with the English language. I opened an essay on Roman history: *Although Augustus possessed a judiciously eclectic faculty...* Years later, we had a competition around a pub table, nominating which first word in a book would most deter the reader. I was voted the winner with 'Although'. Thank heaven I didn't read Dylan Thomas at that time; it might have parboiled my style for life. I wasn't seriously studying English at all, but French, Spanish and Latin. I was in a cohort which, experimentally, was allowed to skip the fifth form and go straight into the sixth for three years. It meant we had to do O-levels (the minimum for university entrance: Eng Lang, Eng Lit, Maths, Latin) at the same time as work for the first A-level year, but the *quid pro quo* was that we had an extra year, after taking A-levels, to work for a State Scholarship. I had a gift for languages and a glibness in writing essays which regurgitated what I had read or been taught. I don't remember once standing back and taking a critical, independent look at Racine, or Lope de Vega, or Tacitus, or being advised to do so by my teachers.

What I do remember vividly is this moment. In the school library, during a free period, I looked for any book by T.S. Eliot, only because I was intrigued and mystified by what my friends studying English were saying about him. They had *Murder in the Cathedral* as an A-level text. I found something, and it fell open and let me first see the lines:

> I should have been a pair of ragged claws
> Scuttling across the floors of silent seas.

My life had been changed in sixteen words. If it hadn't been that it would have been something else, but it was that. I had had no idea that such words could be written, such images offered. What they meant was obscure to me, but as I would later find out, old Eliot himself remarked that poetry communicates before it is understood. To write poetry was my ambition now, as I left the library. Sartre remembered that when he was a boy *the trade of the writer, as a grown-up activity, struck me as being so solemn, so futile, and in the end so boring, that I couldn't doubt it was going to be my trade.* Like him, many writers start to be solemn, futile and boring in their childhood. I was a late starter.

* * *

Gillian lived near me, but we had no friends in common, no connection. Once I had noticed her I was tormented by how I might find an excuse to speak to her. Just going up to her in the street would have called for more wit and courage than I had at 18. I had no chat-up, was sullenly silent when I had my arm around an unfortunate girl's waist in the ballroom-dancing classes that Mr James ran for us with the girls at Lady Eleanor Holles next door. (Only a wire fence separated our playing fields, but on both sides there was a ten-yard zone in which any pupil would be shot by East German border guards, and timetables were so arranged that they were never leaving school at the same time as we were.) I knew nothing useful. Alan Garnett had said he knew a girl called Eileen in Teddington who let him fondle her breasts, and he thought she might do the same for me, but I'd never dared put it to the test. In any case, what the sight of Gillian inspired in me was not coloured sexual but Romantic. I had never had an orgasm.

From her school uniform I sleuthed out that she was at Godolphin and Latymer in Hammersmith, and I made a cunning plan. At Hampton we were off school on Wednesday afternoons, went in on Saturday mornings instead, and so one Wednesday I took the Tube to Hammersmith, and as I'd hoped found a café conveniently opposite the school gates. Following a ruse I'd come across in a detective novel, I bought a newspaper, punched a hole through it, and sat in the café facing the window, newspaper in front of my face, so that through the hole I could invisibly monitor the girls as they came out. She might have come out of another gate, or left at another time, or not travelled home by Tube, or been with a gaggle of friends, or I might have been apprehended as some weirdo peeper, but everything went as plotted. There she was. Fortune favours the chicken. I followed her to the Tube station, got in the same carriage, and all I had to do now was go up to her and chat, as I might have done in the street without going through all that rigmarole, but it seemed easier to meet away from home, with a journey together, and at least the obvious opening line, 'I think you live near Whitton Dene, don't you?'

She had even less small talk than I had, but we got through the first movement, and she agreed to come to the Proms with me. We went more than once, and after the concert we'd go into Daquise, a nice little Polish joint, still there, by South Kensington Tube station, and I rowed her on the Thames at Richmond, and took her out for an espresso sometimes, but I never dared kiss her goodnight, and she never offered her lips. Then I heard that she was also going out with another boy at Hampton, a year below me, with a more worldly way about him than I had. One day I rang her from Waterloo to ask her out, and she said she couldn't, and quite likely it was no more than a family commitment, but I fell down into despair, the ready extreme of the romantic.

I had bought the *Evening News*, and on the train home from Waterloo I started to write my first poem in the margins of the paper, which might have set me on a course of Audenesque inch-wide stuff, but I just wrote wherever there was space, and when I got home went on writing. By midnight I had written quite a long poem. It was whingeing tosh, needless to say, and there was some passing reference to ragged claws. But I was creatively exhilarated, and had got over my disappointment. That was what poetry was for, to evacuate the metaphysical anguish of being stood up by a girl. A week or two later I was mooching around Richmond Bridge, and in the window of an art shop saw a painting of Gillian's lovely face, which fired fresh arrows through my wounded heart. I went into the shop, and the painting – well, print – turned out to be Vermeer's *Girl in a Turban*. I have a postcard of it still, above me as I write this.

Now I was off, a poem or two most weeks. The prevailing tone was miserabilist, the characteristic landscape concrete arterial roads. I was paddling in the existential angst of mid-twentieth century suburban man. I could go on taking the piss out of my younger self because I was full of it, but I'll go easy, because most of us have to write poor stuff before we have drained off the lees and started to tap something better. I had the piece of luck we all need and in time get: an older friend, Peter Robins, who was a published poet for chrissakes, and who coached me. He set me the task of writing two quatrains in imitation of Yeats, and when I had satisfied that, it was Eliot. I know now that imitation is arguably the best training, in poetry and cricket. It is not fashionable among those who believe in virgin inspiration. At Peter's house in Twickenham I met a friend of his who had also published poems, Irving Wardle, later a fine theatre reviewer for *The Times*. The next time I met Wardle was twenty years later at Persepolis, when he came out to write about Peter Brook's production of *Orghast*, and I was there to write a book about the project.

What rescued me from nerdness about girls was that Derek Lawson Hill took me up as a friend and invited me to the parties he gave at his parents' big house in Oxshott, parties that for me had the allure of Gatsby's. Painfully (for them) I started to learn there how to flirt with pretty girls. I slightly knew most of them already, from a so-called Sixth-Form Debating Society that met in an upper room of the Barmy Arms in Twickenham, an arrangement engineered, I believe, by the girls at Lady Eleanor Holles and Twickenham County School; they were single-sex and desperate as we were at Hampton, though at that time what we knew was that girls had no sex-drive, but might be persuaded to put up with ours. At the Barmy Arms, opposite Eel Pie Island, people read out their papers and discussed questions like *What Is Humour?* with reference to Bergson ('Like much else in life, it depends upon the liver,' concluded Liz Woods, who, as Helen Reid, would be a newspaper colleague of mine in Bristol years later.) But everyone knew that the manifest purpose of the debates was not why we all eagerly attended. At Lawson Hill's seventieth birthday party, overlooking a mighty bend of the Dordogne, I thanked him for the growing-up it had allowed me.

In those last school years, and when I was home for weekends during National Service, a high-spirited gang of four coalesced: Lawson Hill, Brian Robins (younger brother of Peter), Paul Lock, and I. I was a year younger than they were and at first played the clown's part, but one night outside the Barmy Arms, doing my yet-again-called-for version of square-bashing, something Hancockian in me squirmed. I was more than a clown, wasn't I? I decided to try grown-up parts, see if I could do cool and witty. If you must self-dramatise, the form to choose is drawing-room comedy. If the others noticed a change in me, nothing was said. We partied together, driven around by Lawson Hill in the car he had, and went to the theatre. At school I was acting – a small part in *Androcles and the Lion* was followed by Lady Macbeth, the big time, though in a parody version, not the real tragedy. By now I was in the lower sixth, a year early, and my voice still had not broken. I was a late developer in that, as in everything, and it would have been for my high voice that I was cast. We were in some sort of competition, so there was an adjudication. It took place not after the show in the evening but the following morning after school assembly, seven hundred and twenty of us sitting there. As a sixth-former I was up in the gallery, among boys who'd started to shave. The adjudicator remarked that my poise was the more impressive coming, as it clearly did, from a junior boy. Any praise he'd given my performance was jabbed out by elbows and sniggers.

With Brian Robins, a gifted pianist, I wrote my first musical, which we performed at an Oxshott party. It lasted about twenty minutes, and was set in the kind of coffee house we frequented.

> Very soon, very soon,
> I shall croon a different tune.
> (Lalalala la la la)
> Every little plastic cup,
> Every little cloth for washing-up,
> Every cactus, every spoon,
> Will be mine...

I filled in applications for Corpus Christi College, Cambridge – recommended by my French teacher Mr Jago, whose son had been there – and for Worcester College, Oxford, where my Classics teacher and form master Mr Mulley had been. I looked at the two completed applications, then tore up the one for Worcester, before Mr Mulley's puzzled eyes, in a surge of love for Cambridge after my teenage holidays there with Margaret. It was rash. If Corpus had turned me down it would have been too late that year to apply to Oxford. Dad once surprised me by remarking that I was impulsive. I had thought myself diffident, like him. Perhaps he wasn't, either, really. I took the entrance exams in the autumn of my third year in the sixth form. The letter from Corpus arrived on Christmas Day. You can tell how long ago it was. It began *We regret to tell you...* I read no further, left it on top of the cistern, since I had started to read it while peeing. Later that day I read the rest of it. They were regretting that they could not offer me a scholarship or exhibition, just a commoner's place. Having had no idea that scholarships or exhibitions were in question, and knowing that my State Scholarship would pay for what I'd need, it was all I had wanted.

2

Smudger

I COULD HAVE GONE TO UNIVERSITY BEFORE DOING NATIONAL Service. I chose not to, and don't regret it. Intellectually and socially, I was much more ready for university at twenty-one than I would have been straight from the sixth form.

At Hednesford, square-bashing, we were drawn up at the side of the square when a parallel universe was faded in outside the perimeter fence, the Cannock Chase hunt in pink coats and full cry. Neither they nor we flickered to acknowledge the other's existence, yards away. There were kids who couldn't take it, one or two suicides a week, a jump from the water tower or a gulped bottle of Brasso. The rest of us got through on camaraderie. My special comrade in the next bed was Maurice Phelps, of the Thames boating family. His laugh darkened his face, and clicked the world back into place for me. A dozen years later, when we were living in Birmingham, I went back with my wife to look at Hednesford. It was abandoned, an expanse of broken hut foundations, overrun by flowering gorse. *Sic transit ingloria.*

At the end of eight weeks I was so fit that I ran two steps at a time up an escalator while toting a full kitbag. I wanted to fly Vampires and be a Pilot Officer but my eyesight test came back 19/20, not quite up to Vampire spec, though probably OK for Snoopy in the cockpit of a Defiant. I was sent to RAF Bicester to be trained as a Clerk (Org), and live with the brown, bumpered lino floor, the cast-iron stove, squat and tall cupboards in pairs down either side, the smell of polish and webbing and dirty pyjamas, the Geordie or Welsh or Brummie accents, the accounts of what was done to this bird and that tart, the same ritual jokes ('I wouldn't kick her out of bed.' 'Not till afterwards, anyway.'), the litter of torn newspapers on Sunday nights. After two weeks you were accepted, cast in a role, signed off with a nickname, mine Smudger, of course, like Dad in the RAF before me. In the next bed was a man called Brian Orchard, who introduced me to the records of Dave Brubeck and Lonnie Donegan, and we went to USAF Brize Norton to hear Chet Baker and Gerry Mulligan. I think Orchard became a radio DJ.

The uniformed, uninformed airmen, pop music, sex, all opening to a new world. How brave a world it was I would soon explore.

Bicester was HQ Maintenance Command, so there was a lot of top brass around and relatively few sprogs like me. The brass couldn't be bothered with time-wasting nonsense like parades and blanco. I didn't polish my badge or press my trousers for the last eight months of my service. In charge of the training registry was Sergeant Houlihan, a cheerful Irish bloke behind his pushy stripes. One day he shouted at me for doing, or not doing, something I hadn't done, or had. A synapse short-circuited. I shouted back at him. I'd never in my life challenged authority so frontally, and this one could have taken me straight to jankers without passing Go. Instead, Houlihan muttered: 'All right, just get on with your work.' Seratonin flooded me. You could shout back and not be squelched.

I was then assigned as clerk to Flight Officer Winifred M. Segger, in an office with half a dozen other clerks. Ma'am Segger's attitude to me I might call materteral, if the language supplied a feminine equivalent of avuncular. She was bossy, as very small people can be, but not unkind. She came to see me when I was at Cambridge, and in her old age I took my family to meet her in Shaftesbury. My work for her took up no more than thirty minutes of a day. The rest of the time at my desk I spent writing poetry and reading the modern poets. I wrote a poem in celebration of Sibelius's ninetieth birthday and sent it to him, and still have his reply. A group of four of us found each other and spent our evenings playing LPs of Brahms, Berlioz, etc and smoking Abdullahs and Black Russian when we could afford them, talking passionately about the poems and paintings we were going to create. Very bohemian clerks we were in our No.2 uniforms, and in garish shirts – worn, my god, outside our trousers – when we went promming in the summer, London being only an hour's train-ride away, and every weekend being a 36-hour pass, every fourth one a 48-er.

After the prom it was Chiquito's dingy coffee dive, off Tottenham Court Road, where we all worshipped a girl called Jo (should have been Mimi), who broke our hearts when she gave in to an opera singer called Alan who finally cracked her by singing beneath her window words he had set to the slow movement of Tchaikovsky's Fifth. Jo, how could you succumb to Tchaikovsky? For our Bicester salons we met in the station library, which I ran as a voluntary activity for one hour an evening, the reward being access to a private space with a key to lock it, a rare asset in the services. The other three were demobbed before I was, but by then I had made a couple more friends for evenings in the library, Peter Comerford, who would become a vicar, and Brian Blessed, a wannabe actor. He mentions me in his autobiography, but when I met him again forty-five years later, at the Cheltenham Litfest, he was anxious not to remember who I was.

A Flight-Sergeant brought a large cardboard box full of books into the library. 'I'm demobbed tomorrow, after twenty-two years. Don't need these any more. Thought you might want them for the library.' I thanked him, and when he'd left glanced at the paperbacks on top. Spillane, Shute. Some days later I got round to unpacking them all. Right at the bottom was Eliot's *Four Quartets*, in hardback. Nothing higher in the box had foreshadowed it. Why had he got it? More puzzling, having got it for whatever good reason, why was he giving it away? My theory was founded on Dad's aspirations: someone had told the Ft/Sgt that Eliot was valuable stuff, so he had gone into a bookshop and bought it, but couldn't get on with it, left it on his shelf and tidied it away now with the rest of what he didn't need any more. You may form a different theory.

Two education officers were among my friends at RAF Bicester. Derek Townend directed several plays in which I acted – nothing serious, Philip King farces to entertain the troops. 'Oh, Penelope!' I hooted as a vicar. Bryn Jones had done an English degree at Oxford, and recognised my literary drift. He invited me to go with him to the inauguration of W.H. Auden as Professor of Poetry. Bryn was an officer and I wasn't, so to drive the few miles to Oxford he could wear civvies but I had to be in uniform, according to some arcane standing orders. Bryn, as an alumnus, had whatever the Welsh for chutzpah is. He marched into the Sheldonian and up to the fourth row from the front, because he'd spotted two vacant seats there. Cecil Day Lewis, Jill Balcon, Enid Starkey and Lord David Cecil were sitting just behind us. At me, in my sproggy uniform, they batted no eyelid, but they did flutter when Auden shuffled in wearing carpet slippers. He'd got something wrong with his feet. Pedal paranoia, it could have been, because from *There Will Be No Peace* we may guess he was affected by the controversy his election had aroused. He opened by asking, 'How can poetry be *professed*?' I should have been sobered by the question. Instead, at Cambridge, I had visiting cards printed:

Anthony Smith
Poet

Printed in gilt, yet. Years later I bumped into Dennis Levy, by now a senior figure at Granada. He opened his wallet and brought out my visiting card, which he must have kept to amuse dinner parties. It is less humiliation than I deserved.

In my twenty-two months at Bicester we played a few cricket matches against other RAF stations, on coconut matting laid on concrete. I found myself ordered to captain the side, though I was the most junior both in age and rank. It was the first time since the 1D putsch that I had been put in charge of anything, so I was happy to comply, but perplexed. I was not the outstanding player in the team. The best guess I can make is that it was known I was going to Cambridge and therefore Senior Aircraftsman Smith *Sir! 2733676* commanded deference on a social scale independent of service rank. Creepy, but nice for me, because I picked up the rudiments of captaining a cricket team without fear, something as hard to do well as writing a sonnet. *The fascination of what's difficult*, said Yeats, in a title. His poem includes:

> My curse on plays
> That have to be set up in fifty ways,
> On the day's war with every knave and dolt,
> Theatre business, management of men.

All that I do know, but will come to it. We had a couple of leaves during our two years. Lawson Hill and I contrived to coincide ours, so that we could take trips to Dublin and Paris. In a B&B on St Stephen's Green we tried every morning to order mushrooms for breakfast, and every time the waiter, presumably covering up for the menu's mendacity, advised us: 'Ah now, I wouldn't be recommending the mushrooms today, sorr.' In the basement bar of the Shelbourne Hotel we discovered John Powers's Gold Label, and that it was possible to go on drinking it till midnight even though we were not residents, something you could not do in the UK. When the boy in a commis jacket brought us our fourth whiskeys on a silver tray, I asked him whether there were licensing laws in Ireland. The boy, about fourteen years old, told me: 'Ah sure, that's a trade secret, sorr.' Lawson Hill remembers that we spent time searching for James Joyce, who had died in Zürich fifteen years earlier. We didn't find him, but perhaps what he remembers is a quest for the haunts of the man.

On September 7th, 1956, Lawson Hill, who had been demobbed

from the RAF a few weeks earlier, drove to Bicester to fetch me back to civvy street, one of a thousand kindnesses. In October we both went to Cambridge, he to read law at Downing. Paul Lock was at LSE and, raised a foodie by his German mother, became a lecturer in transport catering. Brian Robins's life twisted away, entangled with a woman and a daughter they had. He did the traffic news on Radio London for a while, that was all I heard. As a young man he had real talent, musical and comic, and there was professional theatre in the family. Talent is a chemical element. On its own it may remain inert. To combust, it needs to be mixed with perseverance and luck.

3

A Sofa and a Tomcat

MICHAEL MCCRUM, MY SENIOR TUTOR, TOLD ME I HAD GOT MYSELF a place at the college by sitting on his sofa. It was an old sofa, saggy in the seat, so that at the interview with him one had the choice either of perching on the front bar of the frame or lolloping right back in it. McCrum had his doubts about the perchers. As long as the lollopers had performed in the entrance exams, they were favoured. A few years later a tomcat would give me my first job. I was interviewed by Richard Hawkins in the *Bristol Evening Post*'s London office. He always brought Beastie with him from Bristol. Some time in the 1960s, when I was staying with him in the Vaucluse, I started, 'When you first gave me that job...'

He interrupted me: 'I never gave you a job.'

'What do you mean? I worked for you for nearly four years.'

'Yes, but I didn't give you the job.'

'No one else interviewed me.'

'Yes they did. Don't you remember? Beastie got off my lap, walked across the carpet and jumped up on to your lap. That's when you got the job.'

The expectation I had of student life at Cambridge was based on Compton Mackenzie's portrait of Edwardian-era Oxford in *Sinister Street*, and for at least the first year, in collusion with the university itself, that was the lens through which I experienced the place and its buildings, just as, still, every visit I make to the USA is a journey into the land of B-movies, and I am surprised to find it is not in black-and-white. Corpus Christi, the second-smallest college, with a yearly intake of ninety, was overwhelmingly populated by public school boys. Another Mod Lang student in the college, a working-class lad from Lancashire, spent his three years resolutely having no truck with the posh kids, and suffered a nervous breakdown while sitting finals. I fell in happily with them, though not without the sense of being a character making his way through a novel, a bit of a chancer. I made friends who still matter to me, half a century later. However, I don't go to formal reunion dinners because my toes clench at the pretence that we are all still who we were, in the same relationships with each other, and that our collegiateness trumps whatever else we have had in our life. I am who I was, but a lot more than that. The lot more is a discord unwelcome at formal reunions.

I once snapped at my son, then a teenager, for something he'd done, and he levelly replied that I was behaving like a kid. Instead of being offended I was struck by his perception, and went into an analogy with a tree trunk, which grows new rings but still has the older ones inside, and sometimes it is they which are touched by a moment, and yield their older (younger) response. The child is father to the man, and all that. The analogy cheered him up from one of those teenage dread-of-growing-old phases he had been going through, briefly.

My accent altered. I didn't put on drawly vowels, just noticed that my Middlesex ones were being abraded into something nearer classless, the norm nowadays, but not in the less rootless 1950s. A decade on, when I was starting to edge my way into radical theatre work, you were nobody unless you talked like Joan Li'llwood's bruvver innit. I got my vocal timing wrong. I wasn't going to embark on a phoney reversion, though my friend Geoffrey Reeves (Dulwich College and St Catherine's, Cambridge, as they say in the Boat Race) managed to sound like a Dalston butcher when he was working for Arnold Wesker at the Round House. Wesker himself has always had a voice at home in country houses, and so had Harold Pinter, also an East End boy, and John Osborne. It is probably due to their training as actors.

Three weeks into my time at Cambridge, the Eden government celebrated my twenty-first birthday by invading Egypt. I knew which side I was on. I'd marched in my duffel coat for CND, though was disconcerted in Trafalgar Square, as we were leaving the rally, when I heard a woman call to her friend, 'See you next year'. For a CND meeting in the Cambridge Union, E.M. Forster popped across from King's; his address to a packed house began, 'Nuclear missiles aren't really in my line. Unfortunately, I'm in theirs.' Added to the political dismay was a fear that I would be called back to the colours. Our leaving certificate after National Service had warned us that we would be on the reserve for years. Fortunately, the idiocy was quickly smothered by Eisenhower (or, as the *Manchester Guardian* managed to call him, Eisenhowever), Eden dispatched, and the era of Supermac ushered in.

I soon decided that the teaching of French at Cambridge was lamentable. Lecturers read out old lectures or new chapters from their forthcoming books, making no attempt to engage with their audience or to disturb the received canon. Supervisions, just one or two of us face-to-face with the lecturer, were not much better. The essay we had presented was discussed lightly, small points were corrected, good grades were accorded. I had been used to this at school, but after my two gap years with Yeats and Eliot and Auden and Leavis I was ready for something more challenging, more modern. I wasn't complaining, though. My aim was to stay at Cambridge for three years by doing enough work not to get thrown out, nothing more. I had no academic ambitions, so just carrying on where I had left off at school suited me. I stopped going to most of my French appointments. One woman was so dull at the first of our supervisions (which she had scheduled for 9 a.m. weekly, for godsake, and a twenty-minute bike ride away) that I sent her flowers instead of myself for the second, and never saw her again. No one chased us up when we cut things, and neither did anyone question my right to be at Dr Leavis's lectures in the English faculty. I applaud that as a civilised idea of what a university is. The Spanish teaching was better. In particular, I felt stretched by Dr Street, with whom I studied the conquistadors. At school, what I had most enjoyed was Roman history. It was looking as though history might be my avocation, and indeed I would spend much of my writing life parachuted into various pasts.

What I enjoyed most of all, though, was *Don Quixote.* When I read people now chattering about postmodernism, I wonder if they have heard of Cervantes. Part One of his book was so successful that in Part Two, a few years later, he has his characters proud of the fame their author has brought them. Postmodernism three centuries before modernism. Here's a trick question: both Cervantes and Shakespeare died on April 23rd 1616, making it the blackest date in literature, yet Shakespeare could in theory have been at Cervantes's funeral in Madrid and got home for his own. How? The answer is that England had not yet adopted the Gregorian calendar, so Shakespeare survived eleven days after Cervantes.

When I arrived there were two literary magazines, *Granta* and *delta.* The first was smart and urbane, the second seriously literary. I wrote for both, but there was no doubt where my loyalty lay. In my first year, when *delta* was edited by Christopher Levenson, who is still a good friend, I went through the apprenticeship of going the rounds of retailers to drum up ads and invading colleges to sell copies, in my second year wrote poems and reviews, joined the editorial committee, and for my final year was appointed editor by my predecessors, John

Kimber and Michael Carthew. Both were at Downing, as most of their predecessors had been, so it was a departure that *delta* should be edited in a college where English was not taught or recognised as a tripos subject.

I began my editorship with a foreword in which I regretted how spiteful undergraduate reviewers were about literary work by other undergraduates. It reflected an undercurrent of which I had become aware, people jealously eyeing each other as future professional rivals, especially in their final year, small fish biting each other in a small pond. It attracted letters of support from several prominent Cambridge people, including Mervyn Stockwood, then vicar of Great St Mary's. Four years later I chanced to be in Cambridge, reporting cricket, when Leavis was giving his last lecture as a member of the English faculty. I got my colleagues in the press box to cover me for the morning's play at Fenner's, and headed for Mill Lane. Incredibly, Leavis ended his career by advising the packed audience to pay more attention to what their contemporaries were writing, 'in magazines such as *delta*'. Then he ripped his tie off for the last time and walked out through a standing ovation. I rang the *Guardian*, who took a brief news report about it from me.

We published some stuff we could be proud of, but there is no denying that we were outshone by the sophistication of *Granta*, especially in the year of my editorship, where I was up against the American troika of André Schiffrin (later a distinguished book editor in New York), Richard Gooder and Roger Donald, along with John Bird as a guest editor. Bird's talent was unfathomable. He was the leading director at the university's playhouse, the ADC (in the era of Eleanor Bron, Miriam Margolyes, Ian McKellen, Derek Jacobi, Clive Swift, and Margaret Drabble and Janet Burroway, both actors then, novelists subsequently) and a Footlight (with Peter Cook and Jonathan Miller). Bird was reading English at King's, where I was told he would also find time now and then to give the organ scholars some tips at the keyboard. When he wrote a short story in a spare moment it put *delta* in the shade, not that we went in much for fiction. I am glad he has made a good career in satire, but one would have predicted more, an update of the Sistine Chapel, perhaps. My own theatrical activity went no further than the Old Court at Corpus. I was asked to script a sort of pageant to celebrate some anniversary to do with Queen Elizabeth I. It was uncooked stuff, but I did collaborate with a good composer, Mozart.

Sylvia Plath was publishing poems in Cambridge, and Ted Hughes was often around. When I got to know him better, years later, he told me that one job he had was digging up roads, and he was sent to excavate right outside the main gate of his old college, Pembroke. The senior tutor came out, noticed the mighty, sweating, stripped-to-the-waist navvy gripping a pickaxe, nodded, and said: 'Good morning, Mr Hughes.'

In my third year I was also editor of the arts page in *Varsity*. The paper's editor, Charles Manton, was a friend at Corpus. When his arts editor wrote a piddly review of *delta* I returned a stormy letter, which was published, whereupon the man resigned. Charles told me that I owed it to him to fill the unexpected vacancy, with only a day or two before the next weekly deadline. It was then that I was infected with the smell of printer's ink and the pleasure of making up a page on the stone, and journalism became a career I would aim for, remembering Eliot's warning that if you want to write poetry you will have to find another way to earn a living.

I joined a group called Cambridge Writers, where we kicked around each other's poems and stories. I had an advantage. Most of the rest were reading English; unlike them, I was not intimidated by the language of the writers I studied, unworthy to scribble footnotes to their works. Cervantes's fabulation (to use modern jargon) was an inspiration, but I was probably incapable of appraising his prose, and no one would be teaching me to. Through some connection there, I was invited to join the Group, at Teddy Lucie-Smith's house in Chelsea. Each week one poet would read out loud half a dozen new poems he or she (but predominantly he) had written and circulated in advance, and they would be critically discussed by the rest, who usually numbered ten to fifteen. It would have been a waste of time if punches had been pulled, though it was seldom vicious, and occasionally funny. The prevailing tone was Leavisite, and the chief moderator was Philip Hobsbaum, who had read English at Downing and taken over *delta* from its founder editor, Peter Redgrove. When Hobsbaum moved to university positions at Sheffield, Belfast and Glasgow he incarnated similar groups. Among those I met in Chelsea were Redgrove, Martin Bell, George Macbeth, Alan Brownjohn, Peter Porter, Adrian Mitchell and David Wevill.

I went to Italy in my first summer vacation with Lawson Hill, Paul Lock, his girl friend Madeleine Appleby (Lady Eleanor Holles School and the Barmy Arms) and Judith Spero, a family friend of Derek's. It was the first time I'd seen the Mediterranean, and my studies of Romance lang & lit had programmed me to respond deeply to it, as

I still do. When I reach Calais I turn right. We had a seaside holiday at Bonassola, with trips to Florence and Rapallo, where I pretended to be Max Beerbohm. My, what a wag I was. On the beach I wore a green ribbed cotton shirt made for me by Mrs Lock, a motherly kindness I was not used to. I made a desultory pass at Judith, thinking that we both felt it was called for in the hot sunshine, but neither of us was really keen. Far worse was soon to happen, back in Cambridge. A nice girl took her clothes off, joined me in bed and offered her virginity to mine. I bottled. Her first experience of sex ended not with a bang but a wimp. I was callow, the son of a prudish generation. I understand why it was once the custom for fathers to take their sons to a brothel for initiation. To my own son I allowed free rein with his girl friend while they were still at school, and as far as I can judge it did the trick, got him, and her, I hope, over the threshold of terror. But that was in the 1980s. If we believe Philip Larkin, which I am usually reluctant to do, sex hadn't been invented in the late 1950s.

In other vacs I hung around the left bank dives in Paris. If I breathed Juliette Gréco's smoke or spilled Albert Camus's red wine I wasn't aware of it, but I did spend an evening listening to Mezz Mezzrow, his face all pouches – his cheeks from a lifetime of blowing, his eyes from a lifetime of blow. And I found jobs. The best was stacking crates of Guinness ten high at Dad's brewery, learning from those more experienced to build a concealed cave within the stack, in which we took turns to have a Guinness and a smoke and read the paper (*The Times*, brought in daily by a couple of South African world-roamers), and hope we were not caught by the head checker, my Dad. I worked at an ice-lolly factory, where fussy Mr Goody whinged at us in a Kenneth Williams voice: 'Be more careful with the lollees.' 'Right, Mr Goo-dee.' All the first day the chemical used to unfreeze the lollies from the mould trays slopped over my shoes, and when I went to put them on the next morning they had rotted. Mr Goody told me I would be issued with wellies after a week there.

'I'll have thrown away five pairs of shoes by then.'

'A week. That's the rules.' I quit.

I worked in the cuttings library at *The Economist*, a thematic setting I used in my first published novel. I was an invoice clerk at Firestone Tyres. I got a job with the *Kentish Mercury* newspaper group, travelling along the South Coast from Bournemouth to Cornwall, urging hotels and guest houses to buy small ads for the summer season next year. It was July, and the invariable answer was: 'We can't think about next year when we're in the thick of it this summer.' I saw their point. In six weeks I sold six-and-a-quarter column inches. In a final telephone call to the paper I explained the problem, and they were sympathetic in accepting my resignation, while taking the opportunity to mention that the chap covering East Anglia had sold hundreds of column inches.

At the start of my second year at Cambridge I fell in love with a girl who was called Bernardine; still is, probably, though maybe not, since someone told me she became a nun, and don't they take a pseudonym with the veil? No, I just googled her, and she's a psychotherapist in London. I met her at the societies' fair in Cambridge, where the university's interest groups set out their stalls to attract acolytes. I was manning the *delta* stall. She had just come up to read English, which didn't necessarily mean she'd have any interest in new writing, but she did. Her father, Bernard Wall, was editor of the *Twentieth Century* magazine, and her Catholic family background included the Meynells – the poet Alice, her publisher husband Wilfrid and their various literary children.

Bernardine became the first girl friend I had at Cambridge, and the only serious one. She looked at the dowdy clothes on me, sports jacket, cavalry twills, and took me to buy my first pair of jeans. We hatched a plan to dress her as a young man and smuggle her into the Corpus Hall for dinner. She wanted to see inside a chaps-only culture. We tested her disguise by going first to a pub. It was absurd. Nothing could make her face male. In return, nevertheless, she took me to High Mass. I was impressed by the ceremony of holy cannibalism, but any salvation that redeemed me wouldn't be the kind of salvation I could take seriously. That didn't bother Bernardine, unlike Margaret in the same city, years earlier.

Soon afterwards there was a story in *The Observer* which, I thought, encapsulated the reward of religious belief. A man had sat for days in the V&A Museum, gazing at a carved god. One quiet afternoon, he burst out laughing and embraced it, and they never saw him again.

There was only one woman to every ten men in the student population, so I soon had a rival, David Leitch, who went on to be a notable *Sunday Times* journalist. It was never clear to me how Bernardine juggled the two of us, but she found a way, and I was always happy with her, and I hope Leitch was, too. I stayed at her family home in Ladbroke Grove. She told me her father went to sleep with a glass of wine, something to nibble and cigarettes next to his bed, which he would need in the middle of the night.

I also stayed with her for a long summer weekend at Greatham, in Sussex, the Meynell family home. It comprised separate wings around three sides of a square. In a previous generation three daughters had left to get married, hadn't liked married life, and successively came back home, which required two of the wings to be built for them. At supper on my first evening I held forth about D.H. Lawrence. I noticed that everybody around the table went quiet, so I shut up. Afterwards, I told Bernardine that I was surprised that such a literary family would be prissy about Lawrence. She explained that I had not understood at all. About the time World War One was starting, Lawrence and Frieda, skint, had been given accommodation for six months at Greatham in a little summer outhouse, which was still there. One of the Meynells had been scything the lawn, was called away, and left his scythe on the grass. His daughter went skipping down there, and cut her leg on the blade so seriously that she still limped to this day. One of Bernardine's aunts I met that evening walked with a limp. Lawrence had written the incident as a story, in *England My England*, in which he sent the man off to war, where he shrived his guilt by putting his head above the parapet, to be shot dead. The scythe man had indeed been shot in Flanders. Now I understood the silence, but here's an ironic twist. Two years later, Bernardine was called as the last witness in the *Lady Chatterley* trial. *The Independent* columnist John Walsh has noted:

> It brought something important to the trial – the spectacle of a young woman who had read the dirty book and about whom the jury might ask 'Has she been depraved and corrupted?' before looking at her calm, sweet, clever face and concluding: perhaps not. Was this the moment when the British decided they were no longer susceptible to depravity and corruption? And that they no longer needed moral guardians to tell them what they could do, or think, or read, or say out loud?

On our last evening at Greatham there was a party, which we spent smooching to *Songs for Swinging Lovers*. I was deep for her and cannot, now, explain why we went our ways after that. I think she must have taken that decision. I went off and met Sarah, the sister of Martin Lee, my Corpus friend and friend still, and fell for her. Bernardine married a concert pianist, and rang me one day to say he was playing at the Colston Hall in Bristol, why didn't I go to hear him? So I did, and went round after the concert to pay my respects. He asked me if he could stay that night at my place? I told him I'd have nothing to offer better than a shabby sofa. That will be fine, he said. At home, I expressed surprise that a man who had just played a concerto to two thousand people would be glad of a sofa for the night. He said he wanted to save on a hotel bill. A young concert pianist wasn't paid that much, and he was newly married and they were expecting.

The whiff of class at Cambridge never quite went away. There was a posh drinking club in Corpus, the Chess Club, limited to twelve members in their final year. It happened that most of the public-school friends I'd made were invited to join. They were the top-dog social group in my year. One of them hinted to me that my name had been put forward, but I never heard anything more. At the time I minded, but only a little, and rationalised it as I had rationalised not being a school prefect: I was an outsider, a bit of a bolshie, in moments of self-melodramatisation a *poète maudit*, even. I enjoyed that fantasy more than I would have the black-tie drinking. If I had been invited to join, I don't think the outsider feeling would have drained away. For all my willing compromise with the social ethos of the college, indeed of the university, I never lost my sense of where I came from, which was not so much the Middlesex suburbs as the Attlee generation. I was not dogmatic, that's all. I thought it risible when, at an end-of-term *delta* committee meeting, one of the editors, a right-on Labour man, said we should all give each other our home addresses, in case we needed to be in touch during the vacation; after we had announced where we lived he said: 'Well, thank god we all live in houses with numbers, not names.'

I had joined another college society, reputedly the second-oldest in Cambridge. The Gravediggers met to read out plays, glasses of wine in hand. When I became secretary I inherited the minute books, and saw that Christopher Isherwood had been secretary in the 1920s. His minutes were written in a tortured hand, all of it small, but the bodies of letters like b, d, o, or p tiny, perfectly calligraphed with a fine nib. His shade came up in my last week at Cambridge. After finals my director of studies, whom I considered a snob (a view reinforced when I learned that he was treasurer of the university Conservatives) and knew to be a vapid teacher of French, asked me to stroll arm-in-arm with him round the Old Court, past the wonderful set of rooms I had there, Q2. Although I had no respect for him, he was affectionate to me, even after I had stumbled backwards over a sofa at a party at his house and sloshed sherry over the wallpaper. He asked me what I planned to do with the rest of my life, 'now that you are going down'. I mumbled something about writing. 'Writing, eh? Hmm. We've had one or two of those at Corpus, in our time. There was one chap, forgotten his name, sent me a book he'd written, with a most peculiar title. What was it? Yes, *Lions and Shadows*, that's it. Rum title, don't you think?' Mr Isherwood, of course, writing about his Corpus days.

A year or two after leaving Cambridge I was back there, visiting the Green family. On Sunday evening I was walking to where I had parked my car for the weekend and through the dusk came that same director of studies, now hobbling on a stick. He greeted me warmly, and invited me to sherry the next day. I told him I couldn't accept, because I was about to drive back to Bristol. 'Oh, just up for the evening, are you?' Crassly, I said no, I'd been here since Friday. 'Been here since Friday, and didn't come to see me? You shit!' Those words, uttered beneath an angrily waved stick as he departed, were the last ever spoken to me by my director of studies. Maybe he's right and I am a shit, but I couldn't see what he had ever done for me that would have inclined me to go and see him again. Someone I had gone to see was Mike, the groundsman at the college sports field where I had played cricket and football.

My Aunt Val had kept in touch with me through my three years at Corpus, calling in with apples and butter. Dad came to see me a couple of times, and to watch me graduate. I felt awkward for him among all the public school fathers, just as he had felt for me when Harrow had beckoned. Blood is thicker than water, but so is class-consciousness. In the November of my second year he married again. Doris had worked at the Putney brewery for many years, a tough and humorous forewoman. She had always wanted to marry Dad. I think he held her off until I was out of the way, in case I would find it difficult to have a new woman running my home. I was my Dad's best man.

4

The Bee-Humming View

AS EDITOR OF *DELTA* I RECEIVED A LETTER FROM ZULFIKAR GHOSE, at Keele University. He proposed that he, B.S. Johnson at London University, John Fuller at Oxford and I should edit and publish an annual anthology of the best of student poetry. The idea had been tried once before, without much success. *Universities Poetry* was established for some years, publishing the early work of some who would become distinguished. We were able to go through with it only because of support from the Arts Council, in particular their director of literature, Eric Walter White. I already knew him. I had applied for a grant to rescue *delta* from its chronic poverty, and was rewarded with £50, the first grant ever made to a little magazine. A poet himself, and author of books on Purcell and Tippett, he was immensely kind and supportive to me, and would soon be responsible for my moving to Bristol. He was a great one for fixing things. I mentioned to him that it was on my mind to start a new magazine, of which the title, *Scorpio*, was all I had so far, or ever did have. (My zodiac sign is Scorpio, which means that I think astrology is bunkum.) White steamed ahead. He asked Roland Penrose if he would have a word with Picasso about doing a scorpion sketch for me to use as the cover design. Tom Stoppard would later describe White as 'a patrician figure'. At a *UP* committee meeting he looked quizzically down the table at some remark Johnson had made, put his fingertips together, and observed: 'That, I would say, is a point verging on the moot.'

Ghose, Johnson and I, all living in south-west London, became close friends. Ghose and I often wrote to each other daily, men of letters at least in that. When I look through the hundreds from him in 1959-1962, all his talk is about poetry, cigarettes (lack of), cricket (he became a cricket reporter for *The Observer*), beer, poetry, finals, political relations with Keele, and poetry. We sent each other the new poems we were writing, and returned mutual criticism. He was writing a love poem in two voices with the American at Cambridge, Janet Burroway. We engaged in furious discussion about which contemporary poets were any good. He is discovering Stanley

Kunitz, Robert Lowell. In England, *the only poet who promises greatness is Ted Hughes, and he has been writing the same poem all his life.* Hughes's images and narrative exemplified what should be our aim, the *New Imagism... Poets have talked about lean elms and giant oaks, but let's look at the goddam leaves under a microscope and see how and where and why the sap has moved through the veins.* He and I should write a critical book about postwar poetry, *our messianic book, to point to the new direction which poetry is going to take – the new direction being what we want it to be. I want our generation of writers to be truly a great generation.* To promote our credo, we were to publish a joint collection with Johnson and Fuller, start a magazine, found a publishing house. In our spare moments, we were to author a book about contemporary cricketers.

Such youthful enthusiasm was irresistible, and still is when I read it half a century later, but the projects did not come to maturity. I was perhaps to blame, lacking the conviction that Ghose had, always being cool about credos and caucuses. The nearest I was to come to changing literary history was when I hit my brakes in Maida Vale just in time to avoid running down a careless pedestrian whom I recognised, in the headlights, as Stephen Spender. Ghose was the engine that drove *UP2* onwards. He spent weeks of his life on its production. It cost him his job, in his father's oriental fashion shop in Regent Street. *This morning I wandered into office at the staggered and staggering hour of 10.30, had an argument with my father and wandered out, fired. He thinks I can't work for him and write at the same time, so he's given me the freedom to starve... I'm using the last two stamps I have. If you don't hear from me shortly, it will simply be lack of funds.*

We put the word out across the universities, and the poems came rolling in. We had a short list by the time I went to Paris; it included Janet Burroway, Malcolm Bradbury, Francis Hope, Julian Mitchell and Dom Moraes. From a cheap hotel on the Left Bank I wrote to Ghose and Johnson, trying to summarise the selection we had made. At Ghose's suggestion, an edited version of my letter formed our editorial preface to the anthology. I had made sniffy remarks about the Movement, such poets as Larkin, Kingsley Amis and John Wain. Wain was talking to White in his Arts Council office when the phone rang. While waiting for the call to end he picked up a book to hand, *Universities Poetry 2*, and scanned through the preface. When White put the phone down Wain asked: 'Who is this weed Anthony Smith?'

A year or two later we organised a poetry conference in London. Patricia Beer, Christopher Middleton, R.S. Thomas, Michael Hamburger, Stevie Smith, Charles Causley and G.S. Fraser came, and so did William Empson, in full beard. He was scheduled to give us a talk at either 11am or 2.15pm, which was disappointingly precise from the author of *Seven Types of Ambiguity*, but I remember no talk, only that late in the conference he stood up and asked: 'I have always found half-rhyme more difficult to bring off than full rhyme. Do people agree with me?' Wain came too, and was engagingly friendly to my wife-to-be, Alison. He cooked up some nonsense with a pork-pie hat he was wearing, trying it on her, flirty fun. I told him my name, and was grateful that he had not remembered the weed's. In later years, when I was compiling programmes for the Royal Shakespeare Company, Wain's book on Shakespeare was among the first I consulted about any play. I liked him, that time I met him, but I still don't like the mean, oh-come-off-it spirit of the Movement.

Pat Rogers, a contemporary at Cambridge who later turned up in Bristol as an English professor, had a poem in *UP2*, and wrote to me about my preface, mostly in approval. He added:

> I've been pushed alongside la Burroway a few times, & the ensuing mood (tho perhaps good for the soul) isn't very comfortable to live through. She seems to be getting better and better, incidentally; extraordinarily concise and having a sort of packed syntax that British don't seem able to achieve – exc. perhaps Davie, whose line that is.

Burroway herself, when *UP* published a selection of her poems as what was to be the first of a pamphlet series, wrote to me: *I don't think I'm in danger of becoming less serious, you know, but I've been at some growing pains to face what you and I and The Others have always said about my preciousness.*

* * *

Among Corpus's annual awards was the Lazard scholarship. Someone graduating in Mod Lang was given a modest bursary for a three-month visit to France, researching and reporting on a topic to be approved. Toward the end of my third year I was encouraged to apply for it. My proposed topic was French cheeses, which the college thought frivolous. (Had I known it then, I might have supported my case with de Gaulle's lament that it is impossible to govern a country which makes 246 cheeses.) That they asked me to come up with another topic suggests, bless them, they already had me in mind as the recipient of the award, on the strength of my Part I results, a 2(i) in both French and Spanish. I proposed again, French broadcasting this time, and was given the bursary. They were probably not pleased when finals results came out and I had got a Third. I was not unhappy with that. My intention had always been to do enough work not to get thrown out. People were swanking that they were starting jobs in industry at £700. I had no eye on any career that might depend on a good degree, so once I was assured of my third year I could settle for being a poet, and answer a finals question on Proust with a clear mind, having read not a word of him.

My friend John Birch was also heading for France after his economics finals, in which he must have done better than I did, since he wound up as British Ambassador in Budapest. I have seen the carousel there which he paid for, as a farewell present to the country. The Foreign Office had told him to get himself to the Touraine, to polish up his French. John had a little Opel, in which we drove down. Well, he drove; I had not yet taken the test, though Lawson Hill had several times let me drive us home from Cambridge, with L-plates. I stayed with Birch for a day or two, we skinny-dipped in the Cher, then I headed to Paris to start my research. I went to RTF, told them what I was doing, and they arranged for me to meet M. Oulif, their head of public relations. He sat me down in his office and talked fluently for ninety minutes. I took it all down, and that, effectively, was my report written, a week into the summer. I did do a bit of listening to the radio, but nothing more keen-eyed and journalistic than that. I would have been more stretched if I'd been researching cheese. I assume that my report was acceptable, when I presented it months later. The point, after all, was to enable the Lazard scholar to immerse himself in French culture, and that I surely was about to do, for more like six months than three, not to mention two novels with a French setting I would write later, and a libretto adapted from Molière, and numerous visits to France over the years. I am in Arles as I write this.

So here I was in Paris in early July, with a summer ahead of me and enough to live on, frugally. I wanted to get to Provence – I forget what I'd heard about it – and hoped to persuade Sarah Lee to come and stay for a holiday. First, though, I had a curiosity to see something of Spain, where I had never been, despite studying the language. In my final *delta* I had published a very good article by Brian Way about the early novels of Hemingway. I'd thought

Hemingway ought to read this, and as I didn't know how to find out his address I just put it in an envelope marked *Ernest Hemingway, Cuba*, and posted it to the island where Fidel Castro had just taken over. After reading Way's article I had read *Fiesta*, which is a damn fine influence on any young writer's prose. Now, in Paris, I wondered when the fiesta de San Fermín took place. A travel agency checked it and told me: it begins tomorrow. I bought a railway ticket to Pamplona and travelled that night.

All the hotels and pensions were full for the week. Someone at the railway station was touting, and took a bunch of us to a convent, not far to walk from the city centre. I have no recollection of sleeping there, though I must have found my way back a few times. *Durante San Fermín, nadie duerme.* (Or *nessun dorma.*) Amid the 24/7 party that the fiesta is I met a Mexican called Al Carlos. We were talking about Hemingway and he said he's here, you know? I said, you're joking. He said, no, he's here. All over town there were posters for San Fermín, with the quote *Fiesta condenadamente fina – Ernest Hemingway.* Several grizzled Americans with blue-check shirts open to reveal grey chest hair had to stop growling what they thought of the bulls this year and line up behind each other to hide. The real Papa was back, the first time since 1933, and the last time. Al said, do you want to meet him? I said, you're joking. He said, no, I know him. Al was one of the Mexicans I've met who don't lie, he did know Hemingway and took me next morning to the Bar Choko to meet him.

I asked Hemingway did you get the magazine I sent you? He'd got it a week before, and liked the article. He said, sit down, have a drink, and I sat with him on the terrace of the bar, overlooking the plaza. A Spaniard staggered past holding a giant tortoise on his head. There were about a dozen people around the big table, including Hemingway's fourth wife, Mary, and the bullfighter Antonio Ordóñez. Young American men frequently came up to say hi Papa, and offer him a swig from their new bota, which would taste of rancid goat, and then ask him to sign the skin. He was polite to them. On behalf of the Pamplona fiesta he wasn't going to be Hemingway-rude to people, but he was curt, he didn't want them to hang around, and it would have been the same for me, how do you do, nice to meet you, kindly bugger off, if it weren't for Brian Way's article. I sat next to him quietly for an hour or two, with little to add to the conversations around the table. Hemingway himself spoke as he wrote, in short, declarative sentences. 'My name's Hemingstein,' I heard him tell somebody. 'We Jews should stick together.' I fancied that I detected something sad in his demeanour, but what could I know on a first meeting? He held himself straight in his chair. I told him that I was writing poetry, and he said that was a good way to start. I remember no more, except that as we broke up he was shouting to someone: 'Get the bugger down to Málaga for my birthday.'

I ran in the *encierro*. You vault the barricade just before 7 a.m. and wait for a rocket to signal that the bulls have been released, a mile away. They are on their way to where they will wait until it's time for the fights *a las cinco de la tarde*; there is no overnight accommodation for them at the ring, hence they are penned a couple of miles away the previous evening. In the crowd next to me was a short, swarthy chap who looked as though he might be a veteran of this gig, with the red neckerchief and beret that we had all acquired. I said something to him in Spanish. He replied: 'Ah'm sorry, Ah don't speak Spanish, Ah'm over here on a Fulbright.' When the rocket went off, so did I. I may have been close to Roger Bannister's record. You get to the ring, then wait in it, over to the side, while the pace of those still entering accelerates, until finally the cows rumble in through rising dust and then the bulls, with a few young men just ahead of their horns, arching their backs. The arena was packed full, with Spaniards who wanted to see the bulls but couldn't afford a ticket for the fight in the afternoon. The idea is that the cows, who have done this a thousand times, go straight across the ring into the daytime pen and the bulls follow them, as bulls will.

But one bull hadn't read the script. He veered off from the rest, lowered his horns and came charging at where we were lining the barricades three-deep. I remember at one point I had a hand on top of the barricade but couldn't climb over because someone else had planted his shoe on my shoulder. I glanced behind to see whether it was about my turn to receive a *cornada*, but the bull had changed his mind. He followed his fellows into the pen and the gate was closed, and twenty thousand Spaniards were holding their temples in mirth at the sight of fifty gringos fighting to get out of an empty ring. Afterwards, everyone plays at bullfighter with a large, bad-tempered steer with muffled horns, who can give you a nasty knock.

I wrote a piece about my week in Pamplona and sent it to Bernardine, whose father published it in his magazine. It was the first writing I was paid for, £5, and later Bernard Wall invited me to write again for him. I was pleased with myself for the scoop on Hemingway, until I got home, in late autumn. Dad had saved a page from the *News Chronicle* for me. James Cameron had been in Pamplona, too, and he'd been up in the mountains with Hemingway when the car ran out of petrol just short of the descent back into town. Papa emptied his hip-flask of vodka into the tank, and that took them to the slope down to town. At least my scoop had been outscooped by a great journalist. Twenty years later I met James Cameron and ruefully told him that story.

* * *

A girl in Cambridge had told me she would be spending the summer working in Avignon at the *Syndicat d'initiative*, so I headed there. She might be company, at least. They had never heard of her. I explained that I was looking for a place to rent for a couple of months. They suggested I try around Mormoiron. Take that bus to Carpentras, then ask again. I wound up at the Hôtel du Centre in Mormoiron, an amusing name for a little guest house in a small, dusty Provençal village. I asked one or two people about finding somewhere to rent, but got nowhere. I wasn't feeling good, alone. Sarah wouldn't commit to coming out to join me, and she never did.

We Centristes ate our supper on a terrace outside the hotel, and one evening a well-dressed woman at the adjoining table, eating with a teenage boy, spoke to me, since for the first time in several evenings we had shared glances. She said 'You look terribly English.' I answered 'I am terribly English.' She laughed. We'd got off on the right foot. She was Jeanette Friedli, a shrink from Zürich, where her husband was a heart surgeon. The boy was her nephew. She told me she was clearing out a château they had just bought nearby. Would I like to see it? The next day she drove me and the boy in her blue Bentley, glinting in the Midi sun (*to-fro tender trambeams truckle at the eye*, wrote Hopkins), to the nineteenth-century Château de St-Laurent. The boy sat down at a wonky-legged piano and played Chopin. There was a room full of shelves of manuscripts in loose cardboard files. I nosed among them, and all that I read was hand-written book reviews. The old bloke who'd lived there and had died, who had been seen every Thursday riding his basketed bike into Mormoiron for provisions, had apparently spent decades reading and reviewing, for himself. Helping Mme Friedli to clear the place were two East German refugees, Dieter and Manfred, both of them with the ambition to write. She told me they were living at an ancient château on top of a hill, where the châtelaine welcomed young artists to stay. She should take me there.

What happened after that I used in my second published novel, *Zero Summer*. If you read the book, which is self-indulgent, too many notebook jottings folded in like whipped egg-white, you wouldn't have much trouble sorting the fiction from the fabulous fact. Pretty well everything about Marie and Robert (his real name was Sidney Jayewardene) and the château and the village goings-on are from life. The stuff about Muriel, and the climactic episode parodying *The Bacchae*, are made up, for a story's sake. One thing you can say in favour of the book is that a remark that in 1916 Joyce, Lenin, Jung and Tzara were all in Zürich and what if they'd met at the Cabaret Voltaire? was the seed of Stoppard's play *Travesties*. With typical courtesy he asked for my permission to use the conjunction, hardly my literary property, one evening when we were driving across the Cotswolds. After I'd seen the play, I asked what happened to Jung? 'I couldn't work him in,' Stoppard said. 'Too much.'

In Mormoiron I'd started writing a first novel, which the world can be grateful I never got halfway through. Sidney read parts of it, and encouraged me to keep going. He was an educated and fascinating man, half-Sri Lankan. When you offered to shake hands, he had a trick of twisting his left hand out to you, because he had lost fingers on the right hand in a shooting accident. At the outbreak of war he had left an engineering course at London University and offered himself to the British Army as a multilingual spy. They said No, you're not English enough. So he tried the French Foreign Legion, but they said No, you have French nationality. He wound up spying for the French Resistance, and met Marie when he used Blauvac as a hideaway. When Jayewardene died, Richard Hawkins and I tried to place an obit of him, but none of the London papers knew who he was, so he could not be of interest to anyone.

Bernardine read the unfinished novel and said helpful things, but also asked why didn't I write fiction in the satirical style in which I talked to her. She followed her precept by writing two novels with something of the lovely sardonic play of her conversation. Ghose's advice was 'write it as though you were writing a letter to an intimate friend'. I've tried that, starting a novel with Dear –, addressing whomever I was in love with. It has never worked. The crafting of a story is at odds with the digressiveness of conversation, which is what a letter is, an uninterruptible half of a conversation. Philip Hobsbaum also gave me some notes on that first shot. A few years later I reciprocated with some comments on a new, long poem of his, about Chopin. He took my critical remarks so badly that we ceased corresponding for 50 years, until just before his death. I am glad we made it up. His was a generous, prickly soul, in the line of Leavis.

I went on writing the novel once I was installed at the Château de Blauvac, where I stayed until November. It is a fourteenth-century country château, built as a hunting lodge for the Avignon Pope. It stands on top of a hill within the curve of the Basses-Alpes, like a nail fallen from a horseshoe. I found a spot near a spring where I sat every day to enjoy the vast, quiet, bee-humming view across to Mont Ventoux, in the endless summer days of 1959, scented with rosemary and thyme and pine needles, and dream of what a writing career I would have. Our châtelaine, known by the name she had assumed as a water-colourist in Paris in the 1920s, Marie Bonheur, was a child-like, whimsical 60-something, who now created appliqué tapestries on knight-and-damsel themes. Her three boxes were: young, creative, English, so I ticked them all. Manfred and Dieter, with whom I shared outhouse rooms against the garden wall, ticked only two, and had to chop trees down for her, whereas I was required only to fetch water from the spring once a day to make the Earl Grey tea she liked to share with me, pouring it from an oriental teapot. She knew that between the three of us we had only a few francs to rub together, and every evening at seven o'clock a cry crossed the garden, her manservant calling *Potage pour les pauvres poètes!* and we went over to collect our bowls and toasted bread.

Otherwise, I lived on small snacks bought from the shop outside the gate, lavender honey and fried eggs. My Aunt Lucy wrote to me: *I don't know what you're eating out there. Don't expect they have baked beans in France. Eggs, I expect. Don't eat too many eggs. Eggs binds you up.* I thought my diet would be fortified when the postman brought me a parcel from Sarah. I hid in my room to open it. She had found me some Chinese chocolate-coated bumble-bees from Fortnum's.

Marie had an acquaintance with Edith Sitwell, and asked me for some poems to send her. The Dame's response was that I should go on writing. I wonder if she told others that they should stop. I did go on. I would have done in any case, but by now I knew that I felt confined by the single voice of poetry and wanted the space, the multiple voices, of fiction, which later extended to writing for the stage. Marie asked me to do French translations of some of my poems, and they were published, both languages side-by-side as in Loeb editions, in a Provençal literary magazine. She initiated a laureateship, and made me wear a laurel crown at the village fête, of which she was the queen.

In later years, on one of my many return visits after I had started working in Bristol, my friend Derek Balmer was acclaimed laureate for his paintings. During the drive there, he had grumbled Eeyoreishly: 'It's all right for you, all you need is a pad and pencil, but I need paints and brushes and canvases and an easel and whatnot, and I can't get it all in my car.' He had intended to do just sketches, but Marie offered him a couple of turned canvases and other materials he needed, and he wound up doing two fine paintings of Blauvac, one of which hangs over my desk at home. Marie looked at them with admiration, then uttered a sentence which contained all the key words in her lexicon, *Youth, Beauty, Truth, Creativity, English,* and ended by telling Derek that he owed her 75 nouveaux francs for the materials. I tell that story in great fondness for her. She struggled to keep the fabric of her ancient house intact, and as a waged man I used to make a contribution when I visited her.

In the aroma of Earl Grey, one of the topics she and I talked about was Oscar Wilde. She showed me a black cane with a silver knob engraved 'Oscar', and told me how it had come to her. When Wilde was dying beyond his means, in Paris, he gave a token to each of the friends around him who remained loyal. The cane he gave to an *artiste dramatique*, René Véron. In Paris twenty-five years later, Marie had been a friend of Véron, and he passed the cane on to her, with a note explaining how he had acquired it. Another forty-five years on, Marie was dying, and she told Sidney to get the cane to me, with the note. I have tried checking the story on the internet. René Véron is a shadowy figure. There was an Alexandre René Véron in Paris at the right time, but he died in 1897. Hmm. Marie was always full of fantasies; or maybe my memory of what she told me has rusted. Nevertheless, I have no reason to doubt the cane was indeed Oscar's. I am just over six feet tall, but it is a cane for somebody taller, which Oscar was. I have seen a photograph of him in the 1890s with what looks exactly like the same cane. There is Véron's (undated) note, which I have, and the engraved name. None of that is foolproof, and I don't know if DNA tests would apply, but the final credential is that nobody in the story had, as far as I know, any reason to make it up.

When I am dying, to whom shall the cane pass? I have been tempted to hand it to Stoppard, in return for fifty years of generous friendship, since he loves Wilde as much as Marie did and I do. But he is only a year younger than I am, and besides, he already owns many wonderful mementoes. My late editor at Weidenfeld and Nicolson, Christopher Falkus, once asked me to sell my copy of Plum Warner's magnificent *Imperial Cricket* to Antonia Fraser for £150, because she wanted to give it to Harold Pinter as a present. I was worse than broke, but I rejected the offer. Nothing against Pinter, but why should famous people own all the best things? I'd acquired the book honestly, by stealing it, from the shelves behind me at the *Western Daily Press* when I was quitting in protest (see 1963). I would not be getting a gold watch, and in any case, the paper was planning to dump all its library.

Manfred led me to a gypsy café in Avignon. Plastic tables, plastic chairs, beige-tiled floor, chrome counter, a dull joint in a dull corner of town, nobody else there, except over in the corner was a huddle of gypsies, drinking. After a while one of them put a coin in the jukebox, which played flamenco, and a crone with three black teeth in the hole of her mouth rose to perform a straight-backed dance, all flaring skirts and arms twirling and stamped feet and flashing eyes, while the others clapped the rhythm. After it, Manfred and I paid the barman to take a carafe of wine over to them, which they acknowledged with smiles. Twenty minutes later she danced again. We clapped her, and smiled. Then a handsome young man of about twenty, in a red shirt and black trousers, walked slowly across to stand in front of where we were sitting. With a charming smile, he lifted his shirt to show us the pistol stuck in his belt. We left quickly, with charming smiles. My novelist friend Derek Robinson has this advice for novice novelists: *When in doubt, have a man come through the door with a gun in his hand.*

* * *

Marie threw a leaving party for me. We drank wine from Sidney's grapes harvested that autumn. On the night train from Avignon to Paris my stomach became a vat, taking over the interrupted process of fermentation. I groaned into a chemist's shop near my cheap hotel. The man had a good memory. The last time he'd seen this rosbif I'd just left England and, as I always am when I start travelling, was constipated. Now, half a year later, I had the opposite problem. He did his best to hide his chortles. I lay in the hotel in a fever for two days. Fortunately a girl I knew was working in Paris, I got word to her somehow, and she nursed me. The following year we started to go out together, dancing in her high-ceilinged Kensington flat to George Shearing playing *The Folks Who Live On The Hill.*

There will be girls in this story, but I am not going to join up the polka-dots. I have promised myself it is pointless to write a memoir unless I do it with honesty, but you don't need me to name names pedantically where I do not intend to introduce people to you as characters. The years before one gets married are likely to resemble a protracted excuse-me dance. It is the way in which evolution manages its complicated narrative. Many of my Corpus friends had found partners by the time we left, and some of them married. David Harter soon married a very pretty girl from Oxford called Caryl Churchill, who told me she intended to write for a living. I knew enough by then to think, heaven help you. As far as she was concerned I didn't know enough, as it turned out.

Dancing to Shearing in bedsitland, having my hair cut at Trumpers, I toyed with a daft image of myself as one of the fast set around the West End. Equally daft was the lure of being a club drone. Oxbridge graduates were enticed with a £1 fee for the first year of membership of the Oxford and Cambridge Club in Pall Mall. I fell for it, like a dim trout, and was charmed, as I always have been on visits to other clubs, by the Edwardian upholstery and the timeless smell of rich cooking and cigars. Its appeal to me was the same dream as my Compton Mackenzie illusion when I started at Cambridge. It would be a waste of money for me to become a member of one of those clubs. Whenever I am in London, I do what I've come to do and head back home to Bristol. In the O & C, I glanced at the face of a small man at the urinal next to me, and had to stop myself from blurting out my admiration for Clement Attlee. There is a time and a place, especially a place. In the gents' men usually affect solipsism. Not Tories, perhaps. When Butler, Home, Heath and Hailsham were in contention for the Tory leadership in 1964, a senior party member was asked how these things were resolved, in the absence of a constitutional process. 'Well,' he said, 'it works like this. Suppose you were having a pee next to someone you weren't sure about, you might try saying "This chap Heath is stabbing the party in the back, don't you think?" and from his response you could gauge how the wind was blowing.'

Another lark in the West End was the Jermyn Street Turkish baths, to which Lawson Hill introduced me. On my first visit I was physically wiped out by the last, hottest room. A giant attendant asked me if I would like a massage. I nodded, weakly. He worked me on his slab, then put me in the shower and turned on icy water. I jumped out, he was waiting for it, caught me in mid-air and replaced me. When it was over he wrapped me in a towel and carried me to my cubicle, like a baby. 'You want drink?' he asked. 'Hemlock,' I ordered. 'Hmmm?' 'Oh very well, tea.' Back out in Jermyn Street I could have cleared the buildings in a leap, easily, even carrying the Olivetti Lettera 22 I had bought at Ryman's, along the street, with money Dad gave me, and which at once became the most precious object in my life, the poppy for my fantasy. On his deathbed, Henry James asked to hear the sound of his Remington being worked.

I went for job interviews, guided by the Cambridge Appointments Board. My adviser there, I was delighted to find, was the former Kent cricketer J.G.W. Davies. The last time I'd met him he had been a beerbottle-stopper at cover point in my back-garden game of kneel-down cricket. The *Reader's Digest* told me what I'd have to do on their Condensed Books staff. 'First, you read the book. Next, you read it again. Then again, and again, until you can see the spine of the story. When you see that spine, you hew to it. You understand what I'm saying? You just hew to that spine.' The *News Chronicle* interviewed me sympathetically but made no offer; I knew they were not in good shape, having lost many readers over their opposition to the Suez invasion. Applying for the BBC trainee scheme, I was turned down at the final board. Next it was the editor's office at the *Sunday Express*; John Junor seemed to find my jib not badly cut, and sent me out on a trial job. For their series *Would You Like Your Son To Be A...* I had to fill in *Poet?* and get an interview with John Betjeman.

Betjeman told me to meet him at his London home, 43 Cloth Fair, opposite Barts Hospital. I was prompt. The first ring produced nothing. The second brought a light on behind the front door. When he opened it his head was three feet above the ground, sideways. 'Come in, come in, I was just having a quick bath.' He was naked, pink and dripping. All he had brought with him from the bathroom was a small towel, which he used to cover his tits. I followed the future laureate bum up the stairs. He waved me into a sitting-room. 'Go in there, pour yourself a sherry and enjoy the William Morris hand-blocked wallpaper.' I did so. He next appeared in the doorway capering, in a pair of striped combinations. 'Aren't they wonderful? They used to belong to Henry James.' He disappeared, and returned in a three-piece suit. I asked him how come he had a pair of combinations that used to belong to Henry James. 'Oh, quite simple. I'm a fellow of All Souls, and so was he. When he died' (to the sound of his Remington) 'he left lots of his stuff to the college, I asked the warden if it would be all right if I took the combinations, and he said "Of course, John".' At this point, had I been a sharper journalist, my next question would have been: 'Tell me, how vain do you think a man has to be in order to bequeath his underwear to All Souls, Oxford?' Betjeman charmed me, as he charmed millions. From his own experience in journalism he knew what I needed from him. He told me that if he had his life again he would choose to be a station master on a Dorset branch line, so that he could spend most of his time writing poems, not scribbling for a living. He gave me a lift to Trafalgar Square in his taxi, and when I moved to Bristol wrote to congratulate me: 'As that good artist Ld Methuen said to me, "Bath is Bruges and Bristol is Ghent. I like Ghent".' He gave me introductions to several people in Bristol, including 'a splendid fellow called Michael Croucher', with whom I would find myself working four years later.

I handed the piece in at the *Sunday Express*, and took a girlfriend out to dinner. When I told her I was hoping to get a job with the Beaverbrook Press, she said that if I took it she would never go out with me again. Her family were distinguished West Country Liberal people. I started to have second thoughts. I was waiting to hear from Junor when another interview came up. A.D. Peters, generally credited with having transformed the profession of literary agent back in the 1920s, was a straight-talking former naval officer. 'I don't expect to live much longer,' he told me, 'and I need someone to join me in time to learn the job.' A few days later I got a letter from him. He said he liked what he'd seen of me, but he'd appointed Michael Sissons, because Sissons had had a year's experience already in New York. So Peters was sending me to join the publisher William Collins. I just had to go along there and be interviewed, and that would be that. I was interviewed by Wm Collins himself, and then at greater length by Mark Bonham-Carter.

By now, buoyed up by Peters, I had written to Junor saying that I was no longer applying for a job with him. I waited for a confirmation from Collins, and waited, and meanwhile Dad indicated that he would be glad of some input from me to the family budget. At Cambridge I had spent more than my State-funded allowance, mostly on State Express 555, and the bills went to Dad, so my conscience was tender. I got a Christmas job delivering parcels for the Post Office. A little old lady answered the door nervously, her eyes widened, and she said 'For me? But I never get parcels'. At other houses I was watched from next door, through enviously parted curtains, as I delivered the parcel.

Early in January I told Eric White that I still hadn't heard from Collins, and didn't understand why not. He told me there was a crisis at the firm. Raleigh Trevelyan had converted Mrs Collins to Catholicism overnight, and Presbyterian Wm was so shocked that no decisions at all were being made. I was a victim, probably along with several hopeful authors. 'Come to supper,' White said. 'I've got an idea. Bring Sarah.' Sarah was staying in Hampstead, near Eric, but was about to return to Bristol, where she had grown up, the daughter of Sir Desmond Lee, headmaster of Clifton College and later of Winchester. White, a Bristolian himself, beamed down his dining table at the two of us. 'It seems to me, Anthony, that it might be agreeable for you if you were to find a job in Bristol.' Simpering from us two. 'I will arrange an interview for you with Richard Hawkins at the *Bristol Evening Post*.'

I saw Sarah home. She was cool to me on the doorstep, nervous, I guess, of what my moving to Bristol might imply. She watched me go. Fifty yards up the street I shouted back a proposal: 'Marry me!' What we bitterly regret is what we did not do, not what we did. She shut the door and didn't answer. She would write to me some time later. *That is not the explanation I intended; all explanations seem irrelevant. This sort of letter seems absurd... Please have no hard feelings... Pray for fine weather...* The language falls into pentameters at heightened moments. In any case, I knew the explanation. My friend her brother Martin told me. Her mother had advised her: 'Sarah, Anthony is a charming boy, but you won't think of marrying him, will you?' Sarah had taken her mother's advice, which might have been sound. I got on famously with Sarah's mother, Lady Lee, who would clasp me to her bosom, and enjoyed a good joke. She once addressed a crowd of us at Corpus, 'You young people are not promiscuous enough', using the old-fashioned, more innocent meaning of promiscuous, advising us not to be in any hurry to pair off. But she could see I had a deal of growing-up to do before I might make a decent husband. I moved to Bristol on January 20th, 1960, to work for Richard Hawkins's cat Beastie.

5

Arts Page

SARAH MET ME AT TEMPLE MEADS. SHE HAD BOOKED A BED AND BREAKFAST for me. Soon I found a bed-sitting room in Beaufort Road, and lived there most of that year, tapping the chimney to rid it of hooting pigeons, reading a lot (*Lolita, Middlemarch,* Teilhard de Chardin), eating tinned soup, bread and cheese. A boy raised in a working-class family learned nothing about cooking the food he ate, or did much else by way of chores. In a neighbouring room Mr Pickering proudly showed me a boat he was building. It was already far too big to get out through his doorway or window. Sarah was working as an occupational therapist. My room was near where she was living, but she allowed me only occasional, brief meetings. *One must have a glimmer of hope in order to be gloomy,* Stendhal observed. Soon the glimmer went out. Thanks all the same, Eric. It had been a nice idea. My life was lonely for a time. I would parody that period in my first published novel.

I had visited Bristol in my YHA cycling days, but on my first Monday morning as a journalist got lost, trying to find Silver Street at 7.45am, and was told off for being late. I was put on the sports desk, which suited me, to be trained as a sub-editor. Scraps of copy paper in canisters popped down the pneumatic tube, I corrected them and marked them up for the printer, and sent them back up the tube. A few months later I was moved to the features department, still learning how to sub, though now occasionally allowed to write a feature piece, and later on some leaders. One of my jobs was to put together the women's page. One day we had a six-inch space to fill, and I suggested to Daphne Hubbard, the women's editor, that I put in a recipe for aubergines in tomato sauce, which I had been given in France after enjoying them. In 1960 aubergines were exotic. She told me to go ahead, so I found the notes that a French woman had scribbled down for me, and translated them. I committed the solecism of rendering laurier as laurel. Daphne went nuts, understandably, since anyone cooking with laurel might kill their family: 'When the *Daily Express* did this, they had to get the BBC to broadcast warnings all the rest of the day.' The *Bristol Evening Post* could not expect the BBC to be so obliging (no local radio in those days). All we could do was black-surround a front-page warning in the later editions, and hope that nobody had tried my recipe for breakfast.

I was probably the only sub there with a degree. When the news editor spotted me reading a book, I was outed as the office intellectual. Antonio and his Spanish Ballet, Yehudi Menuhin, Ravi Shankar, Ossip Zadkine, all of them I was sent to scrutinize and write eight pars. I became the regular reviewer of exhibitions. I knew as little about the visual arts as I did about ballet. If it was a show of a dead artist, I could confect something from the catalogue introduction. When a living artist was present at the opening, I simply interviewed them. That was how I first met Derek Balmer. It was also how I met Julian Trevelyan, just the once. His Arnolfini show included lithographs of Cambridge colleges, and I mentioned to him that I had been at Corpus, one of those pictured. I wrote a warm review of the show, and got a call from the gallery: there was something there for me to pick up. When I did, it was a print of the Corpus litho, left for me by the artist. If at the end of your life you can reckon you are about all-square in the commerce of kindnesses, you can die feeling decent.

The Bristol Museum and Art Gallery announced the opening of a travelling show of Rembrandts. I went along to the press view, at lunchtime, and found half the walls empty. 'Not many Rembrandts travelling, then?' I asked Hans Schubart, the director. He told me there were more on the way; they had all been sent from London by train, and one carriage must have been shunted into the wrong siding. I wandered back to the office and told the news editor: 'I can't do that Rembrandt review yet. Some of them have gone missing on their way from London.' Only when I saw his braces expanding did I, no newshound, realise how it sounded to him, and I pretended that I had been incredibly cool. Too late. The chief crime reporter dashed to his typewriter, where he was helped by a young freelance who happened to be in the office, Tom Stoppard. Their report led the next edition: *REMBRANDTS GO MISSING IN BRISTOL*. By the final edition it was one paragraph on page 23: *Missing Rembrandts found.*

For social life I often went to London for a weekend, attending the Group meetings, and catching up with friends, especially Ghose. I introduced Ghose and Johnson to the Group. The latter was too maverick to become a regular, but Ghose had poems in *A Group Anthology*, edited by Lucie-Smith and Hobsbaum (OUP, 1963), as I did. *Universities Poetry 2* had been well received in the lit-crit pages. *The New Statesman* remarked that the Labour Party should be supporting that kind of thing. With Eric White's backing, we (without John Fuller, who had apparently lost interest) formed ourselves into a committee, with Arts Council representatives, to oversee annual renewals of the anthology, appointing two new editors each year. It ran on to *UP6*, and would include such student poets as Seamus Heaney, Derek Mahon and Ian Hamilton, not to mention Bernardine Wall and Caryl Churchill.

The last two and I also featured in a special Under-25 issue of Bernardine's father's magazine, *Twentieth Century*, along with Margaret Drabble, David Leitch and Dennis Potter. In what I wrote there I inadvertently did myself an important favour; I mentioned that I was at work on a first novel (still imagining that the poor thing I had flogged at Blauvac had any spark of life in it), and received letters from editors at Chapman and Hall and Chatto and Windus, who said they liked the way I wrote and would be interested to see the manuscript of my novel when it was finished. It was not till four years later that I had any words ready, of a quite different novel, and then I sent it first to Gillon Aitken at Chapman and Hall, since he had been quicker to write to me. My *Twentieth Century* piece also got the nod in a review by John Wain, who still had not remembered the name of the weed, or perhaps was remarkably forgiving, while the *Daily Herald* saw it and asked me to write a young person's take on any subject I chose. When I read it in the paper the subs had greatly improved it.

The Arts Council had their own box at Sadler's Wells. At White's invitation I joined him there for the first performance of Michel Saint-Denis's production of Stravinsky's *Oedipus Rex*. Afterwards there was a party upstairs for the cast and top brass audience. As the Arts Council's man, White felt he should stand near the entrance door and congratulate the cast when they arrived. He knew them by name. Most of them, even after showering, were still sweating, having spent the evening in the spotlights under the heavy rubber masks Saint-Denis chose for the chorus. The last to arrive, with his wife and child, was a singer whom White did not know. Beads of sweat were running down his chin. White was sympathetic. 'It must have been incredibly hot under those masks.'

The singer answered: 'I wasn't wearing a mask.'

'Oh,' said White, 'where were you on the stage, then?'

'I was the one who went off blind at the end.'

White had forgotten that the lead was sung by an Australian making his British début.

Noël Coward was at the party. He spent it leaning elegantly against a pillar, taking a passing canapé now and then, and talking to no one, as far as I could see. I expect people were afraid to go and ask him if he had enjoyed the show, for fear of being scorched by a bolt of repartee.

Another glamorous operatic evening was arranged for me by Martin Lee. We went to stay near Aldeburgh with the Gathorne-Hardy family, friends of the Lees, and were at the opening night of Britten's *A Midsummer Night's Dream*. When we arrived, at dusk, one of the Gathorne-Hardy sons was sitting in a deckchair on a grass badminton court. He apologised for not rising to greet us, but he was preoccupied; now and then, he took a tiny pebble from a bowlful and threw it into the net. He was studying bats. They could be enticed into the net by the pebbles, which they swooped upon as something for supper. He stroked the head of a bat peeping out from his cupped hand.

I was shown to a small, cluttered room for the night, and was woken early by someone banging drawers. When I opened my eyes, the first thing I saw was the bare backside of a stout man bending over to pick something up. It belonged to the Earl of Cranbrook, the head of the family, who had not been at home the previous evening when we arrived, so this was the first view I was offered of the aristocracy. How should I have addressed it – Your Grace? He noticed that he had woken me up. 'Terribly sorry,' he said, 'but this is my dressing-room, do you see?' At dinner that evening one of the guests was David Astor, editor of *The Observer*. Perhaps I missed a trick by not introducing myself as a young arty journalist. *Gissa job.*

Richard Hawkins sent me to report back to him on a weekend conference in Oxford about provincial journalism. I remember a sparkling talk by Hugh Cudlipp, and the editor of *Burke's Peerage* inviting us to consider whether journalists should wear gloves. Wandering around Oxford I struck up with Peter Wollen, who would later marry Bernardine's cousin Laura Mulvey, daughter of the limping aunt, and write for Antonioni, but was at present squatting in a condemned house in Paradise Square. He told me that when the tip-off came from their deep throat in the council housing department that an inspection was due, a herd of artists and poets would emerge, carrying their canvases and manuscripts, and return later in the day when the inspector had gone. But most of all I remember meeting Frank Singleton, editor of the *Bolton Evening News*. He was married, with a daughter, but hedged his bets. He took me to Shillingford in his chauffeured limousine and over oysters and lobster propositioned me. When I declined he offered me a job in Bolton at a higher wage than I was getting in Bristol. He was a Pickwickian figure, with white curls, and in a high voice, like Gerard Hoffnung's, spoke the most orotund English I have heard. I made it clear that I was greatly enjoying his company, and his hospitality, but he was on a loser here. He took it calmly, rode with me back to Oxford, showed me how to break into Wadham after hours, and we remained friends for the rest of his life.

Before the war, during which he worked in intelligence with Empson, he had published a novel or two. 'I had had some success with my first book, and people told me I ought to take on a literary agent, and that a young chap called Peters could be the fellow for me. So I rang Peters, told him that I was thinking of employing him, and arranged to give him lunch at the Reform Club. I arrived a few minutes late, and the lobby was empty, no sign of the fellow. So I went to the bar, and I could hardly get inside the door, it was so crowded. Everyone seemed to be trying to talk to some chap penned up by the bar. When I asked who he was they said "A.D. Peters". I was reduced to sending in pink gins from the periphery.'

Another story he told me I have always suspected was about himself, but he said it concerned a contemporary of his, who had some success with his first novel, dashed off a second, and sent it to Faber and Gwyer. He heard nothing for months, and wrote to enquire if they had received the manuscript. Oh yes, they said, do come in and let's talk about it. He was ushered into the presence of the editor, Mr T.S. Eliot. After some throat-clearing, the young novelist asked Eliot if he had read through the manuscript. Yes, Eliot said, I have read it, yes. Ah, and, er, will you be publishing it? Eliot replied: 'If it is your desire that we publish it then yes, I can assure you that we shall be doing so. However, it had been our impression that it was your intention to write good novels.'

When he was dying in a Bolton hospital, Singleton gave his wife a note he had written in a shaky hand, and asked her to make sure it was posted to me. It is pinned above the desk where I am writing this. It says: *Never can, never will forget you.* It is all the more touching for being addressed to *Dearest ~~Paul~~ Anthony.*

* * *

In December 1960, at the age of twenty-five, I lost my virginity at last, to a friend from my school days, and was invited by Richard Hawkins to inaugurate a weekly arts page in the *Western Daily Press*, a morning broadsheet which, at its own request, had recently been taken over by the *Evening Post* group. The first of those events I remember with eyes closed in embarrassment. The arts page would turn out much better.

The *WDP* was one of the few provincial morning papers left in Britain. It asked the Bristol United Press to take it over because it could not survive independently. Its paltry circulation figure was kept secret even from the hands who ran the printing machine, where the rev-counter had been taped over. The best estimate was that it was selling fourteen thousand copies a day. In April 1960 the BUP took control, and moved the paper into the same building as the *Evening Post*. Richard Hawkins, editorial director of the firm and scion of the family that founded the *Post* in the 1930s, was given a free hand to revitalize the old paper. His most successful move was to appoint a new editor, Eric Price, a foul-mouthed former sergeant-major who came from the *Daily Express* and set about making at least the front page indistinguishable from his previous one. People did buy it thinking it was Beaverbrook's paper. Driven by Price, who edited from the subs' table, its circulation rose to seventy thousand within a few years.

But Hawkins, whose chief love was music, had further ideas about what the newspaper should be. The posh London papers had realised that there was a consumer interest in the arts, and their coverage was blossoming. Hawkins felt why shouldn't the *Western Daily Press* have this once a week? Price loathed the idea, but was not yet powerful enough to oppose Hawkins. I was delighted. The work would be closer to my interests. Morning paper working hours, starting after lunch, suited me better than getting up at 7 a.m. And I would be in a position to commission any writers I could attract. Ghose and Johnson were my first thoughts. Once I'd replied yes (please), Hawkins said: 'When you're thinking about what you're going to do on the page I'd like you to give plenty of work to a young local freelance you might have met, called Tom Stoppard.'

I had met Stoppard once, when I had been sent to review a film, *Battle Inferno*.

'Mein Führer, the Sixth Army has collapsed.'

'Don't be sentimental. It was only an army. Set up another one.'

They don't write dialogue like that for Hitler any more. The only other reviewer at the press view was a tall, skinny, loose-lipped lout in a brown suit. A few years later he would have reminded me of Mick Jagger. He was a freelance for the *Evening World* – Bristol still had rival evening papers, even if they had long been in the same ownership, the BUP group. The *World* at that time housed Charlie Wilson, later editor of *The Times*, Brian Barron of the BBC, and Frank Keating and David Foot, both to become distinguished at *The Guardian*. (A Foot note: thirty years later a woman at the University of Texas would publish a critical biography of Stoppard and, neglecting simple homework, averred that David Foot was a pseudonym for Stoppard, on the ground that Foot was one of his favourite names for a character – Inspector Foot 'of the Yard' in *After Magritte*, for instance. Stoppard has always been something of a foot-fetishist in his naming of characters – Birdboot, Dominic Boot... They originate in his remark: 'I've always been attracted to the incompetence of William Boot in Evelyn Waugh's *Scoop*.') The *World* was a better-looking and more amusing paper than the stodgy *Post*, but that did not save it in 1962, when it folded, and the NUJ father of the chapel, John Coe, told the assembled hacks: 'To put it in plain English, the management are presenting us with a *fait accompli*.'

After the film, the cinema manager offered us a pre-lunch glass of sweet sherry in his office. Stoppard and I exchanged a few cagey words, as rival reviewers do, and neither of us felt any desire to meet again. I went back and wrote that the film was no good, then waited to see what the *World* review would say. Just as I thought, he rated it. Provincial jerk.

Now, six months later, I reluctantly rang Stoppard and through gritted teeth told him: 'Mr Hawkins has asked me to start a weekly arts page, and suggested that you might like to contribute, occasionally.' He said he would like to kick off that very week with a piece on the *nouvelle vague* in French cinema. *Mon Dieu*, I thought, I'll have my work cut out knocking that into shape. When it arrived it was knowledgeable and beautifully written. I didn't change a word. Who *was* this provincial jerk?

We ran the arts page together for two years, 1960 to '62, and spent most of our time in each other's company. I told him I'd had him down as a loose-lipped lout, and he replied that he'd figured me as a poncey graduate. We agreed, later, that our first impressions of each other were not far from the mark. We found we shared literary heroes, most of whom had been in Paris between the wars. Both of us intended to give up journalism as soon as possible and earn our living as writers. I saw myself as a novelist with an interest in the theatre, which would take years to fruit, as it turned out. Stoppard was going to write novels. He did write one. In *Lord Malquist and Mr Moon* he builds a baroque fantasy, full of wit, one strand of it deriving from an idle comment I had made to him, that there are days when the first thing you say on waking up is so sharply honed that you know the rest of your day will be endlessly quotable, and that someone ought to found an agency to supply Boswells for hire by the day, who would take it all down as you said it. In the course of writing it, he remarked in a letter to me that *my hero Moon, quite unconsciously, is becoming a Phipps* (the anti-hero of my first published novel). *Weird. Are we seminal or merely seedy?* But by this time he knew the stage was where he most passionately wanted to work. Writing a theatre column, he enjoyed the company of actors, and formed a close friendship with Peter O'Toole, who had recently made his first reputation at the Bristol Old Vic. There were stronger reasons. Theatre was the going thing. Any new play, in London at least, commanded a lot more column inches than most novels. And, Stoppard observed, he liked to imagine having the total attention of an audience. The most gripping play on television, featuring the dearest friends of his, he would abandon if the telephone rang, and he assumed everybody would do the same.

It really helps a writer to have someone around who responds with generosity, and in Stoppard's case with sharp insight into what's going on. His example was of crucial importance to me. I had the benefit of a good education, a head well stocked, but it was taking me time to find my style. He was fizzing with style, in his conversation as well as in his writing. He is exonerated from what Borges observed about some writers who wrote well *but if you talk with them the only thing they tell you is smutty stories or speak of politics in the way that everybody does, so that really their writing turns out to be a kind of sideshow. They had learned writing in the way that a man might learn to play chess or to play bridge.* When Stoppard is talking, or listening, any phrase might flash itself into a line worth using, and plenty have done. He was a joy to interviewers until he grew tired of his own repertory, which he had developed by interviewing himself in his bath before he became interview-worthy.

He lived with Val and Bob Lorraine and their three children in Clifton, in a secluded, wisteria-wrapped Regency house frequented by theatre people. To me, Grosvenor Lodge smelled like a proper home, where cooking was done. The Lorraines asked for no rent, but Stoppard contributed £2 a week for his keep, all found. Even then, it was absurdly cheap. Val, herself an actress, explained that she wanted to help a young writer in whose talent she had confidence. It's a pity she couldn't have put a few quid on him at Ladbroke's.

Among the freelance jobs Stoppard did for the *World* was that of motoring correspondent. It was an imaginative appointment, because he couldn't drive.

'How do you manage it?'

'I go along to the showroom and review the upholstery.'

I needed a car because, as well as editing the arts page, I had been asked to report Somerset county cricket. I bought a 1937 Series E Morris for £60. It was a convertible, but the canvas hood was so torn that I seldom used it. One January day I was driving to London with Stoppard. It was very cold but sunny, and I had the hood down. Beside me, Stoppard was huddled in a fur coat he had borrowed from Val Lorraine, years before fur coats became fashionable for men. Through the Savernake Forest we were talking about the slight impediment that Stoppard's Czech-born mouth has on the letter R.

'I know you can't manage arrrround the rrrrugged rrrrocks, but can't you find a way to place your tongue on your palate so that you can simply produce the rrrr on its own?'

He experimented for a time, and got it. 'Rrrr. Rrrr.' He was pleased.

I realised that beside me I had a man wrapped in a fur skin and snarling 'Rrrr. Rrrr'. When I stopped the car, because it would have been dangerous to drive and laugh so much, he was furious, thinking I had set him up for a cheap joke.

I got my comeuppance one night at Grosvenor Lodge. Thoughtlessly, I rang a friend, and his father growled: 'No, you can't speak to him, he's asleep, do you know what time it is? Two o'clock. Who are you?'

'My name is Brown.'

Stoppard was weak with laughter, that someone called Smith should grab for an alias.

I spent much of my time at Grosvenor Lodge. Neither of us had a television set or any interest in pubs. We ate cinnamon toast, talked about writing, and we played games. Stoppard loves chess, but I usually beat him. Once, when I moved a piece and announced 'check mate', he looked ruefully at me, not the board: 'It must be irritating suddenly to find that you've won. I feel I ought to apologise for interrupting your train of thought.' At ping-pong we would get to deuce, then he would win. Maybe he was better than I was, but discreet.

It was at Grosvenor Lodge that we planned many arts pages. I was the one who was paid a wage but we made sure he got lots of stuff in and a fee for everything he wrote. Sometimes we wanted to include two pieces by him so something by Tomik Straussler would appear. I had a pseudonym as well, Charles Hockley. We discussed not only the contents but also the layouts. *The Observer* had just revolutionised its use of space, photos and typefaces, and become the first quality paper to look black and white, not grey. We learned what we could from it, and tried experiments of our own. Stoppard had a better visual sense than I have. He loved coming up with snazzy ways of designing the big page. Ghose, too, was alert to the look of it, and would write to me in praise or disparagement of the layout.

The arts page ran weekly in the *Western Daily Press* from December 1960 to February 1963. Most of it was written by outside contributors for tiny fees, but a few staff journalists, frustrated by their humdrum everyday work, were pleased to write about their special interests. We heard that a chap working upstairs was trying his hand at radio drama. His name was Charles Wood, and his job was to lay out display ads and do drawings for them. We got to know him, and his actor and teacher pal Peter Nichols, another would-be playwright, who was doing TV scripts. When the page covered the Cheltenham Festival of Literature, Wood came and contributed drawings of Carson McCullers, Kingsley Amis, Romain Gary and Joseph Heller. The city was full of talented arts people, living there, not just passing through (or at school, like John Cleese). Many of the names would not make much of a thud if you dropped them now, but as well as Stoppard, Wood and Nichols, John Arden was holding a fellowship at the university drama department (the first such department in the country), George Brandt was teaching there, and its students included Alan Dossor, now a leading director, and Tim Corrie, the film agent. No doubt there were other students I didn't know who have gone on to make names for themselves.

Until he became a full-time writer, John Hale ran the Bristol Old Vic, where the general manager was Nat Brenner. Nat later ran the theatre school, where he and Rudi Shelley are revered names among the thousands of actors they've taught, including Jane Lapotaire, Greta Scacchi, Jeremy Irons and Daniel Day-Lewis. At the BBC, John Boorman and Michael Croucher were developing a distinctive school of documentary films. Artists, many of them taught or teaching at the college of art, included Paul Feiler, George Tute, Derek Balmer and David Inshaw. Angela Carter and my predecessor editor at *delta*, Christopher Levenson, were involved in an attempt to set up a writers' group. Bristol had its own dance company, its own orchestra. Even Richard Hawkins's chauffeur at the BUP, Keith Floyd, went on to a different sort of celebrity.

Geoffrey Reeves and Michael Kustow were drama postgraduates working for Centre 42, Arnold Wesker's crusade to disseminate the arts through the trades unions. I wrote some enthusiastic pieces about Centre 42 in the arts page. Reeves and Kustow came to the paper and asked to meet me and Stoppard. When we got to the front office, Reeves started, without a how-do-you-do: 'Arnold's interested in you.' We had been contemporaries at Cambridge, where I had reviewed one of his productions (favourably, as luck would have it) but had not met him. Kustow, who would later run the ICA and then be Channel 4's commissioning editor for arts programmes, had been at Oxford. He was at that time the thin, sinisterly silent partner to Reeves's portly red-faced aggressiveness. 'Clarence's murderers,' Richard Ainley, the theatre school principal, called the pair of them. That first meeting would lead to much else. Its immediate result was that Reeves exploited me for lifts, in return for gargantuan meals.

Stoppard interviewed O'Toole and Albert Finney, wrote about the difficulty of staging new plays in provincial theatres, reviewed cinema (Cassavetes, the new British wave, *Breakfast at Tiffany's*), little magazines, and contributed long articles on Arthur Miller, Lenny Bruce, Wesker, Thurber, Mailer, Chandler. Reviews supplied the pegs for many things in the page, and Stoppard did his share of reviewing. Of Colin Wilson, then a black-clad *enfant terrible*, he wrote: *Mr Wilson, a self-confessed genius, once remarked that he would like to be a household name, 'like Shakespeare'. If history proves to be so commodious,* Adrift in Soho *will be remembered as one of the master's lesser works, the* Titus Andronicus *of the Wilson canon, perhaps.* Just occasionally we had the occasion to go out and be reporters. Stoppard used his news skills to examine plans for a new city art gallery in Bristol, the prospects of the Western Theatre Ballet, and why TWW, then the local commercial TV station, had dropped its arts programme.

In one of our special single-issue pages, he and I surveyed the city's meagre provision for the arts (which entailed less outlay than was spent on the upkeep of the Lord Mayor's ceremonial horses), and proposed the formation of a Bristol Arts Trust. To our surprise we fluttered the civic dovecots. Overnight, three committees – academics, businessmen and trades unionists – came into being to promote the idea. That every regional centre should run its own arts budget is a case I have been arguing ever since. That is how it's done in France and Germany, and it is what the Arts Council itself, before it became a canting bureaucracy, had in mind when Stoppard and I ran with it. Then, there was such a swell of support for it in Bristol that it became a Lord Mayor's motion (a rare thing, by tradition unopposed). It was referred to the finance committee for implementation. They dug a hole and buried it. I was told that the main ground of disagreement was that Labour councillors did not like the seating arrangement at the crucial committee meeting. Thirty years later the city council came up with a proposal to support the arts – in effect, to form a Bristol Arts Trust. It got nowhere.

Zulfikar Ghose wrote mostly about poets for us. When Theodore Roethke visited London (and was involved in a punch-up with B.S. Johnson), he befriended Ghose, and the result was a good interview. In one of the earliest pages we carried a new poem by Ted Hughes to his new-born daughter Frieda, beside a lengthy piece by Ghose. In Allen Ginsberg, Ghose detected 'just loud and prolonged shouting'. Robert Graves was in the habit of bringing out a new Collected Poems every year, it seemed. Tired of it, I headlined Ghose's review of the latest volume *Here again are the main points of the Muse.* Johnson was our man in the European avant-garde: Genet, Brecht, Beckett, Joyce. He thought less well of our home-grown avant-garde, notably Michael Horovitz's *New Departures.*

Philip Hobsbaum was a versatile contributor, writing articles on the significance of provincial rep, television drama, literary criticism, the instruments of democracy and the teaching of English, as well as long pieces on William Golding, Angus Wilson, Joyce Cary, Iris Murdoch, Alan Sillitoe, Peter Porter, Peter Redgrove, and Conrad Aiken. When he attacked the novels of C.P. Snow, he received a letter of support from F.R. Leavis:

> It's a relief to be assured that he has been truly dealt with as a novelist. But has anyone ever supposed – really – that he enjoyed a Snow novel? Our Master, perhaps. The classics, though, don't expect to be exhilarated by modern literature. The classics are my enemies and (or have been) Snow's friends at Cambridge.

David Holbrook wrote features about hymns, Dylan Thomas, youth culture. At the time of the *Lady Chatterley* debate, I found myself involved in a correspondence with Holbrook, who wrote to me that Lawrence is:

> ...up the pole. I say the fullness of physical love counts only in the way it pervades the whole sensibility, chiefly the consciousness, afterwards (and beforewards) – it colours all one's being, and its significance is in all the civilized regions of one's being: not least parenthood, family life, one's relationship with one's children and home. Lawrence says NO. Love counts at the level of being, in areas 'which no consciousness could seize'... but then tries to bring them to consciousness!... In Lady C he must over-anxiously try to know and see what goes on in coition. Which you can't do – if it's good coition. You're too busy!

Holbrook was often vilified as a ranting Puritan, but in person he was paradoxical. He came to Bristol to give a reading, and suggested we should meet. When we did, he got out of his van, with his wife and children behind him, and said: 'Hello, is there a good nightclub in Bristol?' I couldn't say, but I did chortle in surprise. 'We live in the country, nothing to go out for,' he told me. 'I thought, I'm spending an evening in a city, I should make the most of what cities can offer.'

Angela Carter, who had just finished an English degree at Bristol, wrote for the page. So did George Macbeth, who would share an obituary page with Carter thirty years later. To the satisfaction of Stoppard and me, he wrote that Hemingway was *the greatest prose writer since the authors of the Gospels.* He concluded his article by remarking *I should wear a black tie if I were told he'd died.* In London a few weeks later, when I met Stoppard on his twenty-fourth birthday, he greeted me by suggesting: 'Let's go and see if George is wearing a black tie.' It was from *A Farewell to Arms* that Macbeth got the title of his collection *The Broken Places. (If people bring so much courage to this world the world has to kill them to break them, so of course it kills them. The world breaks everyone and afterward many are strong at the broken places.)*

We printed a new poem of Macbeth's, and he was amused to think that so sombre a piece should appear in a newspaper that everywhere else looked like a tabloid in broadsheet size. He wrote to me *Could you possibly send me the whole issue of the paper in which* The Killing *appears? It would be fun to turn over the pages and come on it in its context.*

Certainly, it did not look anything like the *Western Daily Press* with 18-point front page lead headlines which had given Stoppard his first job after he left school. He told me that when he got his first front page by-line, on a story about a caving accident in the Mendips, he felt so fulfilled that he 'wouldn't have minded dying that night'. At that time it had been able to afford four news reporters. Stoppard was there when the Avonmouth oil terminal fire hit the front page of every national paper, and the *Daily Mirror* was rumoured to have twelve reporters and photographers on the job. The *WDP* news editor hesitated a long time, even though the story was only seven miles down the river, before rapping his desk decisively: 'We'll send!'

The boldest stroke we pulled was when we led the page with a review of Martin Esslin's *The Theatre of the Absurd.* The headline was simply the title of the book, but with the word *ABSURD* in six large white-on-black blocks, and we raised the *B* above the line and in the space vacated put *The Theatre of the* in smaller type. It seemed to us appropriate, and it looked wonderful in the proof pulled on the stone. In the paper next morning the *B* had been brought back into line. Our invention had been too much for the editor when he saw it after I had left for the night, and he had put a compositor to the trouble – not just a computer keystroke in the days of hot metal – of editing it with a hacksaw.

We ran a pre-publication extract from Esslin's book. Stoppard went to hear Pinter at a conference in Bristol, and used shorthand to put together a column of quotes. Another conference yielded interviews with Duras, Sarraute, and Robbe-Grillet. Reeves wrote about Cocteau and Duras, Kustow about Piscator and Planchon, Eric White about his friend Michael Tippett's new opera, *King Priam*, and the Moravian composer John Antes, Robert Giddings about Kafka, Rilke, Richard Strauss and Hofmannstahl. Derek Balmer was our painting critic, and when he and I were on our way back from a holiday at Blauvac we stopped in Paris so that Balmer could write for the page about Chagall's twelve windows, on display before being installed in Jerusalem. When Ghose was in Delhi he sent a review of the new Indian painters on show, no doubt the only such review published in England.

With a budget of two peanuts, the only policy we could follow for events outside Bristol was to rely on good writers and good luck. If the page had had a motto it would have been the Dadaist slogan *the*

Corporal Smith, ready to drive Glubb Pasha in Iraq, early 1920s

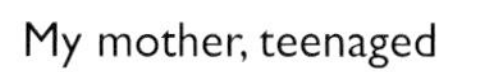

My mother, teenaged

Me, ready to rumble

Walking with my mother and father, at Margate

Dad, fraternising with Belgian girls during the war, and at his ops desk

On holiday in Belgium, 1948

Dad marries Doris in a brewery wedding, 1957

Well badged, with Dad

My education officers at RAF Bicester came to see me at Cambridge. Derek Townend is on the left, Bryn Jones on the right. On my left is my college friend John Garratt

Graduation day, with proud Dad

MA day at Cambridge, 1962. Charles Manton, Ian Barlow, me, David Dew, Chris Manners, Peter Dawkins, and Martin Lee, squatting...

... and the same group met again in 2009, plus Charles Allen, and Christine McCrum, widow of our Senior Tutor

Derek Balmer and I outside Windsor Terrace, in the Arts Page days, 1962

A basket case.
Photo by Derek Balmer in the Vaucluse, 1961

certainty of hazard. As editor, all that I could do to preserve some coherence from week to week was to ensure that the page had a number of preoccupations. One was the meaning of the word 'culture', debated in a series rooted in Richard Hoggart's *The Uses of Literacy.* Another, linked to that, was a desire, perhaps quixotic, to democratize the enjoyment of art, to use a popular newspaper to spread the idea that the arts offered imaginative pleasure to anybody who refused to be cowed by the philistine sneer.

It can only be because of what I was writing in the paper that I received a letter inviting me to stand as a Liberal candidate in the next city council election. I had not met the secretary of the Cabot Ward Liberals, Bob Stacey, and neither could he have known my political views, but I was charmed by his invitation when he told me that party meetings, held in his house, were at irregular times, because he worked in the docks and so was at home only at low tide. A party tied to the phases of the moon had a druidic appeal. A few years later I received a similar invitation from the Redland Labour group, again with no prior acquaintance on either side. Were journalists reckoned to be a hot ticket?

* * *

In a private city with few professional watering holes, the page became a focus of sorts for a talented population. For no reason that is apparent, Bristol had more than its share of the country's creative surge in the early 1960s, which was in part fuelled by the energy of television drama. New institutions sprang up in response, and found accommodation in the dock warehouses that were being vacated as the port trade shifted down river to Avonmouth. It helped that the city is full of fine eighteenth- and nineteenth-century houses. Many were in poor repair. I was paying 27s 6d a week for a garret flat in Hotwells, overlooking the river. By mistake I took it unfurnished, and so I went to Stapleton Road, some distance away, and bought a table, a bed, two chairs, a sideboard and a pantechnicon of a wardrobe for £6 the lot, delivery included. The first night I locked the keys inside the sitting room. The landlord was absentee, so the solution was to break the door open. Before the serious charging I gently pressed my shoulder against the door to gauge the resistance. The doorpost fell flat, and the door crashed open. The whole doorway proved to be rotten with rising damp, the wood spongy, like tobacco.

To get to The Polygon, a little Georgian crescent, you walked the last fifty yards along a grassy footpath. No road reached us, although we were in a built-up district. By day I could look from my window and leap-frog my eye over the bonded tobacco warehouses, like enormous red matchboxes, to Dundry church tower, miles away on the Mendip horizon. Veins of yellow lamps pulsed at night, and Russian timber ships grunted in the Avon down below. I remember in a Duhamel novel a description of the smell of herrings, which licked its tongue into all the corners of a Paris boarding house. Here, it was babies. Every time I opened the front door I was swaddled by a smell of pink and pampered flesh. The sound track was Radio Luxembourg non-stop. The old floors absorbed the treble, but the bass thumped through to the top floor, an endless sequence of facile chords, no melody.

In my previous lodging, a bedsit, the bathwater had been heated by an Edwardian monster that gulped shillings and asked for more, like a ravenous stray tomcat. It had an ingenious arrangement of interlocking levers which ensured you used the controls in the right order. The first time I tried it, it blew up, and I came choking out of a green cloud of copper oxide. In the communal bathroom in The Polygon we had a big copper with a gas ring beneath. It took an hour and three-quarters to heat four austere inches of bathwater, and left the air so acrid that the window had to be open throughout bath time. Then I discovered the luxury of the corporation's slipper baths on Jacob's Wells Road, later expropriated by a dance centre. Sailors used them, and sang together across the cubicles. The public was not considered responsible enough to run its own water. You shouted out: 'More hot in Number Four!' Footsteps, and an unseen hand outside turned a tap, gushing the ordered water through a pipe over your bath. I never raised the courage to try shouting: 'Ass's milk in Number Four!'

To my attic flat Stoppard brought his newly acquired agent, Kenneth Ewing, and with him came another playwright Ewing represented, Peter Shaffer. I was in a nerdish phase of reel-to-reel recording, and in consequence I somewhere have a tape of Shaffer doing a parody of Maurice Chevalier. The derelict house next door was being restored by Martin Shuttleworth, who had succeeded John Arden in the Cilcennin Fellowship at the university drama department. There was no water in his house, so every morning he burgled my place by scrambling along a parapet that ran at fourth-floor level the length of the terrace. He would squeeze in, huge backside first, through the tiny window of the room where I was asleep. 'Thought we could both do with a coffee,' he'd purr. He had no electricity, either, so to keep his house warm enough to work in he chopped up chairs to make a fire.

It would be posturing to pretend that Shuttleworth or I endured bohemian poverty, as opposed to managing on low incomes. The eighteenth-century city of the poetic 'Marvellous Boy' Thomas Chatterton condemned writers to much harder conditions, and besides, there were interludes of fine living. Hawkins, a gourmet cook, sometimes invited me to supper in his flat in Princes Buildings, where the company often included composers such as Peter Maxwell Davies and Alexander Goehr. Once Hawkins took me with him to dinner at Ronald and Linda Avery's house in Saltford, where the famous wine merchant served nine different wines, just to market-research what we thought of them. Ghose, in Putney, was more seriously hard up, though living with his father. The theme of empty pockets runs through his letters to me, beneath the constant subject of how to get good poetry written:

> I had a rather bitter quarrel with my father yesterday: he accused me of being a total waste and a failure, which is probably true; I understand his point of view of wanting me to be yet another machine earning money, and for his sake only feel sorry that I'm not interested in money... If I ever make any money with a book, I think I'll cash it into pound notes and send the whole bloody lot to my father with rose petals strewn in it.

One letter he could not post earlier because, with a few pennies, it had been a choice between buying a stamp or a packet of five Player's Weights:

> Lack of fags makes writing impossible. I bet you're smoking a cigarette right now. When I'm out of fags, I think of all the fortunate millions who must be smoking... Abelard-Schuman have returned my collection without a word. All there was in it was a piece torn off an Olivier cigarette packet which had been used as a book-mark. The man obviously has poor taste... No one really cares about poetry and I don't know why the hell we write it.

He proposes that, as Ted Hughes had done, we should find work as navvies, leaving our minds free for poetry, which reminded me of Betjeman's whimsy about a branch line in Dorset. Ghose was:

> ...fed-up with *The Observer* for not taking any of my poems... After the really bad Enright poem of last week, you'd have thought *Uncle Ayub* was the best thing since *Sailing to Byzantium*; but hell, they sent it back. Fed up too with the Staggers for rejecting and also the *TLS*. It's a lousy situation; I've written so many bloody poems recently, and some of them are, by most standards, good. But there's no one to send them to, and I'm scared of sending too many to *The Listener*. George [Macbeth] told me the *London Magazine* has had a poem of his for two years; they've had mine for ten months only; the reason for the delays I think is that apart from taking a lot of bad poems, any new poem by C. Day Lewis or [Roy] Fuller or Spender is given priority; I suppose I'd do the same if I was editing it and you sent me a poem...

One of the single-issue arts pages was devoted to modern poetry. In the course of reading for it, Ghose wrote to me:

> The young Eliot suffered penury much worse than we do. I'd always thought that as a master at Highgate and working for Lloyds Bank he must have been pretty secure. But his salary at Lloyds was £120 a year, which, allowing for the change of value, is still less than what I've earned over last year. And Eliot had a wife to support. Also, he tried to enlist in the Navy in 1918: that is after the war. He must have been really desperate. This is the time when he was writing lines like:
> *The winter evening settles down*
> *With smell of steak in passageways...*
> I've always found these lines pleasant; it has just struck me with a terrible bang in the brain that Eliot might have been hungry then.

But *we will come through*, he believed, and he was right. Over the next few years his poems appeared in the *TLS, Spectator, Twentieth Century, Listener, Critical Quarterly, Encounter, Granta*, a Penguin collection with Johnson and Gavin Ewart, and several slim vols on his own. The BBC Third Programme sometimes rang him to ask for poems.

While my time with Stoppard was spent talking about fiction and drama, Ghose continued to remind me that poetry had been my first love:

> Kunitz is the greatest lyric poet of the century; the ease with which he flows hurts me into my own littleness... I can see why he is known as the poets' poet in America.

He advised me to read Hopkins's *The Wreck of the Deutschland* aloud. I do read one poem aloud every day. It serves as a reminder that writing is a form of speaking, and should not be separated from the voice. The poet Francis Berry used to argue that what a poet can write is determined by his or her speech.

Ghose has always insisted on technique. In the early Sixties he had, too, the generosity of spirit to talk frequently about 'our generation' of writers, rather than merely contemplating his own practice:

> What's worrying me is that none of us are doing anything new. Our rhythms go back to Yeats or Hopkins, our subject matter is mostly mundane... [Hughes's] rhythms are new and what he says is new. Excited by him, we've all rushed to write animal poems; but looking at some of my own animal poems, they are third-rate imitations of Ted... The trouble is that minor poets see major ones taking certain liberties and consequently think that they can follow suit without any prior formal preparation. It is a great pity that the learning of Latin is in decline. Who learns scansion nowadays?... Except for Yeats, every poet since Hopkins has been like a surgeon operating on other people's bodies; Hopkins makes mincemeat of his own heart and throws it at you.

Ted Hughes liked living near Regent's Park because he could hear the wolves howl in the zoo. A letter of the time from Janet Burroway records that:

> Zulfi and I went to dinner with Ted and Sylvia... Her idea, and I thought he was less than enthusiastic about it, though that may have been my own self-consciousness. He was cordial enough, and no more strained than the rest of us. The baby cried. Sylvia, hassled, tried to cook while holding it, so I eventually offered to hold it. It cried horrifically, and Ted ended up with it, can't remember exactly how. He was pacing, gesturing with one simian arm, the baby held in an elbow-out crook of the other, while he described, intense and intent, how the animals woke him at night and how he lay listening to them. He held his daughter like an alien thing while she cried and he enthused about the animals' howling.

Just as Stoppard would, much later, write an article about finding himself to be Jewish, in 1961 Ghose *woke this morning to find myself British. I absolutely love England. I have an urge to roll in England's grass.* Within weeks he was back in his native country, reporting the 1961-62 MCC tour of India and Pakistan for *The Observer*. B. S. Johnson would soon be reporting soccer for the same paper.

Balmer and I, meanwhile, were driving to Blauvac, where we were joined by Stoppard and Hawkins. Stoppard didn't come back with us. He wanted to explore Spain, and wound up in Gibraltar. Back in Bristol, his brother Peter came to see me. Neither he nor their mother had heard from Tom for some weeks. Mrs Stoppard, who had fled Czechoslovakia with her sons in 1939, had the conviction that the Czech State Security would stop at nothing to recapture its refugee citizens, and now feared that that was what had befallen her younger son. Peter told me, later, that as he sat anxiously in my flat, hoping to glean some clue from me about his brother's fate, I offered him a few reassuring words but spent the time trotting backwards and forwards in front of him, practising the delivery of my leg-break. When Stoppard did finally turn up, he was full of a little fishing village he had discovered called Marbella, which was very beautiful but, he feared, might be spoiled before long.

* * *

From The Polygon I moved to The Paragon. The top floor of No.15 is the highest window on the Clifton skyline as you drive in from Somerset. It cost me about a quarter of my £15 weekly wage. Stoppard and I saw dawns break in that place. It had a triangular balcony, commanding a view from St Mary Redcliffe to the Suspension Bridge, and overlooked from nowhere except the highest houses in Leigh Woods, across the gorge. The *War Requiem* had been premièred at Coventry a year earlier, and I had a reel-to-reel recording of it, and lying on my balcony on a hot afternoon, listening to Britten, the girl with me sighed and stretched and took all her clothes off, to make the most of the sun. I might have said: 'Isn't it a bit early for this? It's only 1962, we haven't got to flower power yet.' What I did say was: 'They could see you from Leigh Woods with binoculars, you know, and they've all got binoculars over there.' 'Let them, if they want it that much,' she answered. I was very impressed. Also, she had a double-barrelled name, and her father made mead. I was starting to get the hang of the 1960s.

In April 1962 Stoppard and I went to New York, both of us for the first time. We joined a charter flight from Bristol. All the other passengers were architects, and had a party booking at a Manhattan hotel, probably one with interesting new modular ideas. We had to find somewhere to sleep. At Idlewild we headed for the telephones. Stoppard made the first call, to a theatre critic whose name someone had given him. The first words we heard on a New York telephone were: 'I'm sorry, this is Mrs Tallmer. Jerry isn't here any more. We're separated.' At that time, the word 'separated' still sounded thrillingly American.

Some calls later we found a place for the night. It was west of Central Park and belonged to a radio engineer who was a friend of someone Stoppard had met once. He was called Herb, or it might have been Hal. He said to come right on over, but when we got to the apartment he had left the key for us, and a note saying that he had gone out but would see us later, and we were to feel free to eat anything in the fridge. We played with his chess set and ate cinnamon bread, and by 3 a.m. it was a long time since we had got up in Bristol, so we tossed up who would use the spare bed and who sleep on the couch. The next morning Herb hadn't returned, but he rang up to say Hi, how're you doing, and were there any messages, and he'd been with his girl friend but he'd see us soon. The second night it was Stoppard's turn on the couch. The third night I was on the couch, and early in the morning half-woke because someone was moving in the apartment. I opened my eyes and Hal or Herb said he was sorry to have disturbed me, and I murmured not to worry and went straight back to sleep. That was the day Stoppard started to use the telephone, and in the evening we complained to each other that Herb had forgotten to restock the fridge with cinnamon bread, and one of us slept in his bed instead of on the couch.

I went upstate for a couple of days to see Janet Burroway and her husband in Binghamton, and chose a tie from Hal's wardrobe. He sometimes rang in for any messages, but there never were any. We figured he was walking around the Park all night, hands in his coat pockets, feeling good about being nice to the limeys. When we left I said, 'We'd better compose a hell of a thank-you note to the guy', and Stoppard said, 'Forget it. There's no way we can thank him for this. We just go.' So we just did.

We saw plays off-Broadway, including *Brecht on Brecht*, a decaffeinated sampler for audiences innocent of the communist ogre, but most evenings we spent off-off. Stoppard had at last made contact with Jerry Tallmer, the 'separated' theatre critic of the *Village Voice*, and he directed us to the best coffee-house satire; one evening we were guided around by a gag-writer called Mel Brooks. In Phase 2 we drank tamarindo coffee and listened to Taylor Meade do a gig in what would later be known as rap. Next it was Vic Grecco and Fred Willard in a sketch about the star who wants to thank everyone who made it possible for him to be up here tonight receiving the Oscar, including the producer, the director, the co-star, the screenwriter, the personal rewrite man, the wardrobe, the dialogue-coach, the make-up team, the doubles, the stunt-men, and finally he wanted us to give a specially big thank-you to the actor who was deputising for him at tonight's Oscar ceremony, thank you. Someone told us that a bird in the hand is worth little or nothing, and someone else lamented the song-writer who had every talent except timing, witness the greatest song he ever wrote, *Bon Voyage, Titanic.*

Second City, Mike Nichols and Elaine May's company, were in town with *The Premise*, scaringly sharp improvisation on suggestions from the audience. They did a sketch in which a weakling gets sand kicked in his face and sees his girl go off with Mr Muscle Man, and the weakling takes the Charles Atlas course, and back on the beach he kicks sand in Mr Muscle Man's face, and Mr Muscle Man is so impressed that the two men go off together arm-in-arm, leaving the girl. (Years later a little Devon theatre group asked me for sketches on a territorial theme, and I plagiarised that one because it merited another outing and what the hell, who's going to know at the Lobster Pot in Instow? The Devon company's director, Charles Lewsen, rang me and said he'd use all my sketches except that one, because it was peculiarly like something Second City had done when he was working for them in Chicago. Be sure your sins will find you out.) At the Village Vanguard, Lenny Bruce wrapped himself around a microphone and jabbered in dark Yiddish. One passage I could understand was directed against the doughty old American socialist Norman Thomas. 'Norm's gonna run his next campaign on an anti-midget platform. Smack a midget a day for Norm. When you were hitching out West in the snow, did you ever get a lift from a midget? Nah.' Walt Whitman's word for New York was 'electric'. The electricity is created by racial friction. What New York has got that I have seldom found elsewhere in the USA is irony. Only people with a historical perspective can be ironic.

I was still wearing detachable collars. One of my studs had broken, and I went into a shirt shop to buy another one. The man squinted at me. 'A what stud?'

'A collar-stud.'

He shook his head: 'We don't stock them.'

'I see,' I said, and felt uppity. 'You don't go in for clean collars in New York?'

'Nah. We go in for clean shoits.'

I looked at the lined-up skyscrapers and told Sandra Schmidt of the *Village Voice* that I had a domino theory about them. She put my theory in the paper. I'd assumed most people would have had the same thought. My favourite domino is the Seagram Building, and I got an interview with Philip C. Johnson, who designed it with Mies van der Rohe. Soon after we got home, Lenny Bruce was at The Establishment club in London, and soon after that he was dead. I asked Stoppard if there was any chance that Bruce would resurrect, but we agreed that he wasn't hot on the New Testament. Another act at The Establishment was a young American folk-singer, with a harmonica hung from his neck. He was called Bobby Dillon, and I am relieved that I wrote an encouraging review.

* * *

I had begun to report cricket for *The Times*, doing a piece for them after filing my staff report of Somerset for the *Western Daily Press*. This was a practice forbidden by all papers, but committed by most reporters. It was the pre-Thomson, not to say pre-Murdoch, *Times*. Uniquely, the paper did not have copy-takers. Instead, the sub-editors took the copy on the telephone themselves, so that they could grill the reporter about anything questionable before he became uncontactable on his way home. To be a *Times* sub involved having got at least a Second in Greats. A.A. Thomson, using the Latin tag or Shakespearean quotation which was a *sine qua non* in a Times cricket report, dictated, 'When Sussex's score stood at 89 for seven it seemed that Lancashire's 166 might prove *multum in parva*.' 'Tsk, tsk. Third declension, Mr Thomson, third declension.' It was the only paper that paid me more in expenses than I had claimed, insisting that tea must cost 7s 6d. You could have bought three whiskies for that, and perhaps were expected to.

My first report for them could only allude to what nowadays would cover the front pages of the tabloids: *Without Trueman, who had arrived too late on Saturday to be included, the Yorkshire attack had no leading edge.* Everyone in the press box at Taunton knew that Trueman had arrived late on account of a chambermaid in the hotel where the Yorkshire team were staying. J.V. Wilson, his captain, had finally had enough, and stood him down. Peter Wight and Bill Alley profited with a stand of 186, and I noted *As the West Indian and the Australian piled up runs accountable to the English county of Somerset...*

On the second morning of the match, when my report was in the paper, a head appeared over the sill of the press box, which was just above ground level. It was the classic head of a peppery colonel, all pink cheeks and white whiskers. 'Is there a gentleman from *The Times* here?' it asked. It took me a moment to realise that he meant me, before I identified myself. 'I wish,' the head barked at me, 'to take grave exception to your report in the paper this morning. That stuff about the West Indian and the Australian – dammit, we've always been glad to give the colonials their chance down here.' One of the umpires was the former Gloucestershire batsman Jack Crapp. When playing for England he had disappointed the press in one respect. Peter Loader, the Surrey quick bowler, had also been in the England side at that time, but Crapp had never batted with him, denying reporters the opportunity to refer to the Loader-Crapp partnership. On the other hand, I have been told that Frank Keating insists that he once heard a radio commentary in which Crapp was dropped in front of the pavilion at Lord's...

I was playing cricket myself every weekend, for Clifton C.C. To join them, soon after settling in Bristol, it was required of me, before any question of performing in the nets, that I should visit the club chairman at his house, so that he could assure himself that I was the right sort of chap. I was also playing for the *Evening Post* in mid-week matches, and was asked to captain them in my second season. Against Mendip Hospital at Wells, I put myself on for the final over of the match. We needed one wicket to win. The batsman was a boy of about ten. I crowded him with fielders, and bowled five leg-breaks. Each of them turned past the edge of his prodded bat. Just in time, I engaged my brain, and sent down a straight dobber, which he pushed into the hands of silly mid-on. At Clifton, between wickets, I once congratulated an elderly slow-left-armer. 'You really think about it, don't you, Eddie?' 'Got nothing to do with it,' he said, 'me thinking. It's when I get them thinking about it that they get out.'

'I fish,' Stoppard wrote to me from Scotland in May 1962, the month after our New York trip. He was staying with his parents:

> The river is by the house, full of trout which stand on their tails and laugh at me... So far I have only caught one trout, from a boat on Loch Ard, 11oz; I ate it for lunch. Fi [his sister] was in the boat, conflict of loyalties between man and fish; got a bit upset, momentarily, when I had to beat the thing over the head to prove my superiority, but decided finally, 'Oh well, that's how it is'. That's how it is. Life. Insect eats microbe, fish eats insect, I eat fish. Somebody, sooner or later, will bring the process to its logical conclusion by eating me, but what or who? Obviously, a microbe. Life, baby.

I had sent him the latest arts page, including a piece I had written about a Michael Kustow production. He commented:

> Probably I would have been much harder on the committed angle; I feel a contempt for it as I do for all simplifications and spoon-feedings; what you said was true (I rather think you wouldn't have felt that a year ago?)

He was right. I had gone into the arts page with a legacy from Cambridge of rather sober-sided moralism, one of many who swallowed Leavis's rigour without his grace of perception (if not of prose). Stoppard's example was that morality was a meal best eaten with wit for ketchup. His own version of it is to claim that in his writing, seriousness and frivolity compromise each other. That is a modest way to put it, as anyone who has seen *Arcadia* might testify. His letter goes on to quibble constructively about the layout of the page.

> MUSIC and FICTION reverse blocks too close to each other; FICTION describes my article sort of, but really shouldn't it have been LETTERS? And Fred's piece was a bit lost, with that right-angled corner. But can't see what else you cd hv done. Christ, I seem to be getting proprietary, but not so; just commenting.

He mentions a poet he'd met in London. He had liked some of her work, and advised her to send me some for the page. She had been taken to a meeting of the Group, and remarked: 'I didn't care for Macbeth much.' (It is true that George Macbeth could abrade, but most people succumbed to the mock-Edwardian charm of the man.) When I had taken Stoppard to a Group meeting he had simply listened with interest, but had made an impression on Hobsbaum, who admired his stuff in the arts page. With typical generosity, Hobsbaum wrote to me:

> I have been brooding over Tom Stoppard... I think it would be a very good idea if he read some of his stories at the Group... Teddy would be keen to get more prose read at discussions... there aren't very many intelligent writers of fiction – there's more cop in writing poetry now.

Despite which, he remained sure that I was a poet rather than a novelist. Stoppard was intrigued by poetry, but all that he ever wrote of it, as far as I know, were snippets in avowed imitation of some famous poet, usually starting lyrical and turning into come-off-it parody. An example was one with the ambiguous title of *TS on his Way Out*. It ends:

and all the things you never did
when you might at least have done the opposite

His letters in the early sixties, like Ghose's, are threaded with penury:

> I did have in mind the sum of £5, but now that you've made it £10 it solves the problem of my getting back to Bristol. I have figured out that I will receive cheques worth £35, and am £36 in debt. That's counting one Y.P. [*Yorkshire Post*] article they hv used to my knowledge (besides Bruce), and they have two more; they may use one more, I hope so – at least I'll have 15 quid to live on. Life's a drag. I don't suppose the V.V. [*Village Voice*] will pay, at least I'm not expecting anything.

His letter went on to warn me that Eric Price, the editor of the *Western Daily Press*, now powerfully rising on a thermal of circulation, was threatening the arts page's survival.

> The Price situation looks bad. I forgot to tell you that just before I left, when I was doing the page on Sunday night, he said to me, 'I've told W.A. [Walter Hawkins, Richard's father] and he agrees with me. It's only that Richard who's for it.'

Price hated what he thought was all arty piffle. Every Monday I had to go into his office for a brief, ritualised editorial meeting. On his desk he would have the paper open at the arts page and be staring at it. He would lift his head, which at times like that always struck me as reptilian, squint at me over his rimless spectacles and enquire: 'What cunt reads this fucking shit?' Ritually, I would reply: 'Your circulation's up by two thousand cunts every Monday, Eric, and there's no other explanation.' In deciding how much space any subject merited in his paper, Price took no account of such data as the comparative figures of paid admissions to theatre and to soccer, in which theatre won three-two. I will not describe his response when, at Hawkins's request, I brought out an arts page entirely in French, to match the theme in that year's Bath Festival.

Hobsbaum gave me advice over the Price threat, reassuring me that if the worst happened I would land some literary editorship in

London. I never tested his assurance. Events kept me in Bristol, where I felt more at home than I expected to feel back in my native city. Neither have I ever really wanted that kind of job. I was learning that it is too hard to get the writing done when I am also doing editorial work. Many people owe Hobsbaum thanks for his encouragement. He promoted my arts page to Richard Hoggart, who wrote to say 'it will be shocking if they let it die' when he heard that the page was under threat. Michael Hastings was another who offered support, telling me that people in London were talking about the page. It survived for almost another year before Price persuaded the management to let him have his way with it. Now in his nineties he still lives in Bristol, on the same side of town as I do, but we're not on each other's Christmas card list.

O'Toole turned up again in Bristol. By now *Lawrence of Arabia* had made him a star, and he was just back from shooting another film in the USA. He headed for Grosvenor Lodge, and arranged with Val Lorraine to have a party there that evening, so that he could see all his friends. He bought crates of drink and food. 'What else do we need? People.' It was arranged that he and I would shuttle between the party and the Theatre Royal stage door, collecting actors as they came off. The curtain call that night must have been depleted. On one trip we talked about Stoppard, and O'Toole said: 'I love fucking Tom.' When I told Stoppard he begged me not to repeat it to anyone, lest the adjective be misconstrued as a verb. O'Toole spent some of the party sitting on a sofa with a beautiful actress, Beth Shepherd, who visibly fell under his spell. Stoppard told me that at that time O'Toole was faithful to his wife. All he was doing was checking that everything still worked, but Beth's boy friend stormed out of the house. Later there was a knock at the front door. A uniformed policeman had come to investigate a report from the boy friend that O'Toole was committing a breach of the peace.

In the small hours a Lebanese girl needed a lift home, and O'Toole offered to taxi her. On Park Street he was confused, after months in the USA, about which side of the road he should be on, so he hedged his bet and drove half-way down on the left and the other half on the right. The police pulled him in. He leaned across his passenger, opened her door and bundled her out. Had she been taken in with him it would have got into the papers, and everyone would have drawn the wrong conclusion. In a police cell for the rest of the night, O'Toole told the duty officer who he was. 'Oh yes?' the sergeant said. 'That's funny. Only last week we had that Laurence

Olivier in here.' O'Toole asked him to call the chief constable, who he knew was a theatregoer and a big fan of his. No dice. O'Toole was up in court that morning, fined and banned. He asked me to look after his car until I could deliver it to London for him. It was a zippy Mini, a treat for me. A couple of weeks later I drove it to London. I took a girlfriend out to dinner in Kensington, and had to ring O'Toole to arrange to deliver the car to him in Hampstead the next day. In the restaurant I asked if there was a telephone, expecting to be directed to one. Instead, the waiter brought one to the table on a silver tray, with a long lead. Not having intended to show off to my friend, I found myself absurdly sitting at a table opposite her chatting to Peter O'Toole.

When I introduced Stoppard to B.S. Johnson it took them three minutes to get into a loud argument, over theoretical strategies in writing. Johnson was for them, as a vicar is for virtue. Stoppard was pragmatic. Johnson was full of his cant that every subject dictates a new form. My experience is that if anything dictates the form it will be the first sentence. Theory can be disabling. The penguin is a bird with a theory of gravity. I go with Albert Camus: *far from obeying abstract principles,* he wrote, *one discovers them only in the heat of battle.* Or Lenin: *reality is slyer than any theory.*

Some writers construct a narrative in order to body forth an idea. Orwell would be an example, Koestler another. But it is more often the case that one comes across some story, or scrap of a story, and it sounds a chord with something already on your mind. After that, it's getting the words right. Shakespeare came across a primitive old Danish yarn called *Amleth*, and it touched some preoccupation he had with prevarication, so, pausing to anagrammatize the title, he came up with five hours' worth of words. They include Polonius's answer to Johnson: *By indirections find directions out.* Incidentally, the most acute analysis I have read of how the words in *Hamlet* work was written not by a drama critic but by Ghose in his book *Hamlet, Prufrock and Language.*

In spite of our arguments Johnson and I had much in common, each of us an only child of an unambitious lower-middle family in south-west London. We fell easily into a cockney mateyness. We were 1950s men who had been educated out of our backgrounds, and would be confused by the social changes of the 1960s. But Johnson had been damaged by a long wartime evacuation, and at school had been given no academic encouragement. He had had to find his own way into London University, after some years of office work. Now, in 1962, he applied for the fellowship in the Bristol drama department, in succession to Shuttleworth. He saw it as:

> ...the only opportunity in the country to do deep research into what the theatre is to become... Wesker, Delaney et al have revolutionised material, subject matter only – useful, but not now (five years later) very important. The really important change must come in technique, to attract an audience specifically to the theatre to see something they can't see anywhere else: this breakthrough in technique I would attempt to achieve (I already have ideas about it that I don't propose to reveal until I am paid to do so) within the fellowship... I do not expect to invent; rather to rediscover through action and the application of deep exploration. Re-thinking form, as I believe I have done in my novel... As you can see, I'm aiming high; but feel I must.

He arranged to stay with me for the interview, but his application did not get that far.

Stoppard, Balmer and I were planning to start a literary/reportage magazine, which we were going to call *The Bristol Review*. It didn't happen, for the usual reasons that such projects don't. (Four decades later a similar project, with the title *Bristol Review of Books*, did happen, thanks to a more sanguine group led by John Sansom, the publisher of this memoir. I have been a contributor.) Stoppard wrote to me:

> Everything draws nearer and I am unprepared. Portugal, Bristol Review, Brennus, visa, money... I am unprepared for them all. Baden-Powell the Unprepared.

Brennus was the name under which he wrote a weekly satirical column in the *Western Daily Press*. A collection would bear reprinting, but he would not sanction it. He prefers to have been born aged twenty-eight and the author of *Rosencrantz and Guildenstern Are Dead*. Actually, he would most of all prefer to have been born aged seventeen and the author of it. He was haunted by what he thought was time lost, before the play made his name. When he read a rave for any new play, all he wanted to know was how old the writer was – if a year younger than himself, he was desperate. Joe Israeli, a young theatre director from Tel Aviv doing a postgraduate year in Bristol, gave Stoppard a fine lecture at a party about how foolish it is to assume that age is absolute. We mature at different rates. Some are burned out at twenty-five, some begin at forty. Stoppard had deaf ears.

In the summer of 1962 Stoppard, Ghose, Johnson and I were planning to go on holiday to Portugal. I forget why it never happened. Instead, just Johnson and I went to Blauvac for two weeks. I gave an account of the trip to Jonathan Coe when he was researching his biography of Johnson, *Like A Fiery Elephant.*

Thanks to an assisted-purchase scheme at the paper, I had the only brand new car I've owned, a red Beetle, and the journey to London, to pick up Johnson, was the first time I had driven it any distance. I found the headlights hard to get used to. I hadn't realised that the offside bulb was dud, though new. Sandra Schmidt, from the *Village Voice*, had been in Bristol. She watched Stoppard and me play cricket at Wells and reported it in the *Voice*, most impressed, as Americans are, that we bravely field without mitts. She had arranged to meet me at Johnson's home in Barnes and get a lift to France. We waited and she didn't show up, and so we were late in leaving, which upset Johnson, who liked to stick to plans. He was already put out by my having said that she could have a lift without consulting him, and then she doesn't turn up and we are running late. So we got off on a bad foot.

In those days there was a service called Silver City. You went to Lydd in Kent and drove on to a plane and flew over to Le Touquet and drove off again. When we arrived at Le Touquet it was dark. It would be an eight-hour drive, maybe ten, to Provence, and we planned to do it through the night, to save money, of which we had little. We had hardly got out of Le Touquet before I went into a ditch. I'd got defective illumination, and there had been no indication of where the road stopped and the ditch started. We weren't hurt, but the car was. We limped back into Le Touquet, got it to a garage and then had to hole up the best part of forty-eight hours while a stub axle was mended, using up most of the money we had.

Johnson took it as a betrayal of his trust in me to give him a good holiday. First I had kept him waiting with this woman who never showed up and now I'd driven into a ditch, leaving us near broke. How much more could I let him down? *Words were scantier than thoughts*, to quote from *Middlemarch.* Also, there were two girls – I didn't know them, they were from Keele, friends of Ghose – waiting for us in Provence. They got there before us because we'd been held up. I got lucky and Johnson didn't. Everything had gone wrong and it was all my fault and yet I was the one who wound up with a nice girl and the other one didn't work out for Johnson. It compounded his sense that when things went wrong people were doing it in order to get at him. He could not handle disappointment. In the USA he'd have sued me. On the way home, at Cherbourg, I locked the keys inside the car, and had to carve the quarterlight open with a hacksaw. Johnson watched me in loud silence.

6

Men of Letters

WHEN I GOT BACK TO THE PARAGON I FOUND A LETTER STOPPARD had left me in my typewriter: *30 Aug 62 – Cher Anthony – I'm in London. For good. Am drama critic/theatre editor of* Scene. He had discovered *Scene*, a new magazine with offices in Fleet Street, to be a subterranean hive of inactivity. The editor was Francis Hitching, *a good looking young slightly dishevelled male model who gave the impression he had been fired by John Michael and spent the summer walking around the Kings Road.* Stoppard continued:

> I showed him a few things like the arts page, and it transpired that his life was a constant stream of people showing him the *Western Daily Press* arts page, i.e. B.S.J. [Johnson]. We got on well and I made a great impression at one point: he mentioned O'Toole but didn't know whether he was back in England, so I picked up the phone on his desk and had an intimate conversation with Sian, re the present whereabouts of the O'Toole, which turned out to be Hampstead. I did it all deadpan and barely refrained from adding, Oh by the way, Albie sends his love. *Scene* had a critic-editor, but chiefy wasn't too happy because he wanted 'news-reviews' à la *Time* Mag, i.e. a bit of superficial knowing news background easing into sub-intellectual criticism. He had plenty of people who were good news-experienced interviewers etc and also plenty of willing and able critics (B.S.J. and the then incumbent) but he wanted someone who had done and cd do both. Me, as it happens. He sent me to review *The Premise* and do an interview piece, i.e. dummies to show my stuff. *Premise* was my sly suggestion. So I went, interviewed them, got a good news angle and sent him both pieces last Sunday. Monday morning he phoned to say I'm it. £12 a week retainer which will be handy in case I'm ill or on hols, or indeed if there just aren't any first nights one week. But I stand

> to make a good £20 working say half the week. Ideal set-up. And every first night in town. Man. Also, the gentleman whom I've apparently replaced will be my second string – presumably for plays which are beneath my attention, heh-heh.

The seed of *The Real Inspector Hound* had been planted.

It was not the first time Stoppard had sought a job in London. He was still sufficiently the journalist to dream about being a Fleet Street star byline. He had previously gone up to be interviewed by the *Evening Standard* for a political reporting job. Back in Bristol, he told me he hadn't got the job: 'The editor asked me "You're interested in politics, then, I take it?" Oh yes. "Good. Good. In that case, could you favour me with the name of the present Foreign Secretary?" Well, I'd only claimed to be interested in politics, I hadn't said I was obsessed with the subject.' Now his letter went on to tell me:

> Ralph Richardson has expressed interest in *Walk* and has sent script to Peter Brook, who may be described as God in the world of which Peter Hall is Mammon. But, Richardson had comments, chief of which was he was worried about the play's shortness. So I am frantically trying to add half an hour without merely padding. I am now in your flat to work on that but took time off to write this. While on the subject – Anthony, whatever you do don't give up this flat – I'll share it with you if you come to town. I'm enchanted with this room and view and it's so fantastic to have it that it would be more fantastic to simply let it go.
>
> I had an extraordinary interview with [Richard] Hawkins. To begin with, I wrote my farewell Brennus on Saturday night, impulsively, mainly because I didn't have anything else to write about and because I realised it was Brennus's second anniversary that week and the damn column seemed to be stretching into a grim future. So I said goodbye in my column – it appeared last Monday. At 11.30 *Scene* woke me up to offer me the job. At 2.30 Hawkins woke me up to ask me to see him.
>
> Until that point it hadn't occurred to me that there was anything odd about writing a farewell column,

> leaving one's editor to get the news when he opens his paper... (it had, as a matter of fact, occurred to Val – she told me off proper. In fact when I said, a little puzzledly, Hawkins wants to see me, she replied I bet he does). Well, I got to the office in a rare state of remorse and terror, burbled apologies before I got into R.H.'s office, but it transpired that he wasn't mad with me. He said it would have bn nice to have bn told in advance, but when I said that I hadn't known in advance myself he murmured acquiescence. He merely enquired re my future. I told him about *Scene*, pointing out incredibly that I'd written the Brennus before I knew I'd got the job. He said that if I intended going to London he'd have offered me more than I'd get from *Scene* to write articles for the *WDP* and *EP*. I double-taked. This was the guy who wdn't give me an extra guinea for West's Week. He said he wanted some really good feature articles and was willing to pay me £1,200 a year, say, for a 60-hour month – i.e. about a seven-day eight-hour week out of every four weeks. So this is still in the background in case I'm fired, or in case *Scene* folds under me or in case I can't stand *Scene*. This idea of Hawkins is presumably hush at the moment, but how about you in London with £1,200 a year?

Ghose, too, had tried to persuade me to move back to London, with talk of sharing a flat. I was not tempted. The gentler pace suited me in Bristol. It is a city you could walk across in a day, a city you can belong to. Stoppard's farewell-to-Bristol letter continued:

> My first piece will probably be *Brecht on Brecht*, which is opening at the Royal Court. I mentioned I'd seen it in New York. At the moment I can't open my mouth without casually impressing the editor of *Scene*. It was a bit unfair on Bryan [B.S. Johnson], but when his name cropped up re Arts Page I circuitously got over the mis-fact that I was one of the two guys Bryan was working for. Incidentally I got in a few plugs for you in case you feel like following up – as far as I could see from the two dummy issues, their book man is a

dud. His piece on Salinger was rewritten from *Time*. Incidentally, I DIDN'T shop Bryan out of his job – Hitching had already said he thought B was 'too intellectual' for *Scene*. So you can see what a crummy magazine it's going to be. For my part, I'm playing it cool because regardless of *Scene*'s intellect it is, at present, the only magazine willing to pay me 20 quid a week for going to the theatre in London. I'll save my best work for the Arts Page...

So, I guess as you're reading this I'm somewhere in London having stone kittens over Brecht, a man whom B.S.J. is clearly better fitted to write about than I. On the other hand, is B.S.J. capable of isolating the really important thing about Brecht and making it easily palatable for *Scene*'s readers – the fact that Brecht – sly-eyed stooping crop-headed Bert Brecht was a notorious communist...?

I got £30 from the bank to buy some critical clothes; and will be in a position to let you have a cheque for £7 far earlier than had seemed remotely possible.

5 a.m. Saturday. Just finished rewriting and typing play. Splendid. Crept down for a pee. Not splendid. Confronted by Mrs S [Ruth Stephenson, my landlady] in dressing gown. 'Good God,' she says, 'I'm going away tomorrow and will have a helluva day, and you wake me up at five o'clock in the morning! Couldn't you use the lavatory downstairs?' Told her I didn't know there was one (True.) So sorry. Though I didn't make any noise, except peeing. What time are you allowed to use the bloody lavatory? Three guineas a week and pee over the balcony.

In fact Ruth was ruthless on anyone who woke her up from her light sleep. Israeli had done it a few weeks earlier, and his penalty was that Ruth turned her radio on full blast at 7.30 and threw her vicious little cur, Jessie, on to his bed. I liked Ruth, but she was difficult. I wrote a catechism to her: *I have cast lecherous eyes along thy daughter... When thou wert on holiday, I have neglected thy hamster... O Lady, let me never be in arrears.*

A week later, Stoppard wrote to me about *Scene*:

I'm very pleased with the set-up generally, and very

> fed up with one or two details, like the fact they cut my *Premise* feature most ineptly so it reads rubbish. Also, the copy date is so advanced that this theatre critic can't review plays; for the first issue I did prelim 'reviews' on two things before they opened. This can't go on. They won't use stuff a week late, so I've either got to do fake reviews or see things in Brighton or somewhere, which is also a fake. In the first issue I have one proper review, short, two fakes, two news stories, several bits of gossip and a letter to the editor (fake). Not bad for the bloody theatre critic. But I've been working here almost full time this week to show willing, and Christ they needed help. I think you'll agree when you see it that it LOOKS good, very clean, a LOVELY sans serif body type for some articles... I loved your ciao-niao, so ciao-niao.

I am lucky in never having felt rivalry with Stoppard. It would be a waste of good envy to expend it on a writer with whom I have for fifty years shared a taste in what writing should be doing, and who at his frequent best has delivered it brilliantly. Another reason, as good, is that his friendship has been generous, with money when I needed it, with critical advice on manuscripts. I have rued how much he is paid for his work in comparison with what I usually get, but that is a resentment of the disproportions of the literary market place. In late 1962, both of us still needed to heed Israeli's admonition. Some of our contemporaries were ahead of us. Burroway had published a novel and a collection of poems. Bernardine Bishop's first novel was at proof stage. *My sharp sense of rivalry with women writers persists,* she wrote to me. And Johnson's first novel had been accepted. When it appeared, Stoppard wrote to me *Its many attributes point to the more important achievement he is, or shd hv bn, capable of.*

The Cuban missile crisis provoked Johnson to write a squib which writers will understand.

> **A Very Short Prayer**
> Please Mr K,
> Don't blow us all
> Up
> Until after my
> Novel's published.

Ghose got a strange rejection slip from the *Evergreen Review*. Scribbled on it in red pencil was: *GET YOUR AUTHORITY FROM THE AIR, where everybody else gets it. Send excerpts from secret personal journal.* I told him about two of my favourite rejections. George Eliot's publisher, Blackwood, on receiving another weighty moral novel: *If you have any lighter pieces, written before the sense of what a great author should do for mankind came so strongly upon you, I should like much to look at them.* And Jack London's *The Call of the Wild* was rejected on the grounds that *Interest in Alaska has subsided to an amazing degree.* Perhaps as a prophylactic, Stoppard played rejection games. For the *Bristol Review* he suggested that we print slips: *We are entitled to reject your work, even if we solicited it, and would not have paid for it even if used.* Later, he came up with a firmer one: *The Editor thanks you for your contribution but deeply regrets that it is a load of shit.* He sent me a whimsy about an oft-rejected writer who finally Saw the Light, offered up a prayer of redemption and received the reply: *The Lord thanks you for your contribution but regrets that it is not quite suitable for the Kingdom of Heaven.* The ironic twist is that this bit of fun was accepted as one of a few short pieces written by Stoppard for his first appearance in book form, Faber and Faber's anthology *Introduction 2.* After some success with the first *Introduction*, in which Faber had given an airing to new writers including Ted Hughes, the editor Francis Pike, whom I had known at Cambridge, wrote to me asking if I could recommend anyone to him for a second volume. I suggested Stoppard and Ghose. The latter was dubious:

> A mate of yours called Francis Pike of the famous firm of Pike & Otter has been writing for short stories. On your recommendation. I might write some but doubt it. I'm annoyed by publishers. They will readily exploit writers to produce anthologies of prose.

Ghose could afford to be sniffy because he had had a poem accepted by Ted Hughes for the annual PEN anthology. After the launch party, *a soaked collection of drunken poets*, he wrote to me:

> The anthology contains none of the established names... This is not because they didn't submit, but it seems Ted rejected them all. Great man. He wasn't there, though Sylvia was and she said that she wakes at four every morning and writes a poem before

> breakfast. Great woman.

He continued to concentrate my mind, that part of it which was still preoccupied with poetry, on the fascination of what's difficult:

> ...a chap like Lowell can twist the heroic couplet, maintain its perfection, and yet make it appear that the couplet doesn't exist. I live in a state of total dissatisfaction with everything I write and everything I read. Poetry, that is. Only Lowell and Hopkins give any satisfaction at present. And Shakespeare, whose erotic poems kill me with their perfection of technique for thousands of stanzas. The chap we should all be studying is Chaucer, of course... The short three-stressed line has been haunting me: it is that much more difficult to control language in it than in the iambic.

Another reason for Ghose's chutzpah was that he was in love, with the Brazilian artist Helena de la Fontaine Verwey:

> Helena and I have fixed September 20th for our wedding. God knows how it shall be managed, but I'm determined that it shall be so. My sister Lily is getting married in the spring which is a terrible burden on my old man, for Pakistani weddings cost the earth. His wish is that I go to Pakistan and get a wife there so that some old bastard there can suffer the same agonies of giving me a huge dowry, but I've told him my phlegmatic mind on this.

Ghose had applied for the Gregory Fellowship, an award Johnson once held. He asked me for a reference, and I promised him: *Sulphur Cargoes, I'll be the best referee since John the Baptist.* He heard that Bonamy Dobrée and T.S. Eliot had recommended he get it, and he was called for an interview, along with David Wevill and Ian Hamilton:

> But the panel, chaired by Sir Herbert Read had discovered during the post-interview deliberations that I wasn't fully British. (I was born in British India, and that was all right, and I am a British subject now,

> which is also all right. But when India got independence in 1947, I lost my British rights until I naturalised.) If they had discovered this earlier, said Read, I'd have got nothing; but now they'd come near to giving me the award and yet to do so would be to go against the terms of Gregory's will. So they were in a fix. By now I had sunk to speechlessness. To get out of the fix, they decided to give me a sum of money (£250) which had nothing to do with the award but which was meant to show their appreciation of my work. At least I'll be able to buy a double bed when I'm married.

But soon, that comforting prospect also receded:

> If you've got Sept 20 down in your diary as my wedding day, you can cancel it for it's indefinitely postponed. Thanks to my mum who's brought a huge debt back with her and has been surprised to discover that like every other responsible son I'm not earning two hundred a month. I went on the wrong and wicked path, she says, when I shd have been an engineer. If I mention the Gregory, I'm told so what, I cd have earned 250 a week as a businessman. The trouble with our – Pakistani – society is that sons are supposed to be an old age pension.

* * *

On December 29th, 1962, I went to Winchester to see Sarah Lee marry her Australian cousin, Francis King, a lecturer in English. For him, of course, I felt contempt, the mask of envy. Forty years later they turned up in Bristol for lunch, and I found him an engaging man. Sarah seemed unchanged to me.

The snow started that day in Winchester, and by the next morning was so deep that in a day's driving I got no further home than Salisbury. The snow stayed for months, in the coldest winter for fifteen years and one still talked about today. Ghose, reporting hockey for *The Observer*, lost eight straight weekends of work, though the paper later gave him a small bonus in recompense:

> So I went and bought myself a pair of trousers and a fancy pair of French shoes. Earning so little, there seems no point in saving.

In February, Sylvia Plath killed herself. Johnson wrote to me: *Rather a handful of dates and contentment than to enter in at the Gate of Peacocks and be booted in the goolies by a broody camel.* He might have written less insouciantly granted the terrible foreknowledge that he would also end his own life, a decade later.

Scene was in trouble. After receiving a piece about the Group that Johnson had written, Stoppard wrote to me: *Hitching says he is making no decisions for 36 hours; our fate is implicit in his remark. But also he said: we are using Johnson's article on poets and I'd like at least two months between articles on poets.*

The last arts page in the *Western Daily Press* appeared at the end of February 1963. The official statement was that it had ended *for commercial reasons*, which was odd, given the increased circulation every arts page day. The truth was that it was gleefully put down by Eric Price, now in total power with his sales of seventy thousand. In the first week after its emasculation, the space where the arts page would have been was occupied by a syndicated feature on the sinking of the *Titanic* in 1912. *Bon Voyage, Titanic.* A vestige of the page staggered on, bleeding, for a few months, as an occasional article, which I had to negotiate with the features editor. Of one of them, by Hobsbaum, Stoppard wrote:

> It's pleasing that despite your curtailment the arts page can still come up with something as good as you will find in any national intellectual mag.

Another article I negotiated was Ghose's review of *Travelling People*, Johnson's first novel. It was an encomium, a eulogy. When I told Ghose that I proposed to tone it down, he protested: *Neither you nor I are obliged to do a favour to B; but we are to literature.* Not many such articles were possible any longer, however, and I determined to quit the paper. I wanted to concentrate seriously on a novel, and, as well as some work for *The Times* in the cricket season, I thought I might earn a regular income from the BBC Foreign Services, for whom I had done a little freelance work in Bristol. As it turned out, I did soon earn a year's living from the BBC, but not from the office I expected.

Ghose had become close to Johnson. Each talked up the other's ambition and shared scorn for most of their contemporaries, a normal attitude in young writers. Ghose wrote to say that the two of them had decided it was time *to revive the short story form by demonstrating the diversity of it, the whole damn range of it.* They were going to write some stories for a joint volume, and invited me to make a third, under their editorship:

> No two of your stories should be the same in technique; this is most important ... We've got to be as good as we want to be.

I wrote some stories and revised some others. Some were accepted, some questioned. I went to London to talk about the project. It became a row with Johnson. What they planned was a manifesto, and I did not have a theory of fiction, or care to have one. I called their formalism pompous; no, they said, just strict, to demonstrate the resources of the form. I argued in favour of vernacular narrative. They opposed it. I returned to Bristol suspecting that I no longer wanted to be in the book, and that they would not want me to be. Ghose confirmed that:

> I hope you're not too pissed off with Bryan and me about the stories. I was hoping that the situation of having to ask you to stand down wouldn't arise by your writing two superb stories soon after that rather disastrous talk at Bryan's... I was talking to Tony Thwaite last night at Dulwich and he said how good your story was.

Anthony Thwaite was literary editor of *The Listener*, which was running a short story competition. I entered one of those I had just written, and won second prize. Another story I sold to the BBC Home Service; the producer, Owen Leeming, invited me to read it myself, which I enjoyed doing, not least because it augmented my fee. Ghose continued:

> The trouble is that Bryan and I are agreed about the end but not entirely about the means. He has got it into his head that a new form for each story is in itself something of a guarantee of its literary worth; I think

> this can lead to absurdity.

Johnson also asked to see Stoppard's stories. He had it in mind to invite him to join the project, though he must have known that Stoppard would be as hostile as I was to a manifesto. They had bumped into each other in London, at an exhibition of the tapestries of Marie Bonheur, from Blauvac:

> B.S. says 'Some of the best short stories I've ever read', whereupon he started picking holes here and there.

When the joint collection was published, under the title *Statement Against Corpses*, it was prefaced with a note:

> These short stories have been written in the knowledge that the form is in decline, but in the belief that this is due to no fault inherent in the form. The short story deserves, but seldom receives, the same precise attention to language as that given normally only to a poem. This book represents a joint attempt, through demonstration of the form's wide technical range, to draw attention to a literary form which is quite undeservedly neglected.

Had I still been part of the project I would have withheld my signature from that benighted declaration. Burroway wrote to me from Ghent, where her husband Walter Eysselinck was working as director of the Royal National Flemish Theatre:

> I thought the joint note on the short story simply unforgiveable, as I told him [Ghose], but the stories on the whole very good. He says it has had 'very mixed' reviews, which I take to mean very bad, and I'm sorry. I think as a critic the statement would have put me off, though, and I probably wouldn't have been fair to it either.

Johnson mistrusted story-telling. He liked to trot out the puritanical observation that, in children's parlance, to tell stories is to tell fibs. I used to answer: sure, and children love stories, and from them learn about the human life they will lead. His argument was: *life is chaos, each life a series of accidents, so writers can extract a story from life only by strict, close selection, imposing false patterns on chaos.* I argued back, and still argue with his shade, that, since *Gilgamesh*, telling stories is how we provisionally make sense of the world for ourselves, and for each other. Religions do it. If you ask people to explain the principles of something, they give you narrative examples. As Nabokov said, *Literature does not tell the truth but makes it up.* Johnson asked *What use are images, anyway? For one thing simply is not another.* My answer is that metaphor is what connects the ghost and the machine.

Johnson was arguing against the third-person, linear narrative. Fine. But the narrative he preferred, exemplified in Laurence Sterne's *sport of small accidents*, is still a story told by a voice that holds our attention, a better kind of lie, perhaps. *Telling stories is telling lies* is equal in insight to *Too many notes, Herr Mozart.* It is inconvenient for a writer of fiction, and it is naïve – as though a reader might not be aware of the contract one signs on opening a novel, or entering a theatre. In Coleridge's famous phrase about *the willing suspension of disbelief*, the crucial word is 'willing'. Of course we know it is just a story and *these our actors were all spirits*, but if we consent to pretend with them that it is true while it lasts we might enjoy the evening, even learn something from a mere story, and only a dolt will leave saying: 'I don't believe a word of it, it's all made-up, a fib.' Picasso said *art is the lie in which truth is told.* Brecht, whom Johnson admired, made a political point of constantly reminding his audiences that they were spectators in a theatre watching actors telling a story, and yet depended upon the sustaining power of narrative. On page 163 of his second novel, *Albert Angelo*, Johnson suddenly drops the pretence of writing fiction and, exasperated, switches to writing about the real people and events upon which he had till now based his story. He calls it *an almighty aposiopesis* (an unwillingness to continue). It struck me as an almighty condescension. We didn't already know that? He liked the trick so much that he played it again at the end of *House Mother Normal.* When I wrote to tell him how much of *Albert Angelo* I had enjoyed, but questioned how productive an experiment it is to punch holes through pages, finding such tricks formalistic in comparison with the linguistic explorations of James Joyce, he replied: *A.A. just* is, *and it's that way because it is that way, and it's no other way because I rejected all the alternatives* [sic] *as being worse, and no one, but no one, can think themselves into the position of the writer and consider those alternatives.* Which disposes of all critical response to anything.

The RSC director Terry Hands put it to me like this. 'Theatre,' he said, 'is like a magician doing a trick, and we say gosh, how did that rabbit come out of the top hat? Then he shows us – look, he says, I've got this false sleeve here, and a distraction technique there, and that's how I create the illusion, and we say oh, I see now, very cunning. And then the magician repeats the trick and we say gosh, how did the rabbit come out of the top hat?'

In Shiraz I was in a tea house when in came the storyteller. He put down a little mat, representing his stage, his home base, but most of the time he went around the hundred or so men – no women, not in an Iranian tea house – telling his story face to face with the listeners, using a few gestures to dramatise the tale. The audience ranged from boys of eight to men of eighty, but it was apparent that everyone was enjoying the story. Their concentration was complete. At the end, while the storyteller went round collecting a few coins for his performance, I asked an Iranian friend to tell me what the story had been about, since I can't speak Farsi. The answer was that it had been about a princess and a wizard and a dragon. What we would call a fairy-tale. My conclusion was not that Iranian tea drinkers must be childish, but that everyone enjoys a story well told, well crafted, and the subject is not what really matters. The traditional storyteller knows his audience socially, even personally. Does the modern novelist suffer in lacking that social rootedness?

B.S. Johnson himself was always a bit of an outsider, chippy. He was afraid to assume the responsibility of telling a story. Perhaps he had a real doubt about who is out there. He was not much interested in what makes other people tick, and that restricted his scope as a novelist. As Frank Singleton once remarked to me: 'We're all egomaniacs, but we needn't all be bores about it.' What Johnson wrote was about himself. From *Trawl*:

> Now I know these rocks only as shapes, that they are rock is of no point, they drop, but how do I know they even do that, they may climb, everything is relevant only to me, relative only to me, to be seen only from my eyes, solipsism is the only truth: can be the only truth: a thing is so only because I think it to be so: if I do not think it to be so, then it is not so: this must be the only truth: belief does not arise.

To which the obvious response is E.M. Forster's: *Only connect.*

7

Getting the Words Right

I LEFT THE *WESTERN DAILY PRESS* IN SEPTEMBER 1963. I HAD JUST got engaged. On one of my days as Geoffrey Reeves's taxi driver I had met Alison Kennedy, a drama and French student from Shropshire. On a spring night the three of us drove to the Somerset coast to see the dawn break over Blue Anchor Bay. They danced together on the beach while I played the *Merry Widow* waltz on my fiddle. The first time she offered to cook supper for me she said it would not be at the digs she shared with two others but at a friend's place. The address was 1, Beaufort Road, the building where I had had my lonely bedsit when I first moved to Bristol, and where I had lost my virginity. I didn't mention that. Soon we were off to Blauvac together, sharing the car with Stoppard and his friend Isabel.

Immediately after I left the paper, Alison, Stoppard and I gave Mrs Stoppard graver cause for alarm than when her son had disappeared in Gibraltar. We went to Zagreb, where Alison was playing half the Polish army and other parts in a Bristol University production of Jarry's *Ubu,* directed by George Brandt, at an international festival of student drama. After Zagreb it would play Bristol and Llandrindod Wells, an appropriately surrealist itinerary. Among an audience from East and West Europe, a group of women from Manchester objected to Jarry as vulgar. They were answered by a Jugoslav: 'It is better to write in the lavatory than in the drawing-room.' Another Jugoslav thought Manchester's own choice, Ann Jellicoe's *The Knack,* bourgeois and decadent, but he was jeered down by his compatriots. The Russian and Czech students were rigorously trained, but in so conservative a method that little came across the footlights. The Russians, asked what modern playwrights they knew, answered: 'Hemingway, and Capek. We have heard of Ionesco.'

From Zagreb the three of us went on to Split and Dubrovnik. The latter seemed like the setting for a Bellini opera: a medieval fortress, perfectly proportioned, its pavements gleaming and lamp-lined, and no cars within the massive white walls facing the Adriatic and the Dalmatian escarpments. We lodged with the leader of the violas in the city orchestra, and went to hear Beethoven's 4th Piano Concerto in the open-roofed Rector's Palace until Wagnerian lightning blacked out the city. The soloist, Jurica Murai, was in the middle of the first movement cadenza, which he extended by improvisation in case the lights came back, then gave up and resolved the key and the problem in two chords. When the lights came on, they finished the Beethoven and were in the middle of the Jupiter when the lights went out again, this time during a tutti passage. The orchestra struggled to keep going from memory, but section by section they surrendered, in a parody of Haydn. The oboes were the last to go. The next week, the streets were crowded with lounging green-uniformed soldiers with Nazi insignia and rifles. There were trucks with swastikas, and a small moustached man delivered a harangue from a flight of steps. Stoppard asked: 'Haven't they heard?' Stewart Granger was rehearsing by the city gate, pointing his fingers and shooting like a kid. Someone said Jayne Mansfield was in town.

Stoppard and Alison went home and I went on to Greece, for the first time. I needed time alone to write. I chose my destination by catching the first boat leaving Piraeus and going as far as it went, which was Lesbos. On the boat I met Mr Axiotis, who misunderstood me and told everyone that I'd come to write a book about Lesbos, and they should all treat me well. He sent me to his good friends at the Hotel Ermes, overlooking the harbour. 'Mr Axiotis sent me.' 'Mr Who?' But they cut the rate from twenty-six drachmas to fifteen. In the dark, high-ceilinged, crowded bars I watched the men drink coffee and play backgammon and billiards and whist, hurling every card down with finality. A balcony ran outside the window of my room, and a young Greek who had been sheep-farming in Australia leaned in every day. 'Hey, Englishman, wanna fock?' I would smile politely, bent over my typewriter, and say: 'No, thanks all the same, I've got to get on with this, you know.' He kept asking. I couldn't decide whether he was offering me his own body or pimping. One day, my English good manners overcame me. It simply seemed rude to go on refusing him. He led me through the little city, where Shakespeare's Marina had preserved her purity in a brothel, and I had no idea what I was going to do when we got there. It turned out he was leading me to a woman who was a ringer for Fellini's whore on the beach in *8½* with mini-skirted thighs like cedar trunks and a rouged smile slashing her huge, round face. I whimpered and ran, back through the market. He stopped asking after that.

I met the Valieris, mother and daughter, who had lived in Paris during the occupation. The daughter – Marina! – had been educated by an English governess, and gone on the family's frequent trips to London. 'We never thought it would be necessary for her to have qualifications,' said her mother, who was over seventy, vivacious and witty in an aristo style. In Paris, the little Marina had usually spoken in English, which her mother said had been punishable by death. 'The chief of Gestapo stopped her in the street and asked, in English: "Is this the little girl who is always shouting in English?" He was said to have murdered many people.' Around 1950 they moved to Alexandria. Then Nasser came to power. Without sentiment, Mrs Valieri observed: 'My husband died just in time, just as we were to be capitalists no longer.' Nasser expropriated 'everything we had – the Mappin and Webb silver, even the cat. We kept the dogs, though. We had proof they were Cypriot.' 'Poor' for the first time in their lives, mother and daughter had come to the Gulf of Yera, where Marina had been left four thousand olive trees, but the Greek government insisted on the use of a spray that had prevented a single olive from appearing.

I stayed a month in what was then the unspoilt Levantine port of Mytilene. The hotel added two more residents to my room. One of them was a devious, gold-toothed little commercial traveller in books. The other was Vassiliou, a holy innocent, unaffected and trusting. He was a fisherman from Molyvos, at the northern tip of the island. I had the room to myself during the daytime, and worked. *Everything else is masks and subterfuge and bribing of sentries,* I wrote to Stoppard. *Only the princess's bedroom, the writing, is real.* Ghose sent me a letter:

> ...the worst thing about being a writer: even when you've sacrificed material comfort and produced a reasonably good work, there may be no reward for it at all. It's only the love and admiration of a few friends which keeps you alive.

In Foutiou's bar on a Sunday morning, hearing the island's political gossip, interpreted for me, and when that bored me looking out across the Aegean and perceiving detail of fishing boats miles out, smelling seaweed and tar and baklavas and coffee, I found the sacrifice of material comfort bearable. As for friends, yes, but most of us would go on writing in solitary confinement. In friendless times there is always the sound of posterity clapping. What I was working on was my first publishable novel. On to my main character, Phipps,

I grafted obsessive-compulsive quirks of my younger self. In the euphoria of arriving at Cambridge I had mentioned them with a chuckle when filling in a medical form; they so alarmed the university shrink that it had taken two visits to to persuade him I was not in need of help. My title, *The Crowd*, was suggested to me by Stoppard, after he had read the first draft for me. The book opens: *An egg that split while he was boiling it always did deject him.* I was plagiarising a poem of my own:

Paranoid Boiling an Egg
It cracked. Jesus Christ, I knew it would.
I hate them when they ooze
Fleshy white ectoplasm
My toes clench tight inside my shoes.
Perhaps, like molten lead dropped into a
Bucket, the shape may
Tell me my fortune.
It looks like burst brains.
There's a nice thought to start the day.
It's soggy to eat, too.
I hack it out, berserk.
My spoon jabs down through
The bottom, like a foot through ice.
The wind picks on me on my way to work.

Any journalist knows that you are more than half-way to writing your piece once you have got the intro right. You have found the tone of voice in which to tell the story. It is the same when you are telling a child a bedtime story. What actually happens, the plot, comes later; the first thing is to set up an atmosphere, a set of expectations, a field of interest, and some sort of convention, which means the relationship of the storyteller to the listener/reader. With a bedtime story, that is usually natural, because you probably know the child very well. It is more challenging with a book to write.

It was a four-day rail journey back to England. Changing trains at Munich I was propositioned by a man eating Würst in the buffet. Railway stations seem to be a favourite location for gays on the hunt. Passing trade, I suppose. From Victoria Station I rang Stoppard to say I was back. He said: 'I don't know if I'm the one who should be telling you this, but Alison is pregnant.'

Alison's parents, both primary school teachers, must have sighed when they heard the news – premarital pregnancy was still in the closet – but they did not reproach us out loud. We had been expecting to get married after her graduation the following summer; her pregnancy simply hurried us up. Bristol University gave her permission to take a year out, the calendar year of 1964, and we booked a wedding at Quakers Friars register office.

* * *

I sent Stoppard what I had written. His response was generous. He told me I was wrong to fear that I was plainly under the influence of Beckett's novels in passages of 'high' writing. I had never set out to imitate Beckett, and it was perhaps more an influence sub-contracted through Pinter. Even if it might be some way from what you think you want to write, there can be a rhythm in the air, a pattern of speech, that affects you. An extreme example is the experience I cannot be alone in having had, coming out from an enjoyable Shakespeare performance and, for a few minutes, while the echoes persist, finding it easy to speak in blank verse. In writing, the effect may go beyond the style of your prose, and start to influence who your characters are and how they behave, because what you can imagine is limited by how you speak.

I sometimes wonder if I should have persevered with the style of that first book, which was fairly well received. Some fifteen books later I did return to it, in an elaborated form; but meanwhile I had been interested in trying out other tunes. When I taught creative writing in Texas, I advised students to forget about finding your own voice, to start with. Think of the job as akin to making chairs. If you want to make a good chair you don't go into a trance and invent the chair. What you should do is apprentice yourself to someone who knows how to make chairs, and learn the craft of it, and only when you know you can make a chair that won't collapse when somebody sits on it do you start to think about making My Chair. It had been my luck, I told them, when I was at school and wanting to write poetry, to have a friend who gave me similar advice. I also told them to skip that advice which is always dished out: write about what you know. That way you will wind up writing about nothing but thoughts at granny's grave, or why I was in tears after the high school prom. Instead, imagine what you don't know, what it would be like to be someone else. Children naturally do that when they make up stories, but by adolescence many would-be writers have been browbeaten into veiled autobiography.

Scene had folded, and Stoppard was:

> ...jobless and sinking. I nearly got on the *Express* – I know you'll be delighted I didn't. But frankly I was looking forward to stopping worrying about what to do next, and merely go through my functions and find £30 in an envelope every Friday for a few months... I am left with nothing. I retired to bed and lay there to save cigarettes till teatime in a slough of hopelessness, sorting out my despair like playing cards into suits...

That phrase I quoted back to him decades later. He denied having coined it. Now, he had:

> ...no money, debts, stuck on play, listless, cigless, starving, rent overdue, Mr and Mrs Smith depending on me for £14 (the first 14 is yours) and mainly the awful too-late feeling of having missed the bus somewhere, leaving me stranded in limbo with the ghosts of the unwritten books and plays to haunt me... very dramatic. In a word, I felt bloody low. The situation hasn't changed, except that I'm past feeling low. I'm going to apply for a job on *TV Times* on Monday. Hack work. Too bad, who cares. Kenneth [Ewing, his agent] keeps on at me about the play which (I lie) I am progressing with. BBC man wants ideas from me with possible commission, and I haven't had an idea in weeks. I've decided I don't give a fuck about anything except to write a full length stage play and at least one TV this winter, but find myself incapable of thought until my grotesque finances are bolstered into at least an illusion of security.
>
> Last night I went to A-R [Associated-Rediffusion] for the first reading of my play, a grisly experience... the cast sat round the board room table and read their lines. I cdn't see the point of the operation. Except that they decided that seven more minutes wd have to come out, and I'm supposed to be cutting it this weekend, which will make it 42 minutes out in all. I'm

> thinking of calling it 'Walk On The' or 'Walk on the Wa'. Cast loves the play, tho.
>
> Did you like West's Week [a *Western Daily Press* gossip column of which Stoppard, from London, had continued to write the greater part]? Price phoned me: Look, Tom, I've decided to cut West's Week to three guineas from now on, okay?/Nothing doing./For fuck's sake, this isn't the *Daily Mail*, you know./If it were it would be ten guineas./Christ, I'm supposed to be cutting down costs./Too bad. Five guineas./Well, we'll see how it goes. Starvation makes one bold.
>
> What I want is an evening with you and Alison in the womb, lots of fags, ingroup jokes, plans and optimism. I'm a slut. I should pore over my immortal works. Meantime Jones cometh for tea tomorrow with vain hopes of picking up his rent owed from Oct 1. When wedding?

The answer was November 16th, with Stoppard as my best man. By then, Supermac's seven years would have closed, and the country would be governed by Sir Alec Douglas-Home, an eldritch apparition in a land raucous with post-Profumo laughter. The Sixties had started by the autumn of 1963. There was a feeling of freedom, of social, if not political, revolution. The old order, what D.H. Lawrence called *the grey ones,* had been discredited, by mockery. *Look Back in Anger*, the Chatterley trial, *Lolita*, Peter Cook, *Private Eye, That Was The Week That Was,* Profumo, *Catch-22* – all of them, and I could ask the printer to go on listing such things until the foot of the page – had aroused a spirit of irreverence, a refusal to be bowed down by pieties. We had seen that the emperor's new clothes were nothing but a grey suit, with an inadequate man inside it. We were impatient to inherit the earth, not meekly.

To Stoppard's critique of my novel, I answered that I was *chewing over yr letter again in case any flesh still stuck to the plumstones.* Another letter soon came back, in a more optimistic key:

> After I wrote to you, I thought up two play-ideas, synopsised one and Ewing, who likes it, is trying to get some tv co to cough up commission. Small hope. But I'll write it anyway, within the month I hope, and

> – well, who knows. I'm not plot-headed about things, as you know, and found it difficult to provide a synopsis as required because I work on a basic idea and the plot 'happens'...

He was paying the rent with hack work:

> The features editor of *Weekend* gave me a True Life Drama (ghosted) to re-write with punch. It took an hour. £10. This was my intro, as far as I remember it:
>
> *The terror struck out of the calm of a windless day and an oily green sea. It began with the fury of whipped-up water – one second I was swimming gently to the beach, the next I was clamped in a giant vice and dragged viciously down and down.*
>
> *And then I knew.*
>
> *Shark!*
>
> *The vice round my legs was the barbed jaw of a great grey killer!*
>
> ... and so on.
>
> Versatile, that's me.
>
> Big news: West's Week is over. Yesterday's, as you read this, ain't mine. At least most of it isn't. I got the inside gen from Keith [the features editor]. Seems Eric Price was furious at my short-shrift treatment of his offer to cut me down to three guineas and immediately started soliciting staff for Week pars with view to making me redundant. He had asked me to do a series on Btl [Bristol] housing for him – I don't think I told you – and I sd I wasn't interested. This annoyed him too.

A year earlier, Price had commissioned Stoppard to write a series on race relations in Bristol. Stoppard was still fixing interviews when the paper came out with a front-page banner heralding *A Searing, Shocking Exposé of Race Relations*. Stoppard was appalled, and went to remonstrate with his editor. 'Listen, laddie,' Price told him, 'this paper is built on bullshit.'

> So Stoppard had to go. I gather that first attempt at Week pars resulted in weak pars, so last Friday's WW

was Stoppard. But the crisis came to its climax when I sent over the enclosed bit for this Friday's lead. Price wrote on it to Turner 'Don't use this fucking rubbish'. Keith told me, so I said 'Okay – I've quit'. Whereupon Keith said, 'Well, actually, Price is writing to you to say you're fired.' An academic distinction. The idiotic part is that this appears to be a bit of sheer pique on Price's part because the scorned item is exactly the same in tone and humour of [sic] other items which provoked Price to tell Turner 'Stoppard is a great writer'. Need I add that flame was added by another item I contributed:

'Mr Charlton (Warwick Charlton, author of Stephen Ward Speaks*) paints a pretty sordid picture of life in the circle in which Ward* [a central figure in the Profumo scandal] *moved, and in which many other people still move,' wrote this paper's reviewer, explaining censoriously: 'There was dust in the flat... Little housework was done by his protégées...' I am one of the people still moving in this sordid circle. If Mr Charlton cares to run his finger along my mantelpiece he will expose a depravity which, if handled right, would put us both in clover...*

I pulled off a major triumph today by sidling into my bank, to which I have given a wide berth, rushed up in a false beard to the newest young clerk, whipped out self-cash cheque for ten quid. He caught it second bounce and I dashed out with the tenner, so am back in fags again...

The play Stoppard had said he was going to write in a month had sounded a difficult trick when he had described it to me, and I told him so. A few days later, he was writing to me again in the highest spirits:

The plain extraordinary beautiful fact is that since I last wrote to you I have written what purports to be a 60-minute tv play (the 60 minute part is pure labelling – I really have no idea whether it lasts 40 or 80). Since I finished it just as your letter arrived, you will not resent my delicious feeling as I read: 'The other awes me: of course it's good but it will need at least 100 fresh gags and I don't know how you sit down and write them.' The chronology was as follows: Sunday, in desperation think up idea of gagman, make notes/Following Thursday, write to you to state idea, without faintest feeling of it ever being done/Friday, first scene done/Tuesday morning, first draft done/Wednesday morning, final draft done/Thursday morning, handed over to Ken Ewing... Oh dear, do I appear cat-and-cream-like? Of course, it was all done at night, and with the flush of it going well I found myself working from 6 p.m. to 7 a.m., finally. I think I've written about two jokes, not 100; the point being, of course, that, as in the case of us two for example, one can be funny for minutes on end without making a single joke. I mean the gagwriter doesn't have to go on about three men in a railway compartment, he just gags with people as we do in conversation, so in fact I merely played 'your' part as well as 'mine' and it went like a bomb. All this presupposes your approval of the result – the opposite may be the case, but at the moment, not having retreated very far from it, I think it's good. If you think so too it will bolster me up; if not then I expect you to say so with force, and by that time I would be gloomily agreeing with you.

The wedding: Anthony, *Walk on t Water* is being recorded on Friday and I'd like to be there if poss, just for the kick of it coming on a screen, otherwise I'd have to wait till March. So I'll have to get the midnight train or a very early one in the morning: obviously if there are no trains to get me to the registry office on time, I'll skip the recording without any feeling of deprivation. So I'll probably catch the train that gets in at 3 a.m., and go to G.L. and meet you at Paragon 9.30 to 10. Or presumably on your pre-wedding night you will be alone [my best man was to be disapproving when he found this not to be the case] so I cd, if you think it's a good idea, make my way to the Paragon from the station. The only thing is that you'll obviously be getting in a good night's sleep, and I'm not sure about burgling the house at 3.30 with that Hound of the Stephensons off-muzzle.

> On wedding (2): my most respectable suit is that brown one, which necessitates brown boots. Clearly this is not going to worry you, but should you feel that reprobation from the assembled Kennedys would reflect on your tastes in best men, tip me off and I'll appear in my second-best-man's grey suiting with Manfield winklepickers, black. (Please strike out all reference to footwear and file under *The Artist as Anarchist – the Stoppard Letters (1959-73).*

He urged me to submit scripts for a new radio series of fifteen-minute plays.

> One can approach something as short as that in the spirit of attacking an article – there is no sense of a great project hanging over one's head, a thing which I find is responsible for many things being left unwritten... [The producer] tells me that if one is weak on plot and good on dialogue, then so much the better – which suits me, of course – I have tremendous difficulty in seizing a 'plot' but am happy to tackle a 'situation'...
>
> I've got 1s 7d in the world and a letter from the bank. However, I'll last the weekend, and by Monday I reckon that Ewing will have read the play. If he considers it easily saleable, I'll be in a strong position to get a few quid advance out of F&D [Fraser and Dunlop, the agency where Ewing worked].

An alternative, he says, is a journalistic piece he has been asked to do, but which would take more research than he feels like doing:

> I might do a think piece with fake interviews and fake facts. I couldn't post this today after all. What happened was that I formulated plan to make another incognito raid on my bank. Unfortunately I slept through alarm and woke up at 2.30 (from 8 a.m.); sailed out, waited for bus, in desperation hailed a taxi which arrived at the bank at 3.1 p.m., leaving me with a taxi and the aforementioned 1s 7d with 2s 3d on the clock. There was a slight altercation, which ended with

me giving him aforesaid 1s 7d and a promissory note.

Stoppard scholars will spot the genesis of *The Dissolution of Dominic Boot*.

Walked back home reflecting on my ruined day, which was to have been pleasant: look in on rehearsal of Walk, wander over to Old Vickers and see O'T and perhaps even get into *Hamlet*. Got home, which was uninhabited by rich and poor alike, and happily remembered 2s in the gas meter which was swiftly converted into Woodbines. And here I am. Tomorrow I shall attempt the bank once more. Depression added to by the Ewing who called. He'd read the play and was curiously reserved, i.e. merely 75 per cent favourable instead of the 95 per cent which I require as a minimum to keep my confidence afloat. So now I'm glumly thinking I've underplayed too much.

Today an offer to have my photo taken by Faber's official photographers, who just had to be called 'Messrs Elliott and Fry'.

[A handwritten PS] And finally – I am now writing a 15-minute play about a man who takes a taxi, broke, to the bank, arriving at 3.1pm, and keeps on the taxi, going from place to place trying to borrow the money to pay the fare, and never quite catching up the clock.

[Later again] Saturday/Sunday – borrowed quid, went to see Peter O'T.

[Later yet, back in typescript] My fortunes have taken another turn – I am just setting off by taxi to the Dorchester to renew acquaintance with the blonde daughter of the ex-President of Guatemala. Also, P, discovering that I was broke, expressed astonishment and dismay that such injustice shd be rife in the world, gave me 'for now' £10 of the £100 which I had just seen him win at chemin, and wrote out a cheque for £100. Said I was too good a writer to 'fuck about journalism'. Some day I'll pay £110 into his account and square my conscience. Taking O'T and my presidential lady to see my *Walk* recording. That about the money is definitely confidential for you two,

> please don't say a thing.

Stoppard and I had not relinquished our notion of a *Bristol Review*. He sent me a postcard about it: As I'm going to Post Office I may as well drop you a line. *The line is: Who is our man in the business suit?* When I sent him another chunk of my novel, he urged me on: *Alison, if you see him doing nothing, hit him.*

> I was woken up today by A-R: because Whiting's *Marching Song* is too close to Kennedy etc, they are putting in *Walk on the Water* tonight ... I lose all the publicity because there is of course no mention of it in the *TV Times* etc, which usually do a write-up of Play of the Week's authors; on the other hand, it may be that the fewer people who connect me with it, the better. This is not phoney modesty; the production, and a lot of Stoppard, depresses me.
>
> My little play about the guy who travels around by taxi trying to raise the money to pay the fare is going to end with the demoniac taxi-driver taking the man's clothes and furniture in part exchange after an all-night search for loans as the meter ticks on and on. I think it ends with Boot walking into a bank in his underwear to raise a loan for the taxi fare. Abandonment of realism.

Just before my wedding I had read the first draft of *I Can't Give You Anything But Love, Baby,* the play Stoppard had written in about six days, which was never produced.

> It was good of you to steal time 'at a time like this' to read and give such detailed report on *ICGYABLB*. I took it to heart and head. The main criticism perhaps boils down to the charge that my characters don't behave coherently: after a couple of hours of depression at your justice, I rationalised it, dragging out my double-action, watercooled, recoilless, muzzle-loading Maxim (a pun, a pun!) – 'Neither do people'... Am having lunch on Tuesday with Mr Collins of Collins re my well known first novel. He somewhere gained the impression that I have a novel 'up my sleeve', an

> impression I have done nothing to discourage. Indeed, I am arranging, when we shake hands, for a cataract of quarto sheets to fall from my soiled cuff.

By the end of 1963 Stoppard had met Jose Ingle, who would be his first wife. They spent Christmas and Hogmanay together in Scotland with his parents. He wrote to me:

> I wilt among the pagan Picts to whom I am bringing Christianity. I end in haste for there are men coming up the drive with a vacant cross and I must go and see what they want.

Back in London, he was asked to see someone at BBC radio:

> ... and found myself closeted with the men behind The Dales... [*Mrs Dale's Diary*] My first reaction of course was one of good grief let me out. The system appears to be that three or four writers do one month's Dales in turn, i.e. 20 fifteen-min progs, for around £500. I know damn all about it, and am only about ten per cent interested, and the ten per cent is all greed. Of course, you will shudder, but be not alarmed, there is no chance of me churning out the Dales for the next five years at the expense of all else... But the situation is at the moment that they want me to do a mock-up dummy run of five progs, i.e. one week's supply, having been briefed on the characters and rough plot lines. Ludicrous of course, but have little objection to going thus far with them as the dummy is worth a hundred quid for a week's work. They want to brief me on Jan 27, and then give me seven days to turn in the five episodes; i.e. the deadline is strict, so it CAN'T take up more than seven days of my time, for the hundred doubloons.

When he did the dummy it was not used. His style *did not meld* with that of the other series writers, though, later, he did pay the rent by writing fifteen-minute serial episodes for the BBC's Arabic Service. He outlined his work schedule:

> Armchair Theatre to be finished by end of Feb

> (deadline in contract), adapt *WOTW* [*A Walk on the Water*] for radio, Dale dummyrun between Jan 27 and Feb 3 (pace Boorman), *Rosencrantz and Guildenstern,* TELLY play for A-R (they want to commission, maybe based on short story in Faber book, the third one), one or two more 15-min radios on request, maybe a novel for Blond or Faber, and let's hope, the stage play which is my new year resolution (1965 maybe). And then in 1970 I'll do... Read 14 books in Scotland – Sitwell memoirs (*Façade* period), *Billy Liar, Lear, Hamlet,* Connolly, James Baldwin, Waugh, Roth, Dover Wilson, *Prater Violet*, John Hale and others. Little or no work. Am bag of nerves, contemplating jobs in hand. In my mind's eye is the Mona Lisa, while in front of me is a block of marble and I keep daring myself to pick up the chisel.

It was acute of Stoppard to see what the Mona Lisa might have been had Leonardo taken a chisel to it.

I sent my novel, three-parts written, to Gillon Aitken at Chapman and Hall. He indicated that he would be accepting it when it was finished, and asked me to meet him at his home in Kensington. Alison came with me. I was impressed to be sharing an imprint with Evelyn Waugh, not to mention Charles Dickens. Aitken turned out to be a very tall Etonian, with a wrong-foot delivery which beat batsmen not sure when his tangled limbs would release the ball. Having written to me in 1960, he had been patient. Now I was sitting, with Alison, in his enormous drawing-room. He charmed us languidly for a while, then his voice changed, became intent, and he leaned forward to tell me what he really wanted me to know about my book: 'You know that silly neurotic habit you've given your character of liking to have the change in his pocket in the fewest possible number of coins? I'm the same!'

Fiction would remain my main road for twenty years. Perhaps not a road, more like a pinball machine. At the outset I could not have said I will do this, and meet him or her, and it will lead to this, and so on. Rather, like a pinball, I hit something, and a few thousand goes up on the screen, and I am bounced on somewhere else, and perhaps earn another thousand or two, and then I disappear down a hole, and for a while nothing at all happens, until I find a handle to get back in play. That is one way of doing it. The alternative, which most writers choose, is to do something else for a steady income. Or to start off with a best-seller. Or, perhaps, to find one form, one style, one slot which pays off, and stick to it. That is what writers concerned with their legacy would do, but my delight in other people's poetry, novels, plays, films and journalism led me to trying out new forms to find out more about how language works. I'm lucky that it was easier to sell my kind of stuff when I had most responsibilities. If there are young writers now with the tastes and models I had, heaven knows how they might earn a living. I am lucky too that I have never found it hard to live frugally when necessary. A wartime childhood conditioned me.

There is this thing called literature. No writer ever got up in the morning and said, I think I'll create some literature today. The word is a badge pinned on posthumously to what, when you're doing it, is just *Getting the words right* (as Hemingway answered interminable probing from George Plimpton, in *The Paris Review,* about what the most difficult thing is in writing). Imagine that Shakespeare's ink were still wet. It was once. If he could come back now he would change lines over which a million scholars have pored, cut this scene, add something there. That is how he worked, how we all work. What was perfect when we finished writing it yesterday has developed cracks overnight. If that never happens to you, your writing, or your sleeping brain, is not in good shape. Perfect art is bad art. It pretends to have an existence independent of the reader.

At editorial conferences now the last word goes to accountants and sales people, *the fool heart of the counting-house* in Yeats's phrase. New titles pour out, seeking short-term turnover. Supermarkets have influence on the choice of titles and jacket design. Sales are hyped by fabricated images of success, not by critically assessed quality. And so writing which might find readers next century, not just next week, which plays and tries things on and changes its mind and delights and challenges, a form in which the English have excelled, is disregarded, and our culture grows more brutal. *When the language goes, everything goes,* said Ezra Pound. My time at Chapman and Hall, which was shortly to merge into Eyre and Spottiswoode, seems like the Garden of Eden before the Fall. It wasn't easy then to get published, or produced on stage; it never was. But it was easy to believe that what it took was to write good stuff. Not any more, in the age of conglomerate publishers and bookstores, an age of which I do not expect my grandchildren to see the end. I will modify Ginsberg's famous line: I saw some of the best minds of my generation wasted by other people's madness for profit.

The rot took hold in the 1980s, and had ruined the crop by the time of the abandonment of the price-fixing Net Book Agreement in 1997, the outcome of which, duplicated all over the country, was that my local bookshop folded. Trevor Hockey, the manager, explained it to me: 'Shops like mine have been delighted to serve minority tastes, to offer personal service, promote local writers, deal in second-hand copies, but in the end we can pay the overheads only by what we earn from best-sellers. When you can go to Asda and buy the latest Harry Potter for less than I have to pay at the wholesale trade counter, we have no chance of surviving.'

Some good books go on being written, and a handful of eye-catching writers make a good living from them, but it is hard to find many of them, like artefacts of a cottage industry. Increasingly they come out through micro-publishing: small houses with no marketing clout, self-publishing, online books. When public library sales underwrote the publisher's risk it was still feasible, just about, for literary editors to keep up with *the best that has been thought and said,* in Matthew Arnold's phrase.

I was taught by Eliot *to care/And not to care*, and have learned to sit still. But not to hold my breath. It ain't coming back. We were just in time.

8

Newcomers

Alison had won a French-verse-speaking prize, worth £10. Added to my £125 advance from Gillon Aitken, that was what we had to live on, at least until the cricket season started in April and I could hope for work from *The Times*. But something turned up.

John Boorman asked me to go and talk to him at his home in Keynsham. I had worked with him before. He had seen my stuff in the *Western Daily Press* arts page about Centre 42, asked me to go and see him at the BBC, and when we met told me that he wanted to make a studio programme about the project, and me to front it for sixty minutes on BBC 1, nationwide, live. I told him I had never looked a TV camera in the eye, did not have a TV set, and had almost never watched one. 'Good,' he said. 'You won't be burdened by preconceptions.' There was no autocue then. The script I wrote was copied on to idiot boards, in large capital letters to be held beside the camera by the PA. Half-way through addressing the nation, I was offered words which I, even though catatonic, recognised had nothing to do with what I was supposed to say next. The PA had got the boards in the wrong order. Idiot boards were operated by an idiot. I ad-libbed a clumsy link into the next item, and am glad there was no video then. I would hate to watch it. In hundreds of TV programmes since then, nothing – not dried interviewees, or wet and unstoppable ones, not a craned camera very slowly collapsing like a giraffe with a broken neck – nothing has matched that first gut panic.

When I met him in Keynsham, Boorman, the new pin-up boy of documentary TV, said he wanted to make a series about Bristol for the about-to-be-launched second BBC channel, and me to script it. In the course of several subsequent meetings I could come up with no format that pleased him or me. To capture a city in six half-hour episodes would be a tough assignment for a seasoned scriptwriter, let alone the rookie I was. In any case, it is not possible to write scripts for Boorman, as other writers, such as Peter Nichols and Alex Jacobs, have found since he became a cinema director. He writes his own nowadays. Suddenly he, as it were, flipped the camera round at me and Alison, and asked us to be the protagonists of the series, the eyes through which he would explore Bristol. It might have been the view from our balcony that gave Boorman the notion, or it might have been the view of Alison.

The series was called *The Newcomers*. We were newcomers to Bristol, and our generation represented the newly-come welfare state, the new Britain invoked by Harold Wilson in the election later that year. It was Boorman who chiefly scripted the series, with his associate director Michael Croucher, of whom John Betjeman had spoken to me some years earlier, and whose obituary I would write in *The Guardian* decades later. Each episode found a form of its own. For the first, a reconnaissance of Bristol and of our lives in it, Boorman borrowed the *Bristol Review* idea, which I had mentioned to him. Stoppard and I, with Derek Balmer as our photographer, were followed around locations on the pretence that we were seeking material for our magazine. Later episodes dwelt on what made for a good life, the city at night, finding a house in which to raise a family, and a party, for which the BBC laid on gallons of neat vodka to ensure spectacular behaviour.

Captured on film, Martin Shuttleworth shows off his best party small-talk: 'What I always say is that history is the black sheep uncle whose debts I repudiate.' That brings a bemused nod from George Brandt, not a man bemused often. The last of the six films (they were later recut as three longer films for BBC 1), about giving birth, presented a problem when, after two months of filming, the hospital discovered that it was going to be twins. To avoid a stagey ending, Boorman decided to announce the facts of the birth right at the start of the film. The rest would be a documentary record of what happened in Bristol during that day, May 30th 1964, an idea that developed from the stepping-stone of someone's remark that anyone would be interested to see the newspapers of the day of their birth. He treated it all as a feature film, with Alison and me and our friends playing the parts of ourselves. But the star, as Boorman intended, was the city of Bristol. Watching it now, you remember how seductively seedy Clifton was then: peeling grandeur, prams and bikes in the corniced halls, real shops.

Cinéma-vérité was in vogue. The term was lazily borrowed for a new, informal style in documentary television, made possible by the development of more nimble filming techniques. So this series was received as tele-vérité. It created interest. One reviewer wrote: *The future historian will be able to tell exactly what it was like to be somebody like Anthony or Alison Smith, in a city like Bristol, in 1964. Television has gained its first diary.* The truth is that the future historian will have no such luck. At best, he or she will be able to launch rough guesses at what it was like to be somebody filmed while undergoing a confusing experience. Another reviewer was more disobliging. *These were not people who make entertainment,* he wrote: *...they were people for whom entertainment is made.* Posterity took a swift sword to that reviewer: one of the people who did not make entertainment was at that time writing *Rosencrantz and Guildenstern Are Dead.* Still, I had some sympathy with the critics. They had little apparatus to help them breathe in the rare atmosphere where documentary and drama overlap. The BBC themselves were more cagey. The series was, they allowed, *something very artful, very created.* Huw Wheldon, then head of BBC documentaries, called it *television's first novel,* which was nearer the mark than *first diary.*

A third reviewer said the series concerned *a real-life couple seen leading their own lives, or at least – as the Goons might put it – a photograph thereof.* But the Goons' distinction is a crucial one. Anyone's life is chiefly interior. When it surfaces, it is usually in words. Hardly ever does it express itself in the kind of neat, significant actions that a 'television novel' requires – so as in a novel, actions had to be invented which would dramatise the invisible real life. We were trimmed into characters. Scenes were staged for the camera on pretexts that few people saw through. We were rehearsed in lines to speak, moves to make, expressions to register. A novelistic realism was maintained. For instance, one of the questions we ask of people we meet is: 'What are you doing for a living?' The true answer, in our case, was: 'We are being paid by the BBC to make these films.' That, of course, would not have done, so work was invented for me to be seen doing. Alison was told privately at the hospital that it was going to be twins, but she was required to use her dramatic training to react with amazement when the scene was set up again for the camera. Hold the front page!

The series had already started transmission, and become news. Boorman pioneered documentaries on ordinary lives, but the tabloids were having none of that. Anyone appearing on TV had automatically become a 15-minute celebrity. When word got out that it was going to be twins, photographers were climbing through the windows of The Paragon. Ruth, our landlady, got rid of them by using her skills, too, as a former actress. She did what she had done to Joe Israeli, picked up Jessie, unmuzzled her and threw her at the *Daily Express*, while shrieking: 'Oh my god, she hasn't got her muzzle on!'

To be trimmed to someone else's pattern was confusing, but so what? Well, any actor in a soap can testify that people wish to tuck him or her inside the character they portray. When that character is ostensibly yourself, a powerful social force has come into play. If we tell several million viewers that we are thus, we may not find it easy to be otherwise, even on our own. Our grasp on what we believed to be our true selves was dislodged by the daily requirement that we should act out feelings that in real life are too complex, tender, and in flux to be squared off in a single sentence. The most searching instance was the climax of the series, the birth of our daughters. Several newspapers had quoted me as saying: *When Alison goes into labour I shan't know who to ring first, the maternity hospital or the BBC.* It was a reporter's quote, not mine, but it hit a nerve. As we held Imogen and Sophie, minutes old, in our arms, we felt called upon to perform the intensity of the moment. Neither of us did perform it, or could. The point is, we felt the demand of being watched.

The Observer gave me a page to describe the experience of working with Boorman. A story I didn't tell in *The Observer*: he wanted to shoot a sequence in a swish flat, and asked if I knew one. I took him to meet Richard Hawkins. In his palatially spartan drawing-room, Hawkins offered us a drink, from the many bottles beside the fireplace. Boorman and I each consented to a whisky. Talking away, on edge with a stranger, Hawkins poured me a glass of the single malt he knew I liked, corked the bottle, uncorked a bottle of cooking whisky and gave Boorman a glass of that. The film-maker was far too inquisitive not to ask: 'Tell me, Richard, why did you give Anthony one kind of whisky and me another kind?' Hawkins realised what, absent-mindedly, he had done, and could see no way out except to tell the truth. 'Well, you look like the kind of man who'd put water in his whisky.' Boorman used to tell that story with delight.

After writing the profile, still the inauthenticity of our experience nagged at me. A novelist, I had allowed myself to become a character in someone else's fiction. Anyone who knows Flann O'Brien's comic novel *At-Swim-Two-Birds* will recognise what happened next. My reprisal, I realised, would be a novel that fictionalised the making of the TV fiction.

* * *

The BBC's regional head of programmes, Desmond Hawkins, heard that a couple of young writers were working with Boorman, and was kind enough to invite Stoppard and me to have a drink with him in his office. 'Writing, eh?' he said to us. 'I've done some of that. Before the war there was a literary magazine called *The Criterion.* I used to review fiction for them, along with T.S. Eliot and George Orwell.' After we left him, Stoppard and I agreed that our question would have been: 'T.S. Eliot, George Orwell and... *Desmond Hawkins?* What happened?' Let the joke stand, but it was a callow one. Apart from being the progenitor of the Natural History Unit, which many would argue is the glory of the BBC, Hawkins had a productive writing life for years before and after we met him, and was an authority on Thomas Hardy.

After that meeting I was asked to write a script for the Natural History Unit about the evolution of the horse. It was a Desmond Morris programme and he had done the research, but was too busy to script it. I was taken to London Zoo to watch the rough cut with Morris, an entertaining man with a surreal sense of humour. Watching Lippizaners prancing around in the sawdust of the Spanish Riding School, he remarked: 'They look as though they didn't like the lunch so they've trampled the furniture to bits.' When the programme went out Maurice Wiggin, the *Sunday Times* TV reviewer, wrote that my script had moved him to tears. Good, I thought, I'll be getting some more work from this outfit. I never heard from them again.

Stoppard went off to Berlin for some months on a Ford Foundation scholarship for playwrights. They were lodged in comfort:

> The man in charge of the accommodation told me that I was free to rearrange my room and decorate it any manner I saw fit because he wanted me to know that I was among people who understood writers and realised that they were individuals who could not be expected to work in an atmosphere unsympathetic to them. I didn't want to tell him I was a middle-class boy who wouldn't get a job and liked the atmosphere fine. Perhaps I will roll up the carpet and hang it on the wall in case he thinks I am a fake.

Sitting in a bar on the Kurfürstendamm, reading a cricket report in *The Times,* he recognised a couple of jokes from Our Correspondent which told him who had written it. Before leaving England, he had met Bryan Johnson. The publication of *Albert Angelo* had been delayed, Johnson had told him, by 'dim printers who have put language into a strait-jacket and don't know what to do when confronted by an innovator'. However, Johnson was feeling bullish about his and Ghose's stories in *Statement Against Corpses*. They were *the best short stories that BSJ has read.*

As part of the Ford Foundation deal, Stoppard's play *A Walk on the Water* was to be performed in Hamburg. He offered to pay our fares there for the opening night. With two new-born babies, we had to decline. We missed a spectacle. At the curtain:

> I was gently told that the actors would be offended if I didn't partake of the German tradition and show myself in the line-up. So indeed I was dragged on, clutching the hot clammy hands of my senile star and my director, whereupon the gallery erupted into a storm of gleeful abuse. Wow. It was a hell of a scene. The gallery booing like crazy and the rest of the audience counter-attacking with bravos (a very self-conscious word, that – I could never shout 'bravo' without feeling like an extra in *The Caruso Story*)... paralysis overtook me: robotlike and blank I allowed myself to be guided by the cast and director not once but twice more back on to the stage to witness the riot, which grew hilariously with my every reappearance... I feel partly fed up and partly furious that I let *WOTW*, whatever its virtues, represent me as a writer first time out. [To his agent, Ewing] I murmured in his ear that if he ever tried to get it put on in London I'd fire him on the spot... may it be only performed after my death as a historical curiosity, assuming, of course, that I arouse any posthumous curiosity, which, the way I feel now, is a large assumption.

In Berlin he had finished, typed out and sent to Ewing *a one-acter in which the characters are 'Fortinbras, Captain, Rosencrantz, Guildenstern, Player, King Lear and Horatio, not forgetting Hamlet. Don't know what on earth Ewing could do with it.* He directed a production of it in a small theatre on the Kurfürstendamm, and remarked *I intend to turn it into a full-length play...*

* * *

Boorman had asked Stoppard and me to think about surreal documentaries, but he shelved the idea when a career in films beckoned. However, something else had turned up for me. Mike Kustow had started working for the Royal Shakespeare Company, and one of his innovations was a new kind of theatre programme, which contained serious critical and historical background material on the play, not just the cast list and actors' biogs and ads for ice cream. It's likely that he had come across programmes of that sort in France, when he was working for Roger Planchon. After a year he moved on within the RSC, to start Theatregoround, and, asked who might take over the programme job, he suggested Stoppard or me. Stoppard was in Berlin, so I found myself being interviewed at Stratford by John Goodwin, the head of publicity and publications. I was no Shakespeare scholar but neither, it turned out, was Goodwin. He was outstanding in the job he did – when Peter Hall moved to the National Theatre he took Goodwin with him – and saw my literary-journalistic experience as fitting the job description better than an English degree might have done. Also, we hit it off straight away, and have remained friends ever since. He offered me the job as a freelance, part-time, and for ten years it brought in about a third of my income. It was a fabulous education in Shakespeare. I saw all the plays done at least once, some of them several times, needed to read all the critics and background stuff, talked to actors and directors, watched rehearsals and learned craft from them. I've had no bigger bit of luck in my professional life.

I had to start work at once, while we were still spending a lot of time filming with Boorman. 1964 was the quatercentenary year of Shakespeare's birth, and to mark it Hall and John Barton had prepared a season of all the history plays from *Richard II* to *Richard III* (in order of history, not composition). I was asked to spend an evening at Hall's house in Kensington, listening to Hall, Barton and the third director, Clifford Williams, argue their way through the themes of the whole season, which would initiate me into the project and also supply some quotes for the programmes. It was a stimulating session for me, and it had begun delightfully when the front door was opened for me by Leslie Caron, at that time Hall's wife.

As well as Shakespeare programmes at Stratford I had smaller programmes to do for the RSC's London operation at the Aldwych. That meant talking to some of the outstanding playwrights of the generation – Peter Barnes, Harold Pinter, David Rudkin and, most remarkably, Samuel Beckett. As a joke, when we were planning to produce *endgame* I remarked to Goodwin that he ought to fly me over to Paris to discuss programme material with Beckett. I was astonished when Goodwin agreed to that, and even more astonished when Beckett did.

I spent the flight promising myself I would not gush out my admiration for him, and it was a promise I kept. What I had not reckoned on was that Beckett was shy of any stranger visiting him, so he too would be keeping his lip buttoned. Why had he agreed to let me call on him? I think the reason was that he was a courteous man, and didn't want to offend the RSC. The spectacularly Beckettian answer to the question 'What do you want in the programme?' was, in effect, 'Nothing at all. The title of the play, and the actors' names if you insist. Nothing else'. The outcome was very long, green silences, during which one of us pretended that we were pondering what the other one had just said, like, no, I won't have another cup of tea, thank you.

> Samuel Beckett once said: 'Every word is like an unnecessary stain on silence and nothingness.'
> – Yes.
> – On the other hand, he SAID it.
> (Art Spiegelman, *Maus*)

Beckett rounded off one lacuna by reaching down a book about a Dutch painter friend of his, Bram van Velde, and talking me through some of the illustrations, just to pass the time until we had fulfilled the two hours we both, tacitly, felt it proper to spend together in view of the cost to the RSC of my trip. The only time we got chatting was when, off the agenda, I asked him about his memories of playing cricket for Trinity College, Dublin. Famously, he is the only Nobel prizewinner to appear in *Wisden*.

'Were you a batsman or a bowler?'

'They used to put me in to open the batting, but I never scored many runs.'

'So you bowled?'

'Not much. I wasn't a good bowler.'

'Why did they want you in the team, then?'

'For short-leg. I was good at snapping up the catches round there.'

I knew he loved to watch cricket at Lord's when he was in London, and asked him if he still went there. He disappointed me by answering no, but then delighted me with his technical reason:

'My eyes are not good enough any more to see what the ball's doing.'

He lived on the seventh floor of a modern apartment block overlooking the exercise yard of the Santé prison. What he saw down there must have fed into the later work, ciphers in uniform. Arriving, I had noticed the makers' nameplate in the lift: Établissements Hamm. One of the characters in *endgame* is called Hamm, and I remarked to Beckett that I saw where he had got the name from. He shook his head: 'No. I've lived here only two years, and I wrote that play nearly ten years ago. It's the names, they won't let you be.' He had been on an Air France flight to London when the pilot came on the intercom: *Messieurs, mesdames, bonjour, je suis votre pilote, Monsieur Godot.* 'I sat there in my seat,' Beckett said, 'and thought, yes, this is how it ends.'

As I was leaving he found a thick typescript file and gave it to me: 'You might find something in there.' I read it on the flight back. It was an American woman's MA dissertation about Beckett, and was singular in its vapidity. He cannot have read it himself or he would have lined his bins with it. He knew that my journey had been profitless, and wanted to be helpful in some way.

Donald McWhinnie gave the play a wonderful production, with Jack McGowran and Patrick Magee, the two classic Beckett actors. The night I saw it there were seven of us in the audience. One of the highlights of my theatregoing life, and the Aldwych was effectively empty. We all knew about the difference that *Waiting For Godot* had made from 1955, yet nine years later a renaissance in the avant-garde theatre was hard to spot.

Other literary work I did for the RSC included editing their audience magazine *Flourish* (another project Kustow had initiated and left), and many interviews with actors, which appeared loose-leaf in the programmes. I got Stoppard in to do some of the interviews. He needed the money. In London he had moved to a more expensive flat than the Blenheim Crescent basement he started in. With Derek Marlowe and Piers Paul Read, both of whom had been on the Ford Foundation 'cultural picnic' with him, he was setting up in Pimlico, and working on the play he had started to develop in Berlin. At that time it concerned what happened when Rosencrantz and Guildenstern made it to England and met the King, who was King Lear. Like my beginnings in poetry, it was prompted by Prufrock: *Am an attendant lord...*

Viewed from Printing House Square, the country consisted of the Home Counties and the rest. I was sent to report cricket from Southampton to Birmingham, Chesterfield to Ebbw Vale, sometimes, on Saturdays, at the same match as Ghose. When I was sent to cover Northants v Kent at Wellingborough School, Reeves told me that I was visiting a shrine to cricket. He had stayed there himself, and remembered rooms called First Slip and Gully, and mottoes on the staircase for boys to ponder on their way to bed: *The lilies of the field, they neither toil nor spin – no, but you should.* And *Ask yourself, are you getting out to the slow stuff?'*

Reporting Somerset v Warwickshire, I was savaged by pink-faced Harold Gimblett. David Foot mentions it in his outstanding biography of that troubled Somerset legend:

> Gimblett... stalked to the press tent and rounded on an erstwhile colleague of mine, A.C.H. Smith, the Bristol writer, because he had dared to criticize in print the state of the wicket at Millfield, where at that time Gimblett was employed. The reprimand was public and condescending and it took some years before I privately forgave him.

Most memorably, I went to Swansea to report Glamorgan's match against the Australians in August, 1964. At lunchtime on the third day I rang Laurie Wayman, *The Times*'s deputy sports editor: 'Mr Wayman, if things go on the way they are going it looks as though Glamorgan might beat the Australians, and that would be the first time a county has beaten them since Surrey in 1956. If they do it, do you still want four hundred words at close of play?'

Wayman, who always sounded as though he was enjoying a fat Havana and sipping cognac, replied: 'Well, Mr Smith, if that were the eventuality, you might consider writing more than four hundred words for us.'

'How many more words, would you say?'

'Well, if Glamorgan do beat them, I think you should probably write all the words you can think of.'

They did, and I did. For the only time, my report led the sports pages. On a turning wicket, Don Shepherd had taken nine wickets in the match, Jim Pressdee ten. The Australian captain, Bill Lawry, had defied national humiliation for four hours and half, blocking it out while less gritty partners came and went, until Pressdee let go a long hop and Lawry could not stop himself from pulling it straight into the hands of Alan Rees. It was ten seconds before Lawry left the crease. He was not questioning the decision but his own sanity.

* * *

In autumn 1964 a lot of us gathered at the house in Cotham to which Boorman had moved his family, to watch the first General Election comprehensively covered by TV. While the results were being declared, and plotted by Robert McKenzie's cardboard arrow known as the Swingometer, the sort of toy you would hope not to get in a packet of cereals, most of us, on Boorman's whim, were playing chess. We cheered as 'thirteen years of Tory misrule' (H. Wilson) came to an end, just. I had canvassed for Labour. In 1966, after eighteen months of Wilson, I wouldn't even vote. At meetings of Tony Benn's New Bristol Group I had imagined something else when Labour came back to power.

John Goodwin asked me for a favour. His stepson, James Belsey, had done a reporting stint in Birmingham and Stratford-upon-Avon and had now been offered a job on *The Observer*, but David Astor wanted him first to get another six months' experience on a provincial paper. Was there anything going at the *Evening Post*? I rang my old news editor there, and by chance they were looking for someone. Belsey was interviewed, came to tell me he'd got the job, and asked if I could help him find somewhere to live. That very morning Michael Croucher had mentioned to me that his basement in West Mall was vacant. Belsey took it – a job and a Clifton pad arranged in a matter of hours. For the rest of his life he regarded me as Mr Fixit, and I didn't disillusion him. He never went to *The Observer*, of course. He liked Bristol too much to leave it, one of a long string of creative people who talked affectionately of the city as 'the graveyard of ambition'.

From January I would be in charge of our daughters when Alison was out, finishing her degree. Till then, I did a share of washing, noshing and cloching, like any self-pitying literary mother. I wrote to Janet Burroway *People say I'm lucky being able to spend so much time getting to know them.* In reply, she told me:

> In spite of or more likely because of motherhood, I have finished another novel, called *Eyes*, that I hope and think much better than the other two... There's less rewriting to do than when I work more slowly. I really do think that I owe this book to Tim [her baby son], as I owed the last hundred pages of *Descend Again* to having a nine-hour secretarial job in Paris. I

> can no longer sit down with coffee and a novel in the morning and get up when I hear Walter at the latch. I have a six-foot-square playpen in my office, and Tim co-operates wonderfully, fantastically, sleeping for an hour morning and afternoon and playing very self-sufficiently beside me for the hour after each nap, giving me four hours that I do use because I know they're all I get.

Stoppard told me *Your élan as a family man living on sheer optimism leaves me breathless. I as a footloose bachelor am juggling financial promises against negotiated overdrafts simply to get a flat established.*

I had delivered the end of my novel, and reverted to poetry. Charles Tomlinson, who taught at the university, helped to arrange a poetry and jazz event, and an anthology of Bristol poets, *The Manoeuvring Sun*, followed. Invitations to give readings of my poetry started to arrive, from Bangor, Bridgwater, and later London and Limerick. I also read poems by Blake and Patchen at a Kevin Ayers concert at the Victoria Rooms in which the keyboard player was David Bedford; years later, as an innovative composer, he ended up living not far from me in Bristol. The event was staged by Arnolfini, where Richard Hawkins was chairman of a very *avant-garde* programme of music, and involved me in several events. A Japanese percussionist spent the day before his performance looking around the city's rubbish dumps, choosing chunks of metal on which he would play that evening.

Entrants to an *Observer* competition were invited to come up with a sonnet on any subject using the line-endings the *O.E.D.* offers as examples: *pig, bat, cat, wig, jig, hat, rat, fig; lie, red, die, bed, pie, wed.* My subject was a drawing by Charles Addams, and the sestet alluded to Robert Lowell. I was joint runner-up with Roy Fuller and, since he was in his superb Faust period, it felt like first prize.

The Last Unicorns
Propped on the last outcrop, with no pig,
porcupine or partridge to combat
our solitude, a far magnificat
pricks our ears, as the dove bears back a twig
and sets the ark's animals all a-jig,
with survival only in their brains. That
new testament appals us. For their Ararat,

posterity, we care not a fig.
Bored by Darwin, on our last bed we lie
awake, by setting sunbeams both dyed red.
Abandoned, having missed the boat, we die
horn by horn and thigh by thigh. Our bed
shrinks to extinction, but our bellies are warm as a pie,
with only ourselves to wed, and once more wed.

* * *

Stoppard told me that *the RSC want to buy an option on Ros and Guil... You remember that I met J. Brooks* [RSC literary manager] *at Kustow's wedding* [where Arnold Wesker had been in the kitchen making pastries] *and arranged to send him my poor two-thirds of a messed-up first draft. Got letter last weekend saying that both he and P. Hall were very keen.* He was split between *my necessity to get away by myself to write like some madman till April, and placating Jose... logic (and frankly preference) indicates Bristol as the spot.*

A one-act play he had written called *The Gamblers* was about a man in the condemned cell. It was a two-hander, and O'Toole had said he would get Peter Sellers to do it with him, but that had come to naught. I had the idea that we could stage it in Bristol, together with a short play about nuclear war Charles Wood had shown me, called *Tie Up The Ballcock*, and some tatterdemalion stuff I wanted to put together on an equally grim-grin theme (*Grim Grin* is French for Graham Greene). The Bristol Old Vic, then and usually, wasn't interested in new plays. They had rejected *Look Back in Anger* before it went to the Royal Court, and they would later give Stoppard short shrift on *Rosencrantz*. After they'd had success in London, Wood and Nichols were each treated by the BOV to one week's run of a play, in the Little Theatre, each filling about 30 per cent of the seats. Wood's *Cockade* took a swipe at military myths and blew up a storm in the local papers. One chap (I suspect it was Wood himself, pseudonymously) wrote to ask why we had to put up with stuff like this when there were *perfectly wholesome* plays begging to be done. As example, he cited *King Lear.*

And so they moved away, inevitably in the direction of London. Stoppard had gone first, then Nichols would go ('I've run out of places in Bristol to take my kids to on Sundays'), and finally Wood. But there was the university drama department, with its own little theatre space, where we saw many student productions of European avant-garde works, and there was the Bristol Old Vic Theatre School. With George Brandt's enthusiastic permission, and Alan Dossor's agreement to direct his fellow BOVTS actors, including Jane Lapotaire and Jeremy Child, we staged three pieces, collectively entitled *The Black Man,* for three evenings in May 1965 in the converted squash court in the Wills Tower that served the drama department as its theatre. It was the first time Stoppard's words were heard in a British theatre, and the extraordinary fact is that it was in the same space that Pinter had been heard first by a live audience, when *The Room* had been premièred in 1957.

Soon, Dossor would be in Liverpool, inaugurating the golden age of the Everyman Theatre, where writers like Willy Russell, Alan Bleasdale and John McGrath were cherished. It was not the only time Liverpool has shown Bristol what the city might have been with a more courageous heart. We have the elements of what they once had in Moscow: an excellent theatre school, a famous repertory theatre, and a leading university drama department. If the three of them would find a way of working together... the fact is they never really have.

Dossor would sometimes show up in Bristol again, once with a young actor called Pete Postlethwaite and a bottle of whisky, which was opened and finished in an afternoon. I asked Dossor how he had spent the morning, and in reply he said he had been admiring *the multitudinous teas in Carwardines.* To unpack the monstrous pun in that, google Shakespeare Quotes.

* * *

Bernardine's marriage, like those of her three Meynell forebears, hadn't lasted. She came to Bristol, staying with friends, Nick and Dinah Wharton, and invited me to call on her. I went with Alison to the Whartons' house in Redland and talked to Bernardine, in the room where I am writing this forty-five years later. Wharton was a history lecturer, the son of Peter Simple of the *Daily Telegraph.* He was about to move to Reading, where he had got a new job at the university. They had bought the house a year earlier, but now had to sell it. We were looking for a family home where we didn't have to schlepp two carrycots up eighty-one stairs. Charles Wood, living two streets away from here, had said: 'Come on over this side of White-ladies Road. It's lovely here, it's cheaper than Clifton, and the houses are Victorian, really spacious. Look.' He'd shown us around his own roomy house so, with help from our parents in raising a mortgage, we arranged to buy from the Whartons. Wood moved across to Clifton three weeks later.

When I saw the deeds recently, I discovered that apart from the Whartons, who were here for a year, only three families have lived in the house since it was built in the 1860s. Under the floorboards I found the remains of a bell system. The shopkeepers who first lived here must have rung for tea and crumpets from the domestic help, who occupied the top floor where we once put three children to bed and now have lodgers.

The house would not be ours to live in until October. Meanwhile, something else turned up. Richard Hoggart had set up a new department at Birmingham University, the Centre for Contemporary Cultural Studies, and invited me to be one of the first researchers there, heading a three-year project to study the popular press, funded by the Rowntree Trust. It's always nice to be asked, but I had never fancied an academic job. My respect for Hoggart, through his ground-breaking book *The Uses of Literacy* back in the Fifties, led me to hesitate, instead of declining outright, and he used my prevarication to hook me like a master fisherman.

'Well, Anthony, while you're thinking it over let me have an application for the post, because they're closing applications three weeks from now and then it would be too late.' I did as he asked, and the next I heard was an invitation to go to Birmingham for a board. Again, I was reluctant to disappoint him, so made an appointment, with misgivings. The board turned out to be Hoggart in shirtsleeves coming round his desk and saying, 'Good to see you. When can you start?' I had three reservations prepared, and thought each of them unanswerable.

'We're just in the process of buying a house in Bristol, so can't move to Birmingham now.'

'That's all right, you don't need to work here all the time. Come in, say, three days a week.'

'We've booked a long holiday in France, with friends, and it could run on into October.'

'Fine. We don't have to work university terms. You could start your three years in November.'

'I'm reporting cricket for *The Times*, and have just started working for the RSC.'

'Oh, we're all doing other work here. It keeps us in touch.'

My quiver was empty. He brought out a form and said we just

had to fill in a few details. When it came to what degree I had got, I detected a flicker on his face when I told him it was a Third. Well, I'd never had academic ambitions. Why he was sure I was his man was because he liked what he had seen in the *WDP* arts page, and above all he wanted someone running the project who had hands-on knowledge of how newspapers worked. He asked me to go and sit behind his desk with him, to interview people who had applied to be junior researchers on the project. Before I left we had made an arrangement for me to go to York with him, to meet the Rowntree trustees.

* * *

Boorman had left the BBC to make his first cinema film, *Catch Us If You Can,* featuring the Dave Clark Five. I thought it was feeble in comparison with *Help!*, which Charles Wood scripted for the Beatles, but Stoppard held the opposite view, as he had on *Battle Inferno*. Boorman got Peter Nichols to script his film, and Nichols was soon in despair as he discovered what I had already experienced, that to Boorman a script is nothing more than a plausible excuse to take his crew to a location, where he makes up the film as he goes along. I was cast as a beach photographer in *Catch Us*, and was called upon to have sand kicked in my face by Dave Clark himself, a piece of acting which he was able to accomplish by not attempting to chew gum at the same time. Boorman's next film, made in Hollywood, was *Point Blank*. After *Catch Us* it was as though the bloke who took one for seventy against Nempnett Thrubwell 2nd XI last week had bowled out the West Indians at Lord's.

Alison, having finished her degree, was spending a lot of time in Boorman's company. Back in the spring, when we were filming *The Newcomers*, I had begun to learn the abrasions of having a beautiful wife when the sculptor Lynn Chadwick, at whose astounding Cotswold house we shot a few scenes, had persevered in trying to persuade her to move in with him. Warning Boorman off was much more difficult, because the three of us had become close friends. Whenever I expressed my unease to either of them, the answer was that Alison was going through a difficult time, perhaps post-natal, and all that Boorman was doing was a talking cure for her.

Because of *The Newcomers* we were recognized in the street. One couple who accosted us were Peter and Miriam Moore-Robinson, he a veterinary student, she, with a brilliant medical degree, supporting them with locum work. They became friends of ours.

Tom Stoppard writing at the well, Richard Hawkins seated,
watching me cheat at boules, at the Château de Blauvac.
Photo by Derek Balmer

Tom Stoppard in 1989. Photo by Ray Fisher

Bryan Johnson with his wife Virginia, who gave me permission to reproduce the shot

PAGE 8

WESTERN DAILY PRESS, Monday, June 4, 1962

THE ARTS

All hands to the shoestring

We didn't actually rub our eyes and flap our ears last Wednesday, because we had an inkling it might happen; but we were very cheered up all the same on hearing Dr. Jeffrey Boss, the new Labour councillor, speaking his open mind to the City Art Gallery Committee.

Gallery director Hans Schubart has worked wonders in the past in the shoestring tug-o'-war that characterises our

Arts Page Notebook

city's patronage of the arts; it makes a change for him to have new support of this articulate quality.

We think he must certainly need it in the face of such connoisseurs as Councillor Philip Nash who, as chief

Val Lorraine reviews 'a book that will be the standard work'..

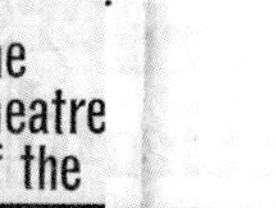

the theatre of the ABSURD

by Martin Esslin, published by Eyre & Spottiswoode at 35s.

Mr. Esslin's book on Brecht, *A Choice of Evils* (1959), was the work of a perceptive disciple, scholarship with enthusiasm. In his latest book on "the type of theatre associated with the names of Samuel Beckett, Eugene Ionesco, Arthur Adamov, Jean Genet (and etc.)," he is no less perceptive, and just as enthusiastic.

At first sight, this makes Mr. Esslin a rather suspicious character, a kind of critic-of-fortune making himself available as professional worshipper to any faction in the ascendant; for Brecht's epic social realism and the "Theatre of the Absurd" are generally supposed to be at the two opposite ends of the theatrical spectrum, and, moreover, in competition against each other.

Mr. Esslin himself acknowledges the fact of this competition, and he quotes at length the celebrated wrangle between Kenneth Tynan and Ionesco in the columns of The Observer in 1958 when Tynan's attack on anti-theatre ("explicitly anti-realist and by implication anti-reality as well") brought a spirited counter from Ionesco ("An ideological play can be no more than the vulgarization of an ideology . . ."

Can Mr. Esslin serve two gods? The critic as acolyte and idolater? An overwhelming question, to which Mr. Esslin has an appropriately heretical answer: The two gods are one.

Mr. Esslin proposes, in fact, that the division is false. He resolves it, finally, thus:

Tynan in quoting Brecht to Ionesco as an example of his socially committed ideal, and Ionesco in attacking Brecht as the embodiment of the arid ideological theatre, are both equally wide of the mark. Brecht was one of the first masters of the Theatre of the Absurd, and his case shows that the *pièce à thèse* stands or falls not by its politics but by its poetic truth, which is beyond politics, since it proceeds from far deeper levels of the author's personality. Brecht's personality contained a strong element of anarchy and despair. Hence, even in his politically committed period, the picture he presented of the capitalist world was essentially negative and absurd; the universe of *The Good Woman of Setzuan* is ruled by imbecile gods, that of *Puntila* is modelled on a Chaplinesque formula of slapstick, and in *The Caucasian Chalk Circle*, justice is done only by the unlikeliest of accidents.

Genet as a witness to this thesis and conclud[illegible] that while Genet's theatre is profoundly a thea[illegible] of social protest, it "rejects political commitme[illegible] political argument, didacticism, or propoganda. [illegible] dealing with the dream world of the outcast [illegible] society, it explores the human condition, t[illegible] alienation of man, his solitude, his futile sear[illegible] for meaning and reality."

Nevertheless, Mr. Esslin has made his poi[illegible] ". . . Brecht's case . . . shows that the irration[illegible] Theatre of the Absurd and the highly purpose[illegible] politically committed play are not so mu[illegible] irreconcilable contradictions as, rather, t[illegible] obverse and reverse side of the same medal."

It needed saying, none the less so because, [illegible] is stating what I have always assumed to [illegible] obvious. Sorry to be pompous, but can anyo[illegible] be aware of a play like *The Fire Raisers* by [illegible] Frisch without seeing that here we have both si[illegible] of the medal presented simultaneously?

And there is one aspect in which the Abs[illegible] has achieved what Brecht dedicated himself and failed to achieve—the matter of alienati[illegible] Brecht did his damnedest to enforce a critic[illegible]

perfect appetiser (an account of a production at San Quentin gaol of *Waiting for Godot*, a play chosen "largely because no woman appeared in it"), Mr. Esslin continues with chapters on the work and biography of Beckett, Adamov, Ionesco and Genet. By the time he has progressed to "parallels and proselytes" (among them, Arrabel, Frisch, Pinget, Pinter, Simpson and Albee), the most modest and unself-confident seeker-after-knowledge will find himself suddenly, painlessly "with it."

Next he traces the traditions of the Absurd, and finally we are taught the "Significance" of all that has gone before.

FROM GREECE TO GROUCHO

On the way, we have the advantage of Mr. Esslin's fluency in several languages (some of his research was carried out in conversation with the playwrights themselves) and he does not presume the fluency of his readers. Nor does he, as others have done, skip the details of little known plays he wants to discuss. It is irritating to be told merely the name of a play performed once in a private theatre in Paris in 1927. One might conceivably have missed it.

His chapter of the tradition of the Absurd (invoking everyone from the Greeks to the Marx Brothers, through the *Commedia dell'arte* and Shakespeare) springs from such a wide knowledge of the history of comedy that one can only hope that this will be the subject of Mr. Esslin's next book. My favourite quote here is from

IONESCO
By implication anti-reality?

BECKETT
At a plotless level

PINTER
An echo from early Brecht

Inside the madman's mind

by B. S. Johnson

AUTO - DA - FE by Elias Canetti, trans. C. V. Wedgwood (Cape, 21s.).

This novel is an object lesson in how to avoid dating a book by its politics. Written in Vienna in the '30s, it triumphantly survives a quarter of a century and on its re-issue appears fresh and relevant because it deals with specifically individual human problems rather than with wide social and political ones.

Auto-da-fé is a study of madness, a terrifying study. Every character who appears in it is mad to some degree or another. Thus the reader is left to pro-

FICTION

vide his own standard of sanity against which to measure them and the events in which they take part, and the result is that he is forced to question such a standard and to defend it.

Elias Canetti achieves this by enacting the events through his characters' minds; almost everything is seen from within them, very little being described by an omniscient author. This is particularly effective and revealing when, as often happens, one character fits a different meaning to the words of another, and the thought-processes of both, diverging and foliating, are followed. Not that Canetti's method results in obscurity; the pattern of his book is always clear to a reader prepared to give it careful attention.

Imaginary library

The story is of a scholar, Peter Kien, whose interest in sinology becomes absorption, then eccentricity then fanaticism, and finally plunges into madness. The titles of the three parts of the

The *Western Daily Press Arts* Page. The layout has been re-edited with a hacksaw

Richard Hoggart at the Cheltenham Festival of Literature. Artist not known

Alison and I got married at Quakers Friars registry office, in 1963. Afterwards we all went for lunch at Marco's

Alison acting in a Drama Department production of Corneille's *Le Menteur*

Derek Balmer took photographs of us for use by John Boorman as stills in *The Newcomers*

Working towards Grade 1.
Everyone needs a pursuit at which they are very bad. Photo: BBC

Baby clothes. We didn't know yet it would be babies' clothes. Photo: BBC

A year later. Alison is about to take her finals

Opposite: Dame Peg's XI at Stratford, 1969. Back row: Umpire, Michael Meyer, Harold Pinter, David Bailie, Anthony Pedley, Peggy Ashcroft, Ian Carmichael, me, Umpire Julian Bream. Front row: Michael Williams was down to play, but this doesn't look like him, so is presumably a stand-in; Tom Courtenay, Tom Stoppard, David Warner, Morgan Sheppard. Photo: *Stratford Herald*

A cricket match at Oxford. Extreme left in the back row is Richard Hawkins, our scorer. Third from right, back row, my cousin Bob Godfrey has a beard. Middle row, on left, Hélène Corrie is servicing her husband Tim's smoking needs. Between them is Miriam Moore-Robinson, later Stoppard. In front of Bob Godfrey is Helena Ghose. On my left is Zulfikar Ghose. At ground level are Alison, John Rudlin, and Clive Barker. My daughters are enjoying the view

Family party at Stuart and Catherine Hall's house, in Birmingham

When we mentioned that we were about to go to the Dordogne for a long holiday with our friends Tom and Jose, Miriam said that they too were taking a car trip around France, and could they call in on us? Thus it was that I introduced Stoppard to Miriam. I remember the moment clearly. For the only time in my life I was making a sauce hollandaise, and had to keep stirring while I performed the introduction, otherwise it would have curdled, too. We were celebrating the publication of my first novel, *The Crowd.* I was scanning the British papers for reviews. Isabel Quigly said it reminded her of early Waugh, which I thought would please Gillon Aitken, then Waugh's editor.

During the days they spent in France with us, Miriam, like the agony aunt she would become, was counselling Alison, over anxieties not disclosed to me. The outcome was that Alison told me she was going back to Bristol with our daughters, and wanted me to stay on in France until she let me know she was ready for me to return to them. I felt I had no option other than to agree, since I did not know why she was unhappy. I drove her and our baby girls to Le Bourget airport, where they joined the queue immediately behind Randolph Churchill. I turned back south, and that night got as far as Chalon-sur-Saône. I drank a lot with my supper, and wandered around the town, talking to myself, as I do when I'm drunk. On the street were whores in various stages of decay and decoy. I was half hoping to be hooked by one of them; I would have taken it all out on her. Cheering came from a hall I was passing. Inside, in dim light, I saw two boxers scowling in a ring, their legs being touched by women leaning under the ropes. A cripple darted around the front row of the crowd. When I left, the rest of the town was fast asleep. I got into my car, I forget why – perhaps to borrow the power of its engine, or simply to park it better. Trying to enter the alley beside the hotel, I hit the corner of a shop window. I don't think the glass broke, but the next morning they were examining a skewed metal column. I reached Blauvac, and after that went on to Cannes, where John Goodwin had lent me his apartment. I stayed there a month, the most miserable of my life. I went every day to the Post Office to see if there was a letter from Alison to say she was ready for me to return. Day after day there was nothing. I rang her once or twice, and got no definite answer. I wrote heartbroken letters to Miriam, not yet knowing that she had encouraged Alison to do what she was doing. I wrote poems refusing suicide. One to our girls included:

> We take delight

> In your guilelessness. You will learn guile,
> And the uses of love, in a little while.

Another I signed: *14 x 65, The worst day of my life. So far.* I looked through the books on Goodwin's shelves and read William Cooper's *Scenes from Married Life*, which did a lot to help me, with its picture of how difficult but feasible it is for two people to enjoy living together. Stoppard wrote to cheer me up:

> My dear fellow (I am trying to perfect a form of salutation implying patronage, insolence and affection in equal parts, so as to leave my correspondents insecure). Jose and I are shortly to leave for Elstree studios where a script not entirely different from the one I wrote is to be taped in the presence of the Lord Willis of whom there is but one. Were it not for the fact that you would find it tedious, I would recommend you to read the final script some time as an illustration and a warning of what is liable to happen to a play if the author is fool enough to go abroad at the critical time. The Lord has decided that the play must be about Mr Blake and not about much else – he calls Mr Blake 'a social problem' – so he has cut the subplot of the reporter's home life... and inserted page after corny page of Scenes with Mr Blake, all of them being laboured, gratuitous and stereotyped. When I read it I toyed with the idea of demanding that my name be taken off it but things had gone too far, so I resigned myself to Lord Willis's fate (accompli). I attended a walk-through in a church hall, and it was impossible to even murmur my misgivings – the production was so far advanced, and everyone was so terribly NICE that to say anything adverse would have been to hit a child... The day was made for me, however, by the Lord Willis's title on the camera-script, namely The Creator.

Finally, Alison did say I could return. I drove from Cannes to Bristol without stopping to sleep. We reached an understanding, but neither of us understood it. We slipped into an open marriage, which the eighteenth-century aristocracy called discretion, and Alison's mother called estrangement. It is better than long indifference or possessive jealousy, but not as good as the more conventional loving marriages I see. If I'd grown up with a mother, would I have made a better husband? I'll never know. Like dancers, we move in steps we have forgotten learning. Had Alison made a bad choice in me? As partners, perhaps. But not as parents of our children. The biologist Armand Marie Leroi wrote in the *London Review of Books* (September 17th, 1998):

> Even baker's yeast, when choosing a mate, is credited with subtle discriminatory powers of a type that one would not normally expect from a fungus.

Don't you love that *normally*?

9

In the Fish Tank

For some months I commuted to Birmingham from Bristol, until Alison said it would be more sensible if we moved up there for a couple of years. We let our place to medical students, and rented half a redbrick-and-timber Tudor house in Water Orton, on the Warwickshire edge of Birmingham. We were near the railway. On the day the last-ever steam locomotive worked the line I took my daughters to the footbridge. As the engine passed beneath us I entreated them to remember the yesteryear smell of coal smoke and steam, but they were too little.

Cultural studies is a worldwide discipline now, but is a grotesque descendant of what Hoggart and Stuart Hall founded. It squeaks in pseudo-scientific jargon. We had one foot in lit crit, the other in sociology, and our output aspired to be as pertinent to the general reader as *The Uses of Literacy*. The dozen or so of us graduates working there, on subjects as varied as James Bond, football crowds, advertising, street crime and press photography, gathered together once or twice a week for joint seminars, run by Hoggart and Hall, which ranged from Forster contrasted with D.H. Lawrence to the sociology of Weber, Tönnies, Marx, Adorno and Durkheim, and as guests we welcomed such speakers as Raymond Williams and E.P. Thompson. I went over to Cambridge once, for a supervision session with Williams. I also wrote to Leavis, having heard that he had conducted a research project into the popular press in his graduate days, but he replied that he did not think highly enough of the work to let anyone see it.

As an educational experience I would class my time at Birmingham as a double-starred first, whereas Cambridge was a lower second, though I was partly to blame for that. Hoggart was a model of integrity and close scrutiny, as he had demonstrated in the *Lady Chatterley* trial, and Hall had the most brilliant mind for synthesis.

Elizabeth Immirzi, Trevor Blackwell and I had to refine our project on the popular press and social change into a manageable vessel. In consultation with Hoggart and Hall, we settled on the contrasting aproaches of the *Daily Mirror* and *Daily Express* to the

General Elections in 1945, 1955 and 1964, plus a consideration of both papers' mediation of what became known in the 1950s as affluence. For me, the most absorbing work was the study of how the two papers behaved in 1945, which, especially in the case of the *Mirror*, could not be adequately explained without following them through the war years. I spent many hours in the newspaper library at Colindale with issues of the *Mirror* that were in my home when Aunt Lucy and Uncle Bub had taken it.

A lecturer in English, Peter Davison, decided that the university should have its own literary magazine, and inaugurated *Alta*. When he asked me if I had anything to offer him, I mumbled that a long poem on cancer had been on my mind. He did what good editors do. Every time he came across me in a departmental corridor he asked how the poem was coming on, until there was nothing for it but to sit down and start serious work on it, to get him off my back. When the poem appeared, I had a letter from R.D. Smith, who worked for BBC radio in London but had seen *Alta* when visiting his mother in Birmingham. Would I consent to having the poem broadcast on the Third Programme? In London for the recording I found Reggie Smith to be excellent company, as some famous writers had done in the post-war years, Dylan Thomas and Louis Macneice among them. He took me round to the BBC's out-of-hours drinking joint, and we formed a friendship that would be enhanced on the cricket field. Everyone who knew Reggie thought him a producer of genius, but his career had always been pruned by the BBC on account of his pre-war membership of the Communist Party. A Christmas tree against his name in the personnel files.

I showed him a radio play I had written, an experimental piece arising from my drunken evening in Chalon; he was keen to produce it, but was turned down at some higher production level. That happened to me several times later on, the producer wanting to do the play but the next-up saying no, and in the end I gave up on radio. A playwright's career conventionally starts in radio, graduates to TV, and aspires to the stage or the big screen. My experience has been the inverse. I've had more than twenty plays staged, a few on TV, been commissioned to write four cinema screenplays, but radio drama is a nut I could not crack. It's a pity, because like most writers I find the radio congenial to language.

After the broadcast I received another letter, this time from the British Homoeopathic Association. They had heard my fine homoeopathic poem, and might they reprint it in their journal?

Having checked in the dictionary what 'homoeopathic' meant, I said yes, of course. Come and see us when you're in London, they said, so I did, on one of the many visits I had to make to Colindale. I was introduced to the BHA director, Dr Llewellyn Twentyman; he was not an imposing figure, a shortish man in a brown three-piece, but when I shook hands with him something happened which I cannot explain. I felt an instant elevation. It has moderated my scepticism about the laying-on of hands.

The new discipline of cultural studies had started to create ripples through the media. I was asked by *New Society* to write a piece about skin magazines, which I decided should entail spending an evening at the Playboy Club in Park Lane. When the piece appeared I received an appreciative letter from John Berger, and a reproachful one from *Playboy*. I became a regular contributor to *New Society*, including what might be the only Marxist analysis of the cover-drive. After watching Colin Milburn, Kenneth Tynan had wondered in *The Observer* why offside strokes attract epithets comparing them to Mozartian rondos, but legside shots, in which Milburn excelled, are thought bucolic. I wrote him a letter, making the case that offside drives do not come naturally but require top-hand training, which would have been given to the young gentlemen in the formative years of cricket culture, the nineteenth century, but not to the lower order, the proletarian fast bowlers, and so a class taste for what is tutored grew up. I got not even a postcard of acknowledgment back from Tynan, so decided not to waste the thought I had put in, and made an article of it. Several of the tabloids picked up on my offside equals toffside argument.

Another piece in *New Society* was about the primitive perception we have of other drivers' behaviour when we are at the steering-wheel. In response I got a letter from Richard Mabey, who wanted to commission me to write a Penguin about national transport policy. It would have been a stretch from my modest article, but in any case I did not have the time. I was asked by Ed Victor's radical paper *Ink* for some articles spinning off from the *Mirror/Express* research, and when Cecil King was allegedly behind an abortive putsch against the Wilson government I was *New Society*'s go-to man. Hoggart set up a series on ABC TV called *Your Sunday Paper*, in which I presented two episodes, and wrote essays to go with them in the accompanying paperback. Harold Evans, editor of the *Sunday Times*, was professionally affronted by the whole series, and published a vitriolic attack, particularly on what I had said. I wrote to him to point out seven errors and misrepresentations in what he had written; in return I got a climb-down letter from him, but no *mea culpa* in his paper. I was also sent to London to be interviewed on the BBC French Service about what we were all doing at the centre. It was hard enough to explain in English; in French, interrogated by a formidably intellectual Senegalese, I was floundering from the first minute, and wound up voicing those oblong abstractions that the French language generates like blank pages from a printer.

All that was fine, and arguably dandy, but I was worrying that I had no inkling where my next novel would come from. I wondered if the theoretical atmosphere of a university, or at least of the CCCS, might be jamming the intuitive wavelength of fiction writing. I mentioned the worry to Hoggart. It interested him, and he asked me to spell out my thoughts about it on paper for him. When I had done so, he added his own insights from a lifetime of studying the relation between writers and their culture, and then asked David Lodge, as a practising novelist and academic, to look at what we had written to each other. Lodge added to the correspondence. Then he showed it to the American critic Mark Spilka, who was visiting Birmingham, and I showed it all to Stoppard, and both of them added their responses. The whole colloquium wound up being published in *Alta*. It produced no aftershocks anywhere, yet the questions remain in the air. They have been in the air ever since Degas asked Mallarmé where he got the ideas for his poetry. *Ideas?* Mallarmé answered. *What have ideas got to do with poetry? Poetry is made with words.* Degas should have replied, *bien alors*, where do you get your words?

Stoppard remarked: *I am disturbed by your immersion in this fish tank.* Ghose had criticised me when I had accepted the job at Birmingham: *It has nothing to do with writing, has it? You haven't been ruthless enough with yourself... in the context of our aims of some six years ago, isn't it an indulgence, a frivolity?* Two years later he was teaching creative writing in Texas. Johnson, likewise, had said *shouldn't you really be doing real writing? I know (!) it's difficult, etc., but there comes a point, no, where the world and money has to look after itself?* Burroway, who probably did not know of my stint at Birmingham, once criticised herself on similar grounds. She wrote to me: *You at least made the serious choice and stuck to it, freelancing, whereas I have done this more usual middleclass American thing, accepted that I can't make a living out of my best talent and gradually gathered skill, except by teaching it.*

With no novel to work on and still a novice playwright, I continued as an occasional poet. I did translations of Baudelaire and Petrarch, and for *Alta* was asked to Anglicize some literal translations from Hungarian. Johnson had become poetry editor of *The Transatlantic Review*, and published a couple of my poems. At Stratford, Peter Hall engaged me as literary adviser – Cervantes's agent, really – on a film of *Don Quixote* that Carlo Ponti had commissioned. Dennis Cannan wrote a fine screenplay, but the project was aborted when Hall and Cannan refused to compromise on the scene in which Sancho Panza shits. 'Peter,' the American producer groaned about the script, 'it's so full of pain. And dirt'. Ponti wound the project up without paying anyone for the work they had done. When I saw his wife Sophia Loren on TV drooling over their new baby I thought, 'Yeah, and I paid for its nappies'.

Friends came to visit us in Birmingham. Jose, hearing something on the radio: 'What is swan-upping?' Stoppard: 'When they get their swan-uppance.' For social life in the city we were dependent on colleagues, especially Stuart and Catherine Hall and David and Mary Lodge. My daughter Sophie, aged four, listened to a conversation about Godard that Hall and I were having, and then asked: 'Stuart, have you seen *101 Dalmatians*?' A teenage Simon Hoggart asked me for advice about a career in journalism. I did my best to point him in a different direction. *Guardian* readers can be grateful that he took no notice. When W.H. Auden came to stay with Richard Hoggart, whose first book had been a study of the poet's work, all the CCCS graduates were invited to meet him. At the centre of the semi-circle we formed around him, with sherry glass poised in his fingertips, and twinkling the relief map of Europe he had for a face, he treated us to a masterclass from the Manhattan cocktail circuit. He croaked story after story. What was admirable was not just the perfection of his anecdotage but his exquisite timing in ending a story, allowing just a beat in which any one of us who dared might comment or swap a story, and then starting the next one promptly enough that no awkward pause had been allowed.

Hoggart told me that he and Mary had decided they should get in some wine, not their usual drink, for Auden's first dinner with them. To be safe, they bought one bottle of red and one of white. With the meal the Bull's Blood went mostly down the throat of Auden, who then insisted on doing the washing-up, at which he was a perfectionist. Announcing that he was on his way to bed, he picked up the opened but undrunk bottle of white wine and took it up with him. For the rest of the week it was tacitly understood that a bottle would be supplied for him every bed-time. Another visitor was Huw Wheldon, by now in charge of BBC1. Emboldened by my acquaintance with him, I was impertinent enough to give him my opinion that Kenneth Wolstenholme was the worst commentator on the BBC. 'Hmmm,' Wheldon mused, in his voice like ripe Brie, 'have you heard Peter West on rugby?'

* * *

Tim Corrie married Hélène, from Bordeaux, and invited us and the Moore-Robinsons to the reception at Château Palmer. Later in the week Hélène's father, Robert, took the men to fish *à la garole*. We lined up along the huge, empty, white beach at Lacanau, in front of a dark pine wood. The white garole net, four feet deep, hangs from a ninety-foot rope, with blue plastic floats along the length of it, and at one end a pole. Half a dozen of us put our shoulders into the nooses knotted into the net and run in an oblique line into the sea. The pole-man stays on shore as anchor while we, in rhythm, ride the waves, curving around to close the net, and come running back up the beach. We had eight mullet in the net. I was behind Robert, watching the broad, brown, energetic back of a middle-aged businessman, who would dry himself off and play tennis, and bridge in the early evening, and take the garole out again at night, when you can hope to catch sole coming inshore. Robert told me: 'The garole is illegal. The commercial fishermen won't have it. Sometimes the police arrest a man. Last week a man said his father had always done it, and he would be doing it again the next morning. Everyone *se grattait la tête* [scratched their head], and we got him off on the grounds that the bye-law was not posted up at the Mairie. We had bribed someone to rip it down before his court appearance. You can't get away with that more than once.'

When I could, I went on visiting Blauvac, until Marie died. I had a letter from her: *Écris-moi, cher bel Anthony, même des mensonges [even lies]*. Once, having as usual run out of money, I hitched from the Vaucluse back to Paris. I had to be at the Place de la République by seven o'clock to catch a bus to Beauvais, from where a plane would take us to Kent, and another bus to Victoria. That was the cheapest way to visit France then. I stood on a hot day for six hours beside the N7, waving a puny little Union Jack I had crayoned at Marie's. One English-plated car that ignored me was carrying three vicars in dog collars. I never was a believer, anyway. At three in the afternoon an English lorry stopped for me. The driver was on his way back from Sète to Cherbourg. I was yearning for something to eat and drink, but for hours he refused to stop. 'Stop in France,' he told me, 'you get your throat cut.' I didn't ask why he had taken that risk with me. The engine beneath us was roaring loudly, but he insisted on keeping up a monologue. A typical passage of it concerned what he had seen in Cairo when he'd been a soldier, the sex clubs there, and what the girls did to themselves with feather dusters. I could hardly hear a word, and didn't want to, but had to pretend to be keeping up, since he was doing me a favour I'd been waiting six hours for.

He did eventually take the risk of pulling in for a quick refreshment, but otherwise he kept grinding north at 40 m.p.h. I kept an eye on my watch, and reckoned we would just make it to the outskirts of Paris in time, and hoped I would find a Metro station quickly. After some hours, he told me about his previous job, at a brewery in Putney, and how the head checker there had got him sacked just because he'd helped himself to a few bottles of beer, as everyone did. I thought it prudent not to remark: 'Good heavens, that head checker, he's my father!' In the middle of the night we reached the perimeter road around Auxerre, about a hundred miles short of Paris, and my driver told me he had to stop for a few hours here, he was knackered. I said goodbye, got out, and looked out across the empty, dark town. Some distance away I could see one building with a light on. I made my way to it, thinking it might perhaps be the police, and I could at least ask them for advice, which was bound to be a shrug. It turned out to be the railway station. I asked the ticket clerk what time the next train to Paris was, and he told me it was about to pull in. How much would the ticket cost me? He told me that, and it was a few francs less than I had in my pocket. The train was packed with soldiers. The small change I had left took me on the Metro, with enough, just, to spare for one coffee at République. Going through customs, I followed an Algerian. He put his suitcase up on the counter but did not open it. 'It is empty,' he said.

'Open it,' the douanier growled.

The Algerian complied. It was empty. While the douanier was staring into it, the Algerian told him: 'It is full of my ideals.' Maybe he had been reading Oscar Wilde.

Another time, I scheduled myself for three nights in a cheap Paris hotel on my way home. The day before I was due to leave I looked at my money. I had the choice either of staying the last night in the hotel, or having a good meal and walking the streets of Paris till seven. I don't get sleepy till two o'clock in any case, so I chose the meal, then started walking, my raincoat collar turned up like the

Sinatra figure's in the old Strand cigarette ads. At three in the morning I was on the Boulevard de Magenta. A café was still open, with tables on the pavement. An old bloke at one of the tables asked me for a light, then offered me a coffee, which I was glad to accept. He told me he was waiting for the early train home to Épernay, from the Gare de l'Est across the street. We talked for a bit, during which I ill-advisedly let slip that I had nowhere to go until seven. What he liked to do through these small hours, he said, was go to a hotel he knew, round the corner, where, for a small tip, the night porter let him rest on a bed for a while. Would I care to join him?

I was still naïve, but now had an inkling I had put myself in a difficult position. I'd enjoyed the coffee and the talk: how could I make up an excuse for getting away? I had not worked out how Sinatra would have handled it when he stood up, to lead the way, and I saw he had a peg-leg. I followed him, not finding the words. At the hotel the night porter opened the door, stared at us, and regretted that there was not a single empty bed that night. Monsieur Peg-Leg was taken aback by that, and I seized my chance to thank him all the same, nice to have met you, and scuttle off without further adieu. I like to think that the night porter had instantly summed up the situation and fed me my exit line, but perhaps he was simply telling the truth.

In London I often knocked around with Stoppard. Walking through Kensington, I wondered who was living behind all those windows. Russian émigrés, Stoppard surmised, and we smiled sadly at all their hopeless expectations that this Communism business would blow over and they could return home. I thought it was a whimsical scrap of conversation we had, but for him perhaps it came from nearer the heart, because he amplified the theme thirty years later in *The Coast of Utopia,* and in *Rock 'n' Roll.* In 1966 he was involved, with Geoffrey Reeves, Charles Wood and Adrian Mitchell in the early talking stages of Peter Brook's Vietnam play, *US*.

When the National Theatre started to get excited about *Rosencrantz and Guildenstern,* he remained penniless. He thought his best hope of making some money, and a splash, was his novel, *Lord Malquist and Mr Moon*, which was published at the same time as the NT opened his play. To the opening night he invited not just Alison and me but also Dad and Doris. In the first interval, I went with him to the Old Vic bar, where he gulped brandy. I asked him what was wrong.

'They're not laughing.'

'They are inwardly,' I told him. 'It's not laugh-out-loud stuff.'

I doubt if he heard me. He was taking a vow. 'I will never write another play without a laugh built in every thirty seconds. Otherwise, how can you tell if it's working?' A few weeks later, with the reviews behind him, he took me into Biba and examined the silk scarves. I saw the prices and closed my eyes. He bought two. Wearing them both, he led me on to Jim Haynes's Arts Lab. Outside, we bumped into Gordon Williams. I forget what was said to provoke his Scots sneer as we went in: 'Pair of fuckin' poofs.'

Through the RSC I was asked to write a calendar on a Shakespearean theme for ICI. When I told Stoppard about it, he said: 'You mean, you start with January 1st, January 2nd...?' I should have agreed a fee before I started work, but ingenuously delivered my copy to the man at head office and only then enquired what he would be paying me. He asked me what fee I had in mind. ICI were asking me how much money I wanted from them. I knew that Paul Jennings had written the previous year's calendar, so made a wild stab at what I thought he might have got. '£150?' The man reached into his desk drawer, brought out a chequebook, and wrote me a cheque for £150, leaving me to reflect that he might have readily written one for £500 if I had asked for it. I never was any use at business. I was later to persuade my children to invest their pocket money in Radio West shares, just before they fizzled, and to withdraw their remnants just before their price soared again.

I went on reporting for *The Times* until 1967, when Sunday first-class cricket was introduced, and I declined to cover it because I played cricket on Sundays. I made the argument that reporters should play the game, at however humble a level, to stay in touch with how it felt out there, but the paper, now owned by Thomson and changed in editorial staff, had no truck with such arguments and dispensed with me.

* * *

Eventually, the fall-out of Miriam Moore-Robinson's week in France with us and the Stoppards was that all three marriages were wrecked. Miriam would leave her husband and marry Stoppard. I was asked to swear an affidavit that the two little boys from Stoppard's marriage to Jose would be better served if they remained in their father's custody, which they did. Jose had to sit in court and hear that read out. She never forgave me. I don't blame her. I hated doing it, particularly at a time when I was feeling paternally shaky myself. But if I cared for the boys, it was the right thing to do. Jose had been ringing me every day for a while, already into her second bottle of white wine by 11 a.m., to tell me that she was more jealous of my friendship with Stoppard than she could have been of a woman's. What she meant was that I had an access to Stoppard's writing mind that she didn't have. To reason back to her that any two writers are likely to have an instinctive understanding, as two deep-sea fishermen or highwire acrobats might have, had no effect beyond hearing her gulp more and repeat the same complaint for the fiftieth time.

The writer she had married had been penniless. She couldn't adjust to his meteoric arc now. It had not turned his head. He is sanguine about fame. He remains an alertly caring man, as I believe he was to her. When she was unwell he gave her all the time with him she needed. They went on a holiday to Scotland, coinciding with the visit there of the Soviet Premier. Stoppard wrote to me: *Kosygin drove past the gate, but luckily he didn't see me.* But, celebrity being an enemy of promise as much as the pram in the hall is, he now had to defend his semi-detachment all the more adamantly. That Jose could not understand why is what produced the figuration of his 1967 radio play *Albert's Bridge*, an early but overlooked answer to those who, until *The Real Thing* in 1982, reproached him for not writing about human feelings. Of all of us who knocked about together as writers in the 1960s, maybe half have remained in their first marriage. Ghose is one who has. He needed semi-detachment as much as the rest of us, but he was shrewd or lucky enough to marry an artist. Two semi-detacheds make one solid house. There's a glib conclusion.

We were not thinking about having more children, but it was as though Oliver was saying: 'Hey, you're not done yet, what about me?' He was born in the bed where he was conceived, two days before my birthday in 1967. I was crouched outside the bedroom door with Imogen and Sophie. We heard the sounds of birth, but the midwife was in no hurry to tell us who had been born. Alison, losing patience, called out to us weakly: 'It's a boy.'

My solitary childhood had left me clueless about raising a family. Fortunately Alison, as women mysteriously do, knew from the start just what was to be done, and did much to teach me about babies and home-making. The practical things were easy to pick up. What I found harder, until they were women, was to feel an inwardness with my daughters. It is rewarding to have it now, developed through a shared sense of humour. With Oliver, a merry boy, I already knew about the father/son vibe. I bonded early. We all did. It was the best thing that could have happened to keep us all together. I have learned a lot from my children.

I don't have a President Kennedy moment about where I was when I heard that they had shot him, but I know just where I was sitting in Bristol Arts Centre on April 28th, 1967 to watch Charles Wood's *Dingo*, banned from public theatres by the Lord Chamberlain, that ludicrous relic, and so performed under a club licence, in a boxing-ring set, directed by Geoffrey Reeves. In North Africa a soldier in a tank has, to quote the stage directions, *been burned to death in a sitting position. He is black; charred, thin as a black, dried-in-the-sun, long dead bean. His arms are bent over his pin-head to open his hatch. Bits of still intact khaki drill flap from the crook of his elbows, crotch, and round his ankles.* Tom Kempinski, playing Dingo with a weary, foul tongue and infinitely compassionate eye, stared at the remains:

> It's not Chalky. Do you think we'd make a mistake like that? Do you think that black, burnt up, high-in-the-sun stinking charred old toothy old jerk of raw material is a British swaddie do you? Do you think we'd risk offending every mother here tonight with unlikely looking material? Highly upset they'd be. That's enemy. People out there lost their dear ones – that's enemy. No British soldier dies like that. That's enemy. You won't find a photograph, a statue, a painting of a British soldier like that.

Dingo transferred to the Royal Court and I saw it there, again, but it didn't work as well in a biggish London theatre.

Charles Wood is admired within the profession as the screenwriter of *Help!*, *How I Won the War,* and *The Charge of the Light Brigade*; he has had plays done at the RSC and the National Theatre and the Royal Court and worked with Peter Brook on US; he wrote the Falklands TV play *Tumbledown,* about which questions were asked in Parliament; and he's done other good stuff on television, like two series of *Don't Forget To Write*, directed by Alan Dossor, who did *Tie Up the Ballcock* for us all those years ago.

But you have to tell people who Charles Wood is. You don't have to tell people who Pinter or Stoppard are, and I doubt if you have to tell people who Wood's pal Peter Nichols is, although his work isn't put on as much as it used to be. Wood doesn't have that imprint. He is a kind of primitive writer, in the sense of primitive painters. His anti-establishment comic genius is there every time he writes, deriving from his birth into a theatrical family (he told me his parents did the sort of three-act touring rep show in which you improvise the middle act according to how the audience is going), and then his early experience in theatre as a scene-painter. When he delivered his script, *H.* (for Havelock) Reeves, who would be directing it at the NT, got Stoppard and me to join him for a first read-through in Stoppard's flat. It took the three of us more than ten hours to get through. Reeves's first job was to hack it down to three hours. Tony Palmer faced a similar problem twenty years later when he received Wood's screenplay for *Wagner.*

In 1968, what the Sixties had been promising seemed close to delivery: in Paris, in Prague perhaps, in Vietnam at a terrible cost, in California, and hesitantly in Britain, including sit-ins at both Birmingham and Bristol universities. At the latter, the cause was the revolutionary demand that students at Bristol Polytechnic should be allowed to use the university's students' union. In Birmingham they had the uglier provocation of a visit from Enoch Powell. Richard Hoggart and Stuart Hall were uneasily divided in their responses, Hoggart committed to democratic reason, Hall more excited (as I was) by the whiff of Sturm und Drang across the western world. Not just protest, but radical change seemed possible. I refuse to feel naïve. What I imagined then is what I still imagine, living in Stalag post-Thatcher/Blair. As far as I'm concerned, the Sixties have not ended. What's been going on for forty years is a dreadful music and frozen caption while we are waiting for normal service to be resumed. The Sixties supplied energy for writers and actors and singers and comedians. It was an exciting and hopeful time in which to grow up as a writer, and I am grateful for it. I am not nostalgic for the Sixties. I leave that to those who were born in or after them, who enjoy the music and fashions of those times but know little of the political imagination. It did at least give rise to the feminist movement, with which I sympathise while feeling uneasy. The real oppression is the capitalist way of thinking, and patriarchy is one of the fungi that sprout in its shadow; but not all the feminists I know would recognise themselves as socialists.

* * *

Our four-volume research report at Birmingham was completed in the summer of 1969. Later it would be my job to turn it into a book. Hoggart and Hall invited me to sit down with them and discuss where, with their help, I might find a lectureship. I had to say thank you but I have no intention of remaining in academe. I would be returning to the challenge of writing for a living. The day we packed our children and chattels into our Beetle and drove back to Bristol was sunny. We stopped in the Cotswolds to buy a paper, and I felt West Country euphoric. Outside the work I did, I had not found much to enjoy in the city of Birmingham – it seems to me a finer place now, forty years on – and had relished every return visit to Bristol.

I had kept my connection with Clifton Cricket Club, playing for them when I could, though I also made shorter trips to Shropshire to turn out for my father-in-law's club, Craven Arms. At Montgomery, the home side had a fearsome young fast bowler, a recent triallist for Glamorgan. In no time he had skittled out us young lions at the top of the order. As a young man my father-in-law, Ivan Kennedy, was good enough to have played for Notts Club and Ground, but he was now in his fifties. He was joined by another schoolmaster of a similar age, with the score at 27 for four. Patiently, technically, they tired out the young quickie, saw him off, and went on to build us to some kind of total, around 140. Our bowlers, chastened by such maturity, then turned in a disciplined performance, and we won the match. I remember my father-in-law, with the modesty of his generation, allowing himself just one gentle chuckle as we drove home. It expressed his satisfaction, but also his recognition of the irony that cricket teaches us, time and again. He was a cool cat. During the Battle of Monte Cassino he played his violin.

As well as club cricket, I played in what cricketers call jazz-hat matches. I organised one myself for about ten years, getting together a bunch of writers, actors and painters to meet, usually, a team collected by my publisher, John Bright-Holmes. We played at various locations, often at a school ground in Oxshott, where Lawson Hill's brother Graham was headmaster, and at Stratford, Exeter, Oxford. The list of those who played, on either side, is evidence that cricket and art share a spring. Stoppard usually kept wicket for us, with tidy gloves and great repartee with the slips. With a production of *Rosencrantz* about to start in New York, he wrote to me that he had decided to travel by the *Queen Elizabeth and miss two days of rehearsal, rather than by the Queen Mary and miss the match.* Ghose and I once put on an opening stand of 130 together, both of us conscientiously playing with bats straight enough to validate the many hours we had spent discussing technique, as we still do. The writers David Hare, John Downie and Ronnie Harwood played, so did the painters Derek

Balmer, David Inshaw and Alf Stockham. From theatre there were Clive Barker, Tony Mathews, Geoffrey Reeves, John Rudlin, Peter Thompson. I felt uneasy when I heard that Michael Croft, founder of the National Youth Theatre, had died of a heart attack not long after I had urged him to bowl just one more over for us, on a hot day.

There were the film makers John Boorman and Bob Godfrey, agents Gillon Aitken, Tim Corrie and George Greenfield. Sam Spoons of the Bonzo Dog Doo-Dah Band turned out for us, so did Stuart Hall, and Reggie Smith, and Michael Freeman, who tragically failed to win the Finchley seat when opposing a little-known Tory, Margaret Thatcher. Richard Hawkins was our scorer, Miriam Moore-Robinson our barber-surgeon, and her husband Peter an unwilling umpire.

I was batting when Christopher Falkus, at second slip, took advantage of a pause in play to remark to me: 'Now that John Bright-Holmes is retiring, you must be wondering how things are looking for you at Eyre Methuen?' We talked after the match, over a beer, and soon he had signed me up for a two-book deal with Weidenfeld and Nicolson. There must be other precedents, but I know of one. In his memoir *Not Prince Hamlet* (yet another Prufrock sprig), Michael Meyer records playing at Marlow in 1947 for a team of writers against the publishing house of Collins: *I had scored eighty including a six over the trees off Billy Collins, the chairman, eliciting from him the splendid non sequitur: 'Magnificent shot. You must write a book for us.'* He did. That was a more chipper Collins than I was to meet twelve years later.

I sometimes played for Bright-Holmes's team against other opposition. Once, to make sure of beating a rival bunch of bookmen, he enlisted another of his authors, Richie Benaud. I stood at first slip to Richie Benaud for ten overs. I will repeat that, in italics. *I stood at first slip to Richie Benaud for ten overs.* (Ghose once kept wicket to Benaud for an innings.) Not an edge came my way. It was a soaked pitch, and Benaud gave up trying to bounce leg-breaks and settled for steady leg-cutters, which did not cut. A Ugandan called John Nagenda, with first-class experience, played him out, maiden after maiden. When we batted, Benaud top-scored for us, with twenty. He was hampered by having been hit full-toss on the foot, by Nagenda. We lost the match.

It was a Sunday, in those days a rest day in Test matches. I listened to the commentary from Headingley the next day. Brian Johnston said: 'I've been joined in the commentary box by Richie Benaud. You appear to be limping, Richie.' 'Yes,' Benaud answered, 'I played in a match at Oxford yesterday and got hit on the foot. By a *Ugandan*.' In my reporting days, at Taunton, an Aussie once told me: 'I dunno about all this Benno business. When he was back in Sydney, playing in the grades, he was plain Richie Bennord.'

Peggy Ashcroft adored cricket. For Garrick's bicentenary, in 1969, she organised a match between the RSC, where she was a company director, and Stratford-upon-Avon Cricket Club. I arrived early, but there before me were Harold Pinter and Tom Courtenay. I found them deep in conversation. Pinter was using a glass ashtray as a bat to show Courtenay how to distribute his weight when playing an on-drive. Courtenay had not played cricket as a boy but now, a famous actor, he was always being asked to play in charity matches, and he liked to say yes. The bug had bitten him. He was going to Alf Gover's cricket school at Wandsworth for weekly coaching. I was in when a wicket fell and Courtenay came to the crease. The first ball he let pass. To the second he played an immaculate cover-drive. Alf Gover would have been proud.

Its only fault was that the ball had pitched on leg stump and gone straight on, at least a foot inside Courtenay's bat. Hearing the stumps rattle behind him, Courtenay closed his eyes in pain. After the match he told me: 'I'd rather have got that cover-drive right than play Hamlet over the river there.' The terrible thing is that he was sincere, and just as terrible is that I agreed with him entirely. Those who love cricket will understand. Those who do not will be thankful that I am ending the chapter here.

10

Persepolis

ALL THREE OF THE AGENTS I MENTIONED IN THE LAST CHAPTER – Gillon Aitken (formerly my editor at Chapman and Hall), Tim Corrie and George Greenfield – represented me at various times, and there were others. I value loyalty, and would prefer to have stuck with one of them, but they retired, or left the country, or moved on, or were defeated by the huckster market that fiction has become. I have paid a price for not having solid representation. So it goes. Along with ten thousand others, according to one estimate I saw, I became a mid-list novelist, which now will increasingly mean self-publication, if not e-books. The Writers' Guild has accepted the situation, and set up a special section for us.

But we are back in the Sixties. I had made a start on *Zero Summer.* Stoppard's agent, Kenneth Ewing, was looking after me for a while, and I went to talk to him. He was just winding up a meeting with Marty Feldman when I arrived. He introduced us, and Feldman looked at me with one eye and said: 'Anthony Smith?' I waited, ready to be conflated again with the author of books about films, or *The Body,* or one or two other Anthony Smiths who were writing then, but Feldman said: 'Did you write *The Crowd*?' Yes, I replied eagerly. 'I loved it,' Feldman told me. 'You *are* a vegetarian, aren't you?' All he remembered was a scene in a slaughterhouse, which I had written partly to scrub off my skin the stink of a visit I had made to one, at the invitation of a friend studying biochemistry. Along with a tannery in Somerset, where I tried to stop breathing, it was the most disgusting place I have visited. When I got home from the slaughterhouse Alison had prepared a special treat for lunch, rump steak. I couldn't eat it.

Three times *The Crowd* was going to be turned into a film. The first producer interested, in 1968, was Oscar Lewenstein, one of the founders of the English Stage Company at the Royal Court. In his Hampstead flat one sunny Saturday morning I sat with Geoffrey Reeves, who was to direct the film, and Charles Wood, who was consultant for the screenplay I had written, and had just scripted the *The Knack* for Lewenstein. We were tossing around ideas for casting.

'If we had Larry,' Lewenstein asked, 'would we have to have Joan as well?' This is the writer's life, I was thinking, pursing your lips over whether Joan Plowright was quite right for it. Before Lewenstein left for Brighton we had agreed that Tony Hancock would be perfect, not Larry. Hancock committed suicide seven days later, in Australia, and I feared that a cable from Lewenstein about my novel might have tipped the balance. What scuppered the project was that Reeves had never directed a camera, and Lewenstein thought it too hard a sell, both a scriptwriter and a director of whom nobody had heard. He told Reeves it would be easy to instal him as assistant director on a BBC film, where he would have no responsibility but to watch what went on, and then Lewenstein would be able to reassure potential backers that his director had film experience. Reeves answered: 'I'm sorry, Oscar, but I don't believe in doing something in order to do something else.' He had preserved his moral virginity. Lewenstein rang me, and said I had a choice: Reeves walks the plank, or we abandon ship. He thought he might get Kevin Brownlow to direct instead. On firmer moral ground than Reeves's own, I believe, I told Lewenstein that I felt unable to ditch Reeves, who had initiated the project, not to mention his having introduced me to Alison.

Next it was Tom Kempinski, who had a dream of moving on from acting to being a film producer, until he settled for writing *Duet for One*. He took the train from London to visit me in Bristol and get my signature on a twelve-month option. It said he would be paying me a nominal £1 for it, since he had no capital at the outset of his new career. Before he left, without troubling to pay me the £1, he asked me to lend him £2 to get the train back to London. I was impressed. I never heard from him again.

Some years later I had a call from Sydney. Michael Robertson had directed *The Best of Friends*, and now he wanted to make *The Crowd* in the booming Australian film industry. I've no idea how the book had found him. He bought an option, for proper money, and renewed it, and we exchanged calls and letters for years, until the boom had trickled into the Australian sand. Even then, he went on vowing he would make the film one day (and maybe you will, Michael?).

In Bristol, HTV had taken over the commercial franchise from TWW. I was asked to do some documentary scripting for them, and then offered my own monthly programme, a 30-minute regional arts review. I guess that Patrick Dromgoole, the head of programmes, knew about the *Western Daily Press* arts page and wanted a TV equivalent. It was called *Gallery*, later *Scene*, and I scripted and presented it for twenty years, which made it, I was told, the longest-running arts programme on the planet. We got surprisingly good ratings, always beating the BBC channels in our 10.30 cocoa-time slot. The first few times I presented it I was very nervous, notwithstanding my experience on *The Newcomers*. An actress once told me that when she was in the West End in a play where the lead part was played by Peter Finch, at that time a world-class film star, he threw up five times every night before going on. It had to be five. If he'd gagged only four times he told them to hold the curtain.

I tried downing a few glasses of wine before going into the studio, and learned that that was not the solution, it just made me slow. No one got formal training in presentation; it was assumed that if you had newspaper experience you knew about journalism, and this was merely journalism out loud. Bruce Hockin, the news anchor, spotted that I needed some help and gave me the only advice I ever got, or needed: 'There are a million people out there watching, but you can't talk to a million people. It's not possible. Tell it to your wife, or your mother, or someone you know. Just one person.' I was also given an occasional mini-series called Cinema Club, in which we showed art-house films, briefly introducing them via a discussion with the critic Derek Hill. I was permitted to rent what I liked from the BFI archive.

Such enterprise was all to the credit of Dromgoole. He had class, and form. On the West End stage he directed plays by Joe Orton and Anthony Shaffer, and for HTV productions he brought in Olivier, Leonard Rossiter, Jackie Gleason. He produced a drama serial called *Pretenders*, about the Monmouth rebellion in the West Country, and generously gave several young local writers their teeth-cutting chance on it. I was one of them, and along with the others I was then invited to write half-hour plays, with Charles Wood as our script editor. Any young writer now, reading this, will think that we were living in TV Arcadia then, beginners being commissioned to write our own single plays.

My first was about an old professional cricketer, modelled on Wally Hammond, the technically great but temperamentally difficult former Gloucestershire and England batsman. When I delivered the script, I warned Wood that I had stuffed the dialogue with jargon (*he had two grabbers up for the cherry*) and I feared that no viewer would understand any of it. Wood said: 'Don't worry. They won't mind, just so long as they're convinced that that really is how cricketers talk to each other.' His experience with army jargon was speaking to me. We filmed at the county ground in Bristol. Freddie Jaeger, an enthusiastic player for Datchet 3rd XI, was delighted to be cast in the Hammond part. His opening shot called for him to lean gently on the ball, into the off side, and take a single. The camera was close on him, half way along the strip. Graham Wiltshire of Gloucestershire C.C.C. was helping us. From behind the camera he lobbed the ball under-arm, Jaeger leaned on it, missed it, and was clean bowled middle stump.

My next HTV play was *The Chef*, set in a restaurant. Again, there was a take I assumed would be binned, when an angry diner, directed in the script to create mayhem by dragging the cloth from the table, instead contrived to do the conjuror's trick. The tablecloth came clean away, leaving just a wineglass teetering. Watching in the box, I waited for the director to stop them, and start again from the break – editing videotape was next to impossible at that time. But he let them run through to the end. 'Using it as an extra rehearsal?' I asked him. 'No,' he said, 'we'll buy that one.' Never mind that it now made a nonsense of the storyline. He didn't want the bother of going again.

* * *

Richard Hawkins had left Bristol United Press soon after I had. Running the newspapers for a few years had been a filial duty, to please his father Walter, whose own father had set up the *Evening Post* in the 1930s, to see off Rothermere's imperialism. Walter understandably hoped to see his son carry it on, but Richard wanted to be a composer. When he left the papers he went to work for the music publishers Schott. He sometimes offered me one of his tickets for a concert. We heard Stephen Pruslin give a piano recital at the Queen Elizabeth Hall. Afterwards, there was a party. Pruslin eventually came in, still slightly sweaty, and was at once clapped heavily on the back by someone tipsy. 'Give us a tune, Steve!' Pruslin, his bow tie dangling, sat down at the piano and rippled off *Black and White Rag*.

Hawkins had a house in the Savoie, and Alison and I, with Oliver in a carry-cot, spent a few days with him there. In my correspondence with John Berger he had invited me to call on him any time I was near Geneva, so we arranged to have lunch with him. With a little help from Mrs Berger IV, and the photographer Jean Mohr, we got through bottles of red wine and much red conversation. Berger did most of the talking, twinkling at Alison, whose mother had fallen for Berger when watching him on TV. Among the niceties of greeting, Berger asked me how our stay in the Savoie had been. I told him we had had a nice time. He frowned, folded his hands together, hunched his shoulders, leaned towards Alison, and asked: 'Time... what has time meant to you in your life?' I didn't think of Einstein's (Woody Allen's?) line *Time is nature's way of keeping everything from happening all at once*, and even if I had I doubt if I would have been brave enough to be flippant. I started to think it might be a testing lunch. I was wrong. The talk, or the listening, was absorbing for about ten hours. I asked him why a committed left-winger would live in Geneva, which I think I called the anus of capitalism. The answer was simple. Their reliable income came from his wife's work at the UN office as an interpreter. On his walls, Britain's most distinguished art critic had only one picture not made and given by a friend, a Léger print. He explained that he did not believe that art should be a private possession. How, then, were painters to earn a living? To that there were answers which did not require the commodification of their work.

We went to Blauvac, joined by Hawkins. He had been there before, with Stoppard, Balmer and me in 1962, but this time he took one look at the Vaucluse and went back and sold his Savoie house. He found a farmhouse in a Byronic valley, a few miles from Blauvac. The agent in Carpentras told him it was his if he paid on Monday, in cash. He raced back to Bristol and went to his bank to withdraw £13,000 in notes. It was Saturday morning, and it was one of those banks that opened on Saturdays in those days. With difficulty, finally driven to ten shilling notes, the bank put a pile together, and Hawkins shoved it into the boot of his Triumph Herald, the lock on which was broken, and drove straight back to the agent. He still lives in the house, with ten cats; in his younger days he also had goats, geese, dogs, and chickens. A gourmet and cook, he wanted to plant a vineyard and make wine, but the French regulations forbade him to grow any grapes other than Syrah, of which he is not fond. We have visited him many times. A few pages of this book were written there. When he grew cherries my daughters went there to pick for him. I once looked after the place for him for three weeks, when he had to be elsewhere. Leading his two puppies for a walk along the top of a cliff I rashly took them to a place where a small jump was needed over a deep fissure. One of the puppies made it over easily, the other one didn't.

Another family trip we made was to Spain, to stay in a house friends said we could use for no rent if we cared to go in March. After two days' driving we had reached Foix, north of the Pyrenees.

On the hotel's wine list I discovered a claret called Château Smith and, perhaps because of our exhaustion, it was the most delicious bottle I had ever drunk. I have bought it in Bristol, but it is never as good as the '60. We were heading for the Mediterranean coast, near Tortosa, and I wanted to take the straight (if that is the word) road over the Pyrenees, not detour through Perpignan. The next morning I made enquiries whether it was safe to drive over a 3,000 ft-high pass on March 3rd, and was reassured that any snow was ploughed away early in the morning. What I should have asked was what if it starts to snow, heavily, while we are driving up there?

We set off in light rain, and soon enough the roads were white, and whiter as we ascended. We came to a fork where I could have detoured down to Perpignan, but by now there was a will in my head, a mad refusal to alter the plan, to be beaten. On we went up the cliff-face, through snow now inches deep, with an unguarded sheer valley drop on the driving side. Our children wanted to stop and make a snowman. I kept the Beetle to a steady 10mph: any faster and we might skid, any slower and we could stall and be unable to get moving again. I was saying to myself, over and over, *grace under pressure*, and another Hemingway line, *each man retained now, better than any citation or decoration, the knowledge of just how he would act when everything looked lost.* What I retained was that I felt anxiety, but not fear. That came afterwards, and still does.

We went around a bend in the corniche and had to stop, because ahead of us was a car athwart the road. Its front wheels were over the drop. Its rear doors were open, where the passengers had climbed over the seats to reach the road. Alison murmured: 'We haven't got any rear doors.' I don't know how the message had reached them but men with a rescue vehicle had come down from Andorra and were dealing with it. When the road was clear they gave us a push to get going again. In Andorra happy skiers with woolly hats were strolling blithely. How safe their world was. I had just been through what was starting to feel like the most frightening experience of my life. With three small children in the back, my irresponsible choices had put us all in peril. And yet, three months after her husband Walter had been in a car crash, Janet Burroway wrote to me: *I'm a little alarmed at how quickly the terror is fading.* I sank two brandies, and bought snow-chains, which were never used because the road on the Spanish side was clear. It was a good holiday. In Tortosa market the women made a fuss of little children. Ours learned three words of Spanish: *naranja, chocolate, galleta.*

We returned by way of Cannes. John Goodwin had said we could stay in his flat, where, a few years earlier, I had been wretched. I wanted to go and play roulette in the casino, just for the experience of it, and had kept a fiver to lose in a few spins. I had a clean shirt, a sports jacket, a narrow tie and a pair of pressed flannels, and I put them on and jaunted along the front. I knew how things worked in the foyer of the casino because I had just seen *La Baie des Anges*, in which Jeanne Moreau is a compulsive gambler in Cannes. I went over to the guichet and presented my fiver, for chips. The man asked what I wanted and I told him, to play roulette.

'Un moment, m'sieu.'

He beckoned, and a vision glided towards me, a man in the most perfectly tailored suit, who bowed, and repeated the question, 'Qu-est-ce que Monsieur veut?'

I told him: 'Je veux jouer à la roulette.'

With an elegant gesture of regret, he told me: 'Mais Monsieur est habillé pour le sport.'

You don't get a more exquisite put-down than that. I was laughing all the way back to the flat.

'Did you lose it?' Alison asked.

'No, they didn't let me in.'

'Why not?'

'They said I am dressed for sport.'

'What sport?'

I shrugged. "Fishing? They might let me on the towpath.'

* * *

Richard Hoggart had left Birmingham to work in Paris for Unesco as assistant director-general. It tickled him that a boy from the hard backstreets of 1920s Hunslet had risen to 'outrank the British Ambassador on reception lines when there's an official do'. He had to produce discussion papers for very political international conferences on cultural subjects, and in his kindness to me, concerned at how I might make a living wage, he brought me in to draft them a couple of times. I became briefly an authority on comparative state provision for support of the arts, and on what contribution the arts make to environmental concerns.

In the Unesco library I was digging my way through files with the assistance of a delightful student who worked there to pay her way through the Sorbonne. She told me that she was being taught by the philosopher Roland Barthes, a name I knew from our Birmingham work. At my wide eyes, she asked if I would like to go with her her to a Barthes seminar? 'Of course,' I replied, 'but won't he mind?' 'Oh no, he won't even notice you're there.' She took me to where the seminars were held, a dilapidated semi-detached house in the suburbs, its front gate hanging on one hinge, the lawn a foot high. In a dimly lit room some seventy students were crammed in, most of them perching. I was expecting a small, bespectacled academic, but when Barthes strode in he was over six feet tall, bronzed from skiing and smoking a fat cigar. One student read her paper, and Barthes swiftly demolished it. Another one read his, same result. End of seminar. Only three people had opened their mouths. Not the way we do it in England. I introduced myself to Barthes, and we had a talk about the work at Birmingham. He was hard-nosed, as American academics had been when they visited us. All this lit-crit stuff, reading for tone and so on, was simply not rigorous. He wanted an analytic approach, the Americans wanted numbers. If you can't count it it doesn't count. I was told Barthes died when he was struck by a milk float, and thought how perfect a signifier for him – milk when you are entering the world and when you are departing it. I understand now that it was a laundry van, not quite as apt, speaking poststructuralistically, which I do seldom.

Hoggart invited me to a book launch at W.H. Smith's in the rue de Rivoli, with the come-on that Mary McCarthy would be there. She never showed up, but I did start my affair with Edna O'Brien. It has had three chapters, so far:

1. I have been talking to her for all of a minute when a waiter with a tray of drinks passes between us, and it is like one of those trick wipes in films, when a bus passes through the frame and the next shot is somewhere different. The flame-haired temptress is yards away, talking to someone else.

2. Years later, I am at a poetry festival at Nell Dunn's castle in Somerset. I am walking alone at twilight, through a gothic courtyard, and O'Brien, also alone, in a flowing frock, comes walking towards me through the long shadows, and as she approaches a smile lights up her face, and I am astonished that she remembers our fleeting moment together in Paris. When she has reached me she says: 'Oh, I'm sorry, I thought you were someone else.'

3. More years later, at a party at Weidenfeld, I am introduced to her. I say we have met before, and tell her the first two chapters. She replies 'That is the saddest story I have ever heard', and turns to talk

to someone else.

Hoggart offered me an editorial job on a Unesco journal. It was tempting, a well-paid life in Paris, but Alison had been invited to start acting professionally, with a group in Devon called Medium Fair, and we were not going to split the family up. Her need trumped mine. For me, a new journalistic job would have been another enemy of promise.

* * *

When I had completed *Zero Summer* I told Bright-Holmes that I had a question for him, probably the one that publishers dread most. He nodded me on. I had been looking at the poems I had written over the two previous decades, and thought the best of them would add up to a collection. Might I show them to him? He gazed fondly at me through his horn rims, and said: 'Anthony, you are like all authors, you understand nothing about publishing.' I began to murmur my apologies for having even mentioned it. I was inviting him to squander Eyre and Spottiswoode's money. 'No, no,' he said, 'you've got it wrong. You think we see ourselves as being here to publish books. But we don't. We are here to publish authors. You are one of our authors, so yes, please do let me see the poems.' I went home and looked at the poems again and never did send them to him. There were not enough good ones to respond to the generosity of what he had said. The story is unimaginable in commercial publishing now.

He was right about something else. A girl I had used as the model for a swinging Londoner in *Zero Summer* was a graphic designer, so I was keen that she should design the jacket, out of house. Bright-Holmes said: 'It will end in tears, it always does, but go ahead and ask her, if you must.' I did, and yes, she messed around, kept asking questions, getting nowhere, till the deadline blocked out the sun and in panic I found a photograph that did the job, and the in-house designer did the rest. The book got a few decent reviews. The one I appreciated most was from the *Daily Telegraph*'s William Cooper, whose own novel had done something to save my sanity when I was alone in Cannes in 1965.

At an Arnolfini show of David Inshaw's paintings I struck up a friendship with him. He was living at 15 The Paragon, which I had recently left. One afternoon there I watched him paint about one square inch of canvas, three hours of painstaking pointillism. He liked to work to the sound of a Test Match commentary, and had recorded an entire day of it, which he replayed every day. When Alison took part in a presentation he gave of the influences on his work – Thomas Hardy, Elgar – it gave me an idea for my arts programme. The producer took some persuading, but we devoted the entire half-hour to one painting Inshaw had just finished, *The Badminton Game*, which is now in the Tate. Using some of the presentation material as background, we filmed the painter talking at places that had contributed elements to the painting – a tower at Evesham, the topiary at Montacute, Arnos Vale cemetery.

Stoppard's radio play *Albert's Bridge* had won the Italia Prize, the European radio drama award, and been published, like all his work, by Faber and Faber. (They must owe me a hefty finder's fee after my introducing Frank Pike to him, back in 1962: I have been told that a successful playwright will earn more from the publication of plays than from their staging.) One day his agent got a letter from a producer in Hollywood called Al Brodax; he had just produced *Yellow Submarine*, was looking for his next hot property, and somehow he had come across this British radio play, and wanted to buy the film rights, and commission Stoppard to write the screenplay. Stoppard asked me to co-write it with him. There were three reasons. First, he was short of time, being in the early stages of writing the play we now know as *Jumpers*. Second, he knew I was broke and could do with the payday. He is a generous friend. Third, it's strange now, but the fact is that at that time I had more screenplay-writing experience than he had, so at least I could be relied upon to know how to lay out the characters' names and the stage directions. We set to work, gearing up to collaborate on a Hollywood screenplay.

Stoppard knew how such collaborations proceeded. He rented Troy Kennedy Martin's vacant smart apartment in west London, got in two typewriters, two ashtrays, two shot glasses and a bottle of whisky. Neither of us was a serious drinker, or any use at writing when drinking, but he knew that was how writing collaborations looked when you saw them in the movies. The first day we tried sitting each at a typewriter, but nothing got done, so we went out for lunch, and afterwards we tried it with one of us at a typewriter and the other one strolling around shooting out lines, but still nothing got done. So we tried a shot of whisky each, and that did us in for the day. I think we got through a couple of hours the next morning before we both admitted this was never going to work. We each went home and got the screenplay written like tennis, one of us doing a draft and posting it to the other for a re-draft, and so on, back and forth, until it was done as well as we could do it.

The agent posted it to Hollywood, dollars came back, and that was the last anyone ever heard of *Albert's Bridge the Movie*. Or of Al Brodax, for that matter, in the UK at least. We called him Al Brodaxident. I was in touch with him just afterwards, about a film he had told us he was trying to set up on a modern Quixote theme. I offered him the Cervantes research I had done for Peter Hall's project, if it would serve him. Then that film also sank without trace, like *Albert's Bridge* and Hall's *Don Quixote*. I don't *think* I was the Ancient Mariner responsible for all those fine vessels sinking. It's just the way it goes in Hollywood. You can make a living out of movies not made. Since then I've had a lot to do with *Albert's Bridge*, having first turned it, with Stoppard's agreement, into a stage play for the Edinburgh Festival, and more recently adapted it again as a Sondheimish stage musical.

You will already have jumped to the point of this story. Neither of us is the kind of writer who can work in company, so to speak. Few writers are, though there are examples, of course, particularly in TV comedy. A great deal further back, Beaumont and Fletcher come to mind. Who knows how they worked? To get the words right, hear the characters speaking, most of us retreat inside our heads, swim around in our imagination, and somehow we find the words or they find us, it's never clear which. Stoppard and I could not sit there in that London flat and come up with the words to order. It's not that we're dilatory. We are both of us pretty reliable deadline meeters. It's that we couldn't do it with the other one waiting for it. Maybe there's an analogy with the difficulty people have in producing a urine sample.

* * *

Reeves had directed at the National and the RSC, and would go on to run the Northcott Theatre in Exeter and the Nottingham Playhouse. In 1968 he had started working in Paris with Peter Brook's newly formed International Centre for Theatre Research. Brook had been invited by the Shahbanu (Queen) to take his company to Iran in 1971 for a three-month development period, culminating in performances of the outcome, entitled *Orghast*, at the Persepolis Festival. He wanted someone to go with them and write a book about the project, since the object of the trip was research, and it is no good doing research if your findings remain inaccessible in the Iranian desert. Reeves proposed me, which was some compensation for his sinking of the Lewenstein film. Brook knew me from the programme I had done with him in 1968 for his celebrated *A Midsummer Night's Dream* at the RSC, and invited me.

Together with Ted Hughes, who was writing the experimental material for Brook's actors, we left in heavy rain in June, and exited in oven heat at Tehran airport to the flash of press-camera bulbs. I don't know whether they were there because Brook's international celebrity went beyond theatre, or because the Shah's régime was intent on getting maximum PR mileage. We spent three months in a beautiful country as oppressed then as it is, by a different absolutism, now. What we did is recorded in the book I wrote, *Orghast at Persepolis*, which came out from Eyre Methuen in 1972. Finding a title gave me trouble. I got a telegram from Brook suggesting *Teahouse of the Orghast Moon*, a pun that older readers will decode. I thought it too flippant, a product of the hilarity that lies well hidden beneath Brook's magisterial public presence.

For three months I watched a great director at work. One lesson from that privileged education was that I am not a director. When, twenty years later, a company called Simply Theatre invited me to direct *The Witch of Edmonton*, I accepted because I was intrigued to see what I might bring to it. The answer was what I predicted. I am at home with language, and in the few bits of directing I have done I could work with the actors on inflections, pauses, emphasis, rhythms, but I am not imaginative in the visual and physical. When the stage manager asked me questions about the lighting, the set, the costumes, I had to do what Stoppard told me he did on his one venture into film directing, of his own *Rosencrantz*: admit from the start that I had no competence in these technical areas, and depend upon those who had it to interpret what I was doing. It is not a bad way to work, but it misses the conductor-like integrity that a maestro like Brook brings. When he is working hard, Brook hardly sleeps. Some nights I kept him company into the small hours, mostly hearing him reflect on his long experience. One night, I forget why, I brought up the subject of *Irma La Douce*, a small-scale French-import musical I had enjoyed as a teenager. I shrugged in apology for the triviality. Brook twinkled.

'Do you remember who directed it in London?'

'I'm afraid not.' Directors had not meant much to me at the time.

'I did.'

He had seen the show in a little Paris theatre and persuaded an English producer to let him try it out in translation. It ran in the West End for three years.

Later on, when it was necessary to work at the Persepolis tombs where the show would be performed, the company rehearsed there at nights, to avoid the heat of the desert day. There was a problem: vipers came out in the darkness. One night Hughes caught four of them and skinned them. He told me he would have the skins made into a pair of shoes for his wife. A no less poisonous problem in the night were the trigger-happy soldiers guarding the site, adjacent to the tombs, where the Shah would soon be staging his extravagant celebration of 2,500 years of Iranian monarchy. I was sitting next to Brook in a car when we found ourselves staring at the pointed muzzle of a rifle. Another night I stopped, more from instinct than observation, two paces short of falling a hundred feet from the side wall of Darius the Great's palace. This place was as hazardous as the Pyrenees in snowfall.

As well as the book, I had been commissioned to write articles for British newspapers. For the *Sunday Times* I included some photographs I had taken of Brook at work, and when one of them appeared across five columns my boyhood hobby of photography was consummated. I ate lunch most days, and sometimes supper, with Hughes. His public image was a Yorkshireman, but in conversation the Celtic roots in that name, Hughes, came through warmly, in amused stories about the dissipation of poets, or observations of the sometimes absurd behaviour of westernised Iranians. Seeing me filling up my notebooks, he said: 'I hope you're going to make lots up.' When he learned that I follow horse racing, he offered me his system: 'Top-weight winning two-year-olds.' In Hemingway's phrase, he was *small-spoken, the way a leopard is.* From the work that Brook and Hughes did with the actors I learned that a person's voice is an anthology, if you can read it, of their life. Hughes's life, at that time, was one of being persecuted by those who held him solely to blame for Sylvia Plath's suicide. It was one good reason why he had accepted Brook's invitation to get away from it for three months, bringing his wife and two children out. He told me a story that epitomised the problem. In Massachusetts recently, Plath's mother had been upstairs in a house where she didn't lock the doors. She heard noises from below, and found two women students had let themselves in and were looking around, as though Plath's childhood home were now a public shrine. 'Oh look, that's where Sylvia ate her breakfast. And that's where she did her homework.'

Brook's children also came to Iran. Those of us with a family at home were cheered up by the company of kids, but reminded of what we were missing. Alison used to read my letters to my children. When I told them I had been swimming in the Caspian Sea, she got out the globe. Three-year-old Oliver looked at the map of the Caspian and asked: 'Which is the deep end?' Stoppard and Miriam came out to visit us, and so did Hoggart, representing Unesco. Alison asked friends to mind our children for two weeks, and joined us in Shiraz and the magnificence of Isfahan. Seeing the prosperity of the middle-class in Tehran, and the fashions they wore, including miniskirts, I reckoned that in a few years the country would be completely Europeanised. Political prediction is clearly another area in which I have no competence. We had next to no chance to talk to the labouring millions, who might have altered my vision.

The book came out in hardback and paperback, and in foreign editions in the USA, Italy, Germany, and, weirdly, Bulgaria. I told my agent that I'd heard about Bulgarian book deals. You couldn't get the money out, so you spent it all on flying over for a Black Sea holiday. When I finally got the foreign royalty statement it told me I had the equivalent of just over £5 in a Sofia bank. It might be £6 by now, with interest.

11

A Thatched Interlude

After ten years of doing RSC programmes I completed the Shakespeare canon in 1973, with *Cymbeline*. By now I was editing them, as well as researching and compiling, since John Goodwin had been tapped up by Peter Hall to rejoin him, at the National. I am delighted to see that one or two of Charles Hockley's pithy insights are still being requoted in programmes, decades later. They must wonder where I found him, since he has published no books of Shakespeare criticism. The answer is that I invented him. In the critical books I now and then came across an argument which struck me as a necessary entry in the programme, but it was made at academic length. Hockley was the man to boil it down to a sentence or two.

Goodwin, with typical cheek, persuaded the Trevor Nunn régime to allow him back as a guest editor for the *Cymbeline* programme, so that he too would have completed the canon. In the course of our work he called a meeting in the theatre between George Mayhew, our graphic designer, himself and me, and told us he was negotiating with a publisher to have our collected programmes brought out in book form. As we broke up I mindlessly asked: 'When shall we three meet again?' The book deal broke down, and Mayhew died within months. Do not smirk if you see me touch wood or salute a magpie. I once had a watch which could not tell me when we had reached New Year midnight because the glass had just been brushed off and both hands with it. A bare-faced watch. At Stratford, had I known *The Wire* then, what I should instead have said to wind up the meeting was Stringer Bell's wonderful dismissal of the 'hood: 'Adjourn your asses.' It felt like time for me to call it a day at the RSC, too. It was not an easy decision. Under Nunn, the company was producing exciting work, but the old question was nagging. Unless you make time for your own writing there will always be something else to do.

In the late Sixties and through the Seventies it was a good time to be a playwright in Bristol. As well as HTV there was Avon Touring Theatre Company, set up by the actor Tony Robinson and the playwright David Illingworth in collaboration with the director Howard Davies and another actor, Chris Harris. It was one of a bloom of small companies all over the country, most of them radical in outlook, in response to the politics of the 1960s and, now, the cold fish of Edward Heath. I was invited to contribute to some of their early shows, written by divers hands, and later on to write two full-length plays, *Prostitutes* and *Face Value*. The first was adapted from a book by Jeremy Sandford. He had done his research on women on the game; I localised it by talking to prostitutes in Bristol. The second was a commission for a play about race relations, and was directed by George Brandt of the university drama department. Brandt carried the history of European theatre (and Balinese, and other traditions) in his head, and was generous in sharing his learning. That would not necessarily have made him a fine director, but in the event his intelligence was doing the job on my play until, a week before opening, we reached one of those crises that became endemic in right-on groups, when the collective spirit fatally blurred the distinctions between the different skills and responsibilities of director, writer, actors.

It turned on the last line in the play, which I had modelled on Brecht's *The bitch that bore him is in heat again,* from *Arturo Ui*. My intention was to throw the problems of race back in the face of the audience as they left. A couple of the actors were concerned only that their own position on the question of race be perfectly clear, and who gives a damn about dramatic ambiguity? A company meeting was called, in the rehearsal room at McArthur's Warehouse. For ninety minutes we argued about the one line, a vote was demanded, and it went against my line. Although Brandt had been a Jewish boy in Hitler's Germany, his attitude to racial discrimination was adjudged unsound, and he was told to leave. He asked me to stay for the last week, and direct the rehearsals. I secretly reported to him every evening at his home. All of that was a more entertaining play than the play. If I had it to do again, that is how I would set it, actors in a rehearsal room arguing with each other.

The founders of the company had left by now. Tony Robinson was working at Chichester, where actors who did not have a lot of main-stage work had got permission to run their own pub theatre group in their spare time. Robinson invited me down to write a play for them about the Battle of Britain, since Tangmere aerodrome was close by. I spent some time talking to retired fighter pilots. They were breezy, wizard-prang chaps, except for the one who had scored by far the most kills. He had haunted eyes, and spoke in single, terse sentences, closely watched over by his nervous wife. I went to have a look at Tangmere. It was deserted, so I drove into the camp, prepared to sing out *Sir! 676 Senior Aircraftsman Smith* if arrested. But nobody was there. I drove through to the runway, and Snoopy could not resist it, gunning my car across the tarmac at 90mph, only 40mph short of a Spitfire's take-off speed.

David Illingworth had died at thirty, unflinching to the end. His funeral promised to be unbearably sad, but his widow, Kate, from the political Foot family, spread her courage among us. At Canford Cemetery she had arranged for a 'cellist from Avon Touring to be seated by the open grave as we arrived, playing Bach. It turned out to be a rainy day, and to protect the 'cello someone had to stand beside him with a huge umbrella, and had chosen one panelled in red, green, blue and yellow. Pure Fellini. Kate arrived in a minibus and, followed by friends, tripped down the path in a floral smock.

* * *

Alison was acting full-time in Devon with Medium Fair, while I looked after our children at home with the help of au-pair girls. In 1973 the BBC asked us to make a half-hour follow-up to *The Newcomers*, ten years on. It was called *Deadly Serious Smith*, and the director was our friend Colin Rose, who had been a drama student with Alison, and later our lodger. This time I undertook to script it myself, in the third person. Alison, in the same spirit, simply invented a character for herself, and played it unremittingly. I still find it an entertaining film, as I hope impartial viewers did, but what I most of all hope is that we alerted them to the falsity of fly-on-the-wall that pretends to be unmediated by performance and editing. The western world is running out of scepticism as fast as it is of oil.

In the film we quoted Frederick Raphael: *Truth is stranger than fiction, but fiction is truer.* It is another answer to Bryan Johnson's *Telling stories is telling lies.* Johnson himself was making a short film at the same time, *Fat Man on a Beach*, for HTV. Full of self-referential humour, it was shot on the Llyn peninsula, a place he loved. The first I knew of it was when my arts programme producer, Terry Harding, told me that this month I had to link to a film made by some chap called B.S. Johnson.

Later in the year Johnson ended his own story with a razor blade in a warm bath, choosing the noble Roman manner. From Jonathan

Coe's brilliant biography of him we may infer sexual perturbation in Johnson, but I am sure the literary world's refusal to value him as highly as he believed it should had manured the ground. In *Middlemarch* George Eliot speaks of *That melancholy embitterment which is the consequence of all excessive claim.* If I sound acerbic about a friend whose reputation has survived him, and whose best writing has had influence, on Coe among others, it is because suicide is an act you commit once upon yourself and then perpetually upon others. A corrective is available in an obituary appreciation Ghose wrote in *The Review of Contemporary Fiction.* Ghose, Coe and I sat together on a platform at a British Library conference about Johnson in 2009. I told the audience that there had been a bonhomie between Johnson and me, but he was fundamentally a lonely man, lacking deep-seated fellow-feeling. *I have failed as a member of all groups I have ever joined,* he confessed. His melancholy humour was like Tony Hancock's. He was doctrinaire. Beware of the dogma. I respect those who seek truth, mistrust those who say they have found it. Chekhov advised writers to live with questions open, but Johnson needed QEDs. He didn't think his way in, or out. He was no good at what William Empson called argufying. Ghose said that Johnson never got over the initial praise, with allusions to Beckett and Joyce, which his first book attracted: 'He was formally interesting but intellectually naïve, drawing attention to his own modernism. He simply had not read enough.'

* * *

Hoggart and Hall had gone to Chatto and Windus with the popular press project, and I had to turn the four-volume research report into a book people might enjoy reading. When it was published, with the title *Paper Voices* (it came to me when Oliver was singing *Paper Roses* at the top of his voice), three top dogs in management at the *Daily Express* invited me to lunch with them in London. I accepted, because I was curious to hear what they thought of it. We had not concealed our distaste for most of what their paper had been doing in the postwar years – in the 1945 election the Labour Party had been represented as *a Gestapo under another name* – and I wondered if they might slap a libel writ on me over the pudding. Not at all. They were, I think, simply intrigued, perhaps slightly flattered, that a popular paper could reward intense academic scrutiny, and wanted to see what kind of weird ocean denizen I was. The book got a lot of review space, for much the same reason. It was unusual for popular culture to be the subject of serious study.

As when I had been working in Birmingham, eventually Alison said it would be more sensible if we all found somewhere to live where she was acting, in Devon. We let our house again, spent a few months in a semi in Exeter, then saw a newspaper advertisement for a fifteenth-century farmhouse to rent in Christow, on the edge of Dartmoor, quite cheaply. Whenever I returned to it I smiled at the sight of it: thatched roof, roses around the front door, a stream trickling past the gate, a two-hundred-year-old pear tree in the quilted back garden, sheep baaing on the hillside, it was a corny Christmas card in three dimensions and gorgeous Technicolor. However, the winter was hard, quickly blowing away pastoral drapes. We saw what a tough life the local people led.

Not far away in Devon was Ted Hughes, farming, with his wife Carol. We met a few times. Eric Walter White, still with the Arts Council, was concerned that Hughes had not produced a new book since *Crow* in 1970, and came down to Devon to do a little geeing-up. He found Hughes stripped to the waist in the middle of a tupping pen. When a sheep had been seen to by one of the two rams, it had to be removed from among those still waiting their turn. Hughes asked White, a silver-haired, elderly mandarin in a suit, to stand just outside the fence of the pen and catch the sheep as he hurled them out to him.

Midwinter Day, 1974
for Imogen, Sophie and Oliver

On midwinter day we went looking for holly,
tramped through the old year's decaying ground.
We found a bush by the stream, with red berries,
and walked home the long way round, holding bunches.

Were met by a man with three dogs barking.
Private road, he said, *all mine, no right of way.*
Leaving, Nolly leaned to smell the witch-hazel.
The man bellowed *Get away!*, slamming his man-trap mouth.

You three said we should call back *Merry Christmas!*,
but I thought the irony had entered his soul enough.
We noticed the spikes of living green holly are gentle,
not like the barbed stuff you buy on midwinter day.

I was working on a novel, *Treatment*, about the experience of a young married couple subjected to television documentary manipulation. The first section of it was all right, I think. Alan Coren thought so, in the *TLS*. The second section changed gear and headed in the direction of magic realism, and wound up lost in Pirandello territory, receding levels of truth. But I did enjoy my last reality flip, sending a copy to John Boorman, now a Hollywood director, and offering him the film rights.

John Goodwin, now in charge of publicity and publications at the National Theatre, asked me to compile a few programmes there. One was for *Who's Afraid of Virginia Woolf?* We agreed that thematic content would be impossible. I was simply to interview the four actors and the director, Nancy Meckler, the first woman to direct at the NT. Everything was set up for me. I was given an office for the day, and the appointments were made. The last, with Joan Plowright, would be two hours after the others, because of her rehearsal schedule. I was warned that she could be prickly. The first four went smoothly enough into my tape-recorder. Paul Eddington was particularly charming. Then, with a couple of hours to wait, I wandered off around the building and chatted to one or two people I knew. I was back in good time for Dame Joan, hit the recording button, and found her entirely pleasant. She had had a good day's work. Once it was over and she'd left, I breathed in relief, went under the desk to unplug the recorder, and found it already unplugged, by some jobsworth during my absence. I had not made any written notes, and the tape was still virgin.

I spent the train journey back to Exeter sweating, ransacking my memory for what she had said, any characteristic phrases, and trying not to imagine how she would react when she was asked to do the whole thing again. The arrangement was that all the interviewees would read my versions of what they had said, and could amend it if they chose, since it was in-house reporting. I posted them off, and waited in trepidation for what Dame Joan might say about my garble. She signed it off with no demur. I could have taken that as a tribute to my memory, but I think the truth was that it was so bland, without the spikiness of word-accurate quotes from her, that she found it too dull to bother her.

On a visit to the NT Goodwin bought me supper and invited me to fill a new post he was creating, editing all the theatre's publications. I would be paid four times the income I was used to. I caught the late train to Exeter, and was so elated that I chose to walk home from the station, under the midsummer stars, and got to bed at about 5am. When I woke up I rang Goodwin and turned him down. One short night's sleep on it had been enough to remind me why I had resigned from the RSC, and declined Hoggart's offer to find me an academic position, and before that left the *Western Daily Press*. Living in London, in heady theatrical air, and doing a full-time job, I would have found just about no time for real writing. When I told Alison, a little apologetically, she understood, and in fact agreed with my decision. We loved Bristol, where we would soon be returning, and did not want to bring our children up in London.

By the time we did return, in the autumn of 1975, there had been an addition to our household. Alison had asked me how I would feel if John Hill, the roadie for Medium Fair, moved in to live with her. I answered that I didn't know, but was willing to find out. We explained the situation to our children. The girls were briefly upset. Oliver said, 'Okay. Can we play football now?' It was an eccentric arrangement we were asking them to accept, but not as damaging as if we had announced we were divorcing, or told them lies. In Christow, and then back in Bristol, it all worked well enough. I found Hill easy to get on with, and he had practical skills in the house that I lack. Unfortunately, I also started to find bottles of whisky hidden around the place. Alison had to ask him to move elsewhere until he had dried out. He lived rough after that, and soon he died, not of drink but of Weil's disease, which he probably picked up from dock rats in the rehearsal room at McArthur's Warehouse. He was the sort of man who would pay no attention to a cut hand.

Southwood Farm had been an idyll, hence it could not last. Alison had had enough of fit-up performances, and Medium Fair would soon have run its course. I am a city boy, and was glad to be back in the streets of Bristol, few of which are mean. I had played village cricket for Teign Valley C.C. on Saturdays, but on Sundays had been driving up to play for Clifton. For about fifteen years I was captain of what turned into an extraordinary team, extraordinary not in its strength but in the sociability of a mix of arty, legal and business types, bearded academics, scientists, and schoolboys. We were the Sunday 2nd XI, but when the Sunday 1st XI were short our regulars often declined to be promoted, which led to our being known at the selection committee as Smith's Bloody XI.

We did have some good players. Until the age of fifteen Andy Pott had batted right-hand, but then turned himself into a left-hander, for political correctness we suspected, since he was leader of the Avon Labour group. Richard Lee played in a Cambridge Blue sweater; we never told the opposition that his Blue was for boxing. Our leg-spinnner, he was the architect of Broad Quay House. Stand on the Centre and look the other way and you see the Colston Hall extension, architected by our slow-left-armer, Axel Burrough.

Jeremy Mulford had played representative cricket during National Service. He talked me through to my first century. It was a very hot day and we were playing a local derby at Westbury-on-Trym. I won the toss, and went in to open with Mulford. I got to 50 quite soon, and he came down the wicket to remark, 'You've never scored a hundred, have you? Keep going. Today's the day' I took his advice, though knew I was starting to play loose shots, and eventually I got there. He was still in, with seventy, so I told him to keep going, too, to add to the centuries he had scored before. So he did, and when he got there I declared at 220-0, which was later established to be a record in the club, founded in 1819. (The name of W.G.Grace appeared in some of our 1860s teams, but he was an old tart and turned out for several other Bristol clubs, too.) Mulford, who carries a little condition, as racehorse trainers say, was so exhausted that all he had for tea was orange juice and salt tablets. He was our best off-spinner, but told me that bowling was out of the question for him after that. With an hour to go we still needed five wickets, and I asked him if he was up to it by now. He took the last five wickets in 5.5 overs. It was a day when everything insisted on going right. Westbury's last man was doggedly blocking it out, and we had only a few overs to go before close of play. I didn't want such a day to end in a draw. I told Chris Coleman at second slip to come up close. Mulford said no, leave him back. It was absurd. After our partnership, we were having a tiff on the pitch. I exercised my captain's prerogative, brought Coleman up, and he caught the next ball.

The club used to open its season with a double fixture against Bristol University at Coombe Dingle. One year I opened the batting for the 2nd XI, in the first over got one down the leg side, flicked at it, expecting it to go to fine leg, but inadvertently picked it up on the half-volley and saw it go over square-leg's head for six. As the 1st XI were fielding in their match, my fluke was the club's first scoring shot of the season. In September the last fixture was for the Sunday 2nd XI at Dinas Powys. It had been a late arrangement, and the Welsh groundsman had already installed rugby goalposts, one of them directly behind the bowler. Mike Segal, a high-powered scientist and one of my bridge-playing friends, was batting in the last over before tea. Remembering how I had started the season months earlier, he picked his ball and converted it straight between the goalposts.

Another regular in the Sunday 2nd XI was my editor at Weidenfeld and Nicolson, Christopher Falkus, a good batsman. For several seasons he drove down from Earl's Court on Sunday mornings for the matches. Through the Nicolson connection, he had access to the gardens at Sissinghurst Castle, and the use of accommodation. He invited me to take Oliver there for an autumn weekend with him and his son Justin. I was billeted in what had been Harold Nicolson's library. I grazed the shelves and came across a book of which I had heard but never expected to hold, Wyndham Lewis's *Hitler*, which in 1931 presents the Führer as *a man of peace*. Nicolson had the habit of scribbling notes on the fly-leaf of a book he was reviewing for *The Observer*. With some difficulty I deciphered what he had scribbled in this one: *of course fascism has no chance in this country because of the bloody British sense of humour*. I am still fascinated by the ambiguity of *bloody*, given that Nicolson had once been in Oswald Mosley's New Party.

The next morning, a Sunday, we had all been invited to a lunchtime party at Stoppard's. On the way, Falkus asked me to drive my battered Beetle into Lord Longford's country seat to give a lift to another of his authors, Antonia Fraser, who was also invited to the party. That she would be pleased to see Pinter there was by that time no great secret. At the Stoppards' house I noticed a change. Miriam had been writing articles in the national press on the evil of smoking. Stoppard had made a concession. He had bought ashtrays with lids.

12

A Carpathian Walnut

AS SOON AS I HAD DELIVERED *TREATMENT* TO WEIDENFELD, MY agent at that time, Jackie Baldick, told me that they were looking for someone to write a biography of Dickens to accompany a new TV series, *Dickens of London*, scripted by Wolf Mankowitz. He had said he would write the book too, but now had run out of time. I knew little about Dickens's life, and told Jackie I did not fancy the job. Not my kind of thing. 'They're offering a thousand pounds,' she said in her engaging Baltimore voice.

'That's not much for a biography.'

'It is for five weeks' work.'

'They want it in *five weeks?*'

'Ant'ny, you're always telling me you're broke. How often can you make a thousand pounds in five weeks?' She had a way with her, Jackie. 'Oh, and when it comes out it will be by Wolf Mankowitz. Okay? You don't tell anyone that you wrote it.'

I did it. Dr Johnson wrote *Rasselas* in a week, to pay for his mother's funeral. I could not allocate a lot of the five weeks to original research. I depended on Edgar Johnson's superb two-volume biography. I did not plagiarise his words at all, but accepted his chronology without question. My spare time from writing two thousand words every day I spent dipping around in other books about Dickens, and consulting one or two Dickensian friends. The result was better than it might have been, and was sumptuously illustrated. On page 82 of the UK edition is a sentence that starts: *Bentley yielded again, controlling his sullen mood in the hope (not one that was obviously ludicrous for...* which read acronymically reveals: 'By A C H Smith not Wolf.' Mankowitz was beyond acronymising.

On the day the book was published I was rung, in Bristol, by someone in Weidenfeld's publicity department. 'Just want to check one or two details with you, before the launch this evening.'

'There's a launch?'

'Yes. Oh, haven't you been invited?'

'No.' I'd only written the book. In five weeks.

'Sorry about that. You know how things are. Do come, if you'd like to. It's at George's place, in Cheyne Walk.'

When I had answered her questions I put the telephone down in a seethe. But it was a party at George's place, one of George Weidenfeld's legendary parties, it would probably be my only chance to see one of them for myself. I went to Temple Meads. In Cheyne Walk, the first three people I saw were Harold Wilson, just retired from Downing Street, Peter Sellers and David Frost. It was legendary all right. I stayed clear of the celebrity end of the salon, so cannot report what any of them were talking about, but Sellers kept them all laughing. The whole evening Mankowitz, seated next to a woman with orange hair, accepted a parade of congratulations. I kept clear of him too. In his position I would have been acutely embarrassed to be confronted by the real author. But I underestimated him. When it was time for me to leave, it occurred to me that if, the next day, he happened to be told that the chap who had written his book had been at the party but hadn't even said hello to him, it would strike him that I had been uncomradely, disrespectful.

I hedged my bets. I went over, didn't identify myself, shook his hand, wished him luck with the book and the series, and said I had to be going now, to catch the last train back to Bristol. My final word had given the game away. 'Bristol?' he asked. Someone must have mentioned that his jobbing hack lived in Bristol.

'Yes.'

'What's your name?'

'Anthony Smith.'

'Excuse me,' he growled to the woman with orange hair, and rose, for the first time in an hour. He was a few inches taller than my six feet. He put his arm around my shoulders, and quietly assured me that I had written 'a wonderful book'.

'Thank you.'

His arm squeezed me. 'This series is going to be a very big hit, Anthony. They will want more from me. I'm going to write them and you, you are going to write the books. We are going to make a great deal of money, Anthony. I'm going to give them Robert Louis Stevenson, Paul Gauguin, and – you got any ideas for a third?'

From nowhere, I suggested, 'Victor Hugo?'

Hole in one with my eyes shut. 'Victor Hugo! Perfect.' An extra big squeeze. He told me we had to stay in touch. 'We are going to make a great deal of money, Anthony.'

'Good. Good. I'll tell my agent about it.'

His manner altered. 'Your agent? We're writers, Anthony. We

understand each other. We don't need any fucking agents getting between us. It's you and me.' Nevertheless, the next day I rang Jackie, and told her. She said she would get hold of Mankowitz and firm things up. She rang back later the same day. 'OK, Ant'ny, I've spoken to Mankowitz, and here's the deal. You do all the research. You write the books, then give him the manuscripts, and he uses them to write the scripts. He gets half the book income, and all the TV money.'

'That's a terrible deal, Jackie.'

'Damn right it's terrible. That man would charge his grandmother half a crown for a rotten grapefruit.'

If Mankowitz had ever written his autobiography, I could have suggested the title for it: *Great Exploitations*. In the event, the Dickens series was derided by the reviewers, and Mankowitz faded over the horizon. The book got some good press, however. In the *Financial Times* C.P. Snow said that those who had known Mankowitz since he had sat at the feet of Dr Leavis had always known he had a good 'literary' work in him, and here it was. Poor old Snow. I had to resist the urge to drop him a note putting the record straight. Leavis was having the last laugh on him.

Knowing my fondness for horse racing, Falkus suggested that I should write a racing thriller. I blinked. 'What, compete with Dick Francis?' Falkus replied: 'You think Dick Francis has cornered the market. The truth is that he has created the market.' Having never sat on a horse, I decided to write it from the point of view of a small-time punter in Bristol, like me. I came up with the idea of fixing races by using a sonic gun, and consulted a university physicist about the plausibility of it. He was an Australian, and had been working on the puzzle of why Concorde, coming in over the Severn, delivered a sonic bang on Bristol but not Clevedon. He explained to me how such a McGuffin as mine might be built and operated, and what it would look like. My last question was, would it work? 'I'm not sure,' he said,'but if you like I'll rig one up for you, and we can go up to Cheltenham and give it a try.' He meant it. 'Oh no,' I simpered, 'I'm a novelist, I'm not for real.'

The Jericho Gun came out in 1977, sold out its paperback reprint the following year, and was twice optioned for film rights, which as usual came to nothing. Encouraged, I suggested to my batting partner Falkus that I follow up with a cricket thriller, using the same pair of anti-heroes. He agreed. *Extra Cover* did not work as well as the racing book. Ted Dexter had just published a thriller in a Test match setting; I felt it unwise to challenge him in the arena of professional cricket, so again I wrote from my own experience, in club and village cricket. The cricket bits of it I liked, but I could not work up a satisfying plot.

Some years later I was rung by a solicitor. Would I be ready to be a witness in a trial at Southwark Crown Court? *The Jericho Gun* was to be called in evidence in a case involving an alleged drugs dealer. Asked by the police why he had been found with half a million pounds in notes in his car, his defence was that the money was to be used to develop a sonic gun to fix horse races, like the one he had read about in my book. What I was supposed to say in court is beyond my conjecture, but in the event I was not called. However, the prosecution did arrange for trials of such an instrument, in which Greville Starkey rode the horse. They were not conclusive. More sinisterly, at Royal Ascot a horse called Ile de Chypre unaccountably veered violently off course as it was coming to win its race, and something similar happened in South Africa. I was interviewed in *The Independent*, with no hint of villainy on my part but some question whether I might have inspired villains.

My publishers had established from the Dickens job that I could write this kind of book quickly, and needed the money. I was commissioned to write the novelisation of *Edward and Mrs Simpson*, in seven weeks this time. Simon Raven was writing the television scripts for Thames TV, locked in a room in Deal, at his own request, so that he could not get at the booze. As it came off his typewriter, each of the seven episodes was rushed to me in Bristol, one a week. I had time to do some cursory research of my own, and found little sympathy in myself for the aristocratic protagonists. Dad told me that people at Christmas in 1936 had been singing *Hark the herald angels sing, Mrs Simpson's pinched our King.* With TV marketing behind it the book came out in several languages, and was serialised in the ever patriotic *Daily Express.* Auberon Waugh, who had previously been kind enough to invite me to a *Private Eye* lunch after I had interviewed him on my HTV programme, publicly vented his disgust at the whole *Edward and Mrs Simpson* project, but I didn't mind, because at the launch of the series, at the Dorchester, I got to dance with Cherie Lunghi. When she writes her memoir, I do not think she will record having danced with me.

* * *

At a writers' conference in Exeter the guest of honour was Henry Williamson. Aged eighty, with a gorgeous young woman beside him feeding him his notes and clearly doting on him, he spoke from the platform, and then in conversation, with a sparkle brighter than any of the several hundred other writers who attended. I knew he had got it wrong about fascism, as Wyndham Lewis had, and perhaps Harold Nicolson, and definitely Ezra Pound, and there was some question about Yeats, and Eliot... Detestation of a writer's political views should not corrupt our response to their work, though it almost always will. This man had written *Tarka the Otter*, and was now the charming proof that age need not wither us – only two years before his death, as it turned out.

It was in Exeter, too, that I met Colin Wilson, when we sat together on the literature panel at South West Arts. Twenty years earlier, when he had been lionised for *The Outsider* and lumped in with the Angry Young Men, he had come to speak at the Cambridge Union. Dressed head to toe in black, sesquipedalian, aggressively serious throughout, he had struck me then as a star speaker at Pseuds' Corner. The man I met now was warm, sometimes humorous, and just concerned, as I was, with how to be a writer and yet pay the gas bills. He told me I had made a mistake in choosing my writing name. The initials were a turn-off, notwithstanding T.S. Eliot, W.B. Yeats, W.H. Auden, not to mention D.C.S. Compton, P.B.H. May. I explained that I knew of four other writers called Anthony Smith. When I had published my first book, *The Crowd*, I could not settle for being just A.C. Smith, the only initials on my birth certificate, because I was reporting cricket then and A.C. Smith was a Warwickshire player. (Once, reporting at Cardiff, I found myself standing next to him. I said 'Are you A.C. Smith?' 'Yes,' he replied. 'So am I,' I told him. He looked at me nervously, and backed away.) I perhaps should have invented a *nom de plume*, but why shouldn't the Smiths put their name on books? So I added H, for Hockley, my grandmother's maiden name, and now it was too late to emend it.

The literature panel was chaired by Eric Walter White, although he still lived in Hampstead. He invited me to succeed him in the chair, but before I could do that I had resigned from the panel altogether. We had about £4,000 to distribute in annual funding, and it was going out in little parcels of £50 here, £200 there. Already, in the mid-1970s, it was becoming obvious to me that London publishing houses were turning their faces against writers whose distinction was literary, not commercial. Richard Hoggart thought the same, and was advocating the establishment of a state-funded national publishing house, equivalent to the national theatre and ballet companies. My argument to SWA was that, rather than dressing the wounds of many, we would do better if we confronted the blade by applying the whole of our funding to publishing and promoting three or four literary books a year ourselves, inviting submissions. When the panel voted against it, I felt we were appeasers, and quit.

I was invited to apply for and was awarded the Cilcennin Fellowship at Bristol University drama department, a sort of resident playwright position lasting three years. It was the one John Arden and Martin Shuttleworth had occupied, and Johnson had eyed. After being interviewed, I bumped into Mike Costeloe, who opened the bowling for the Sunday 2nd XI, and was professor of Spanish. I told him I'd just been appointed a colleague of his, so looked forward to lunching with him in the senior common room and enjoying cross-disciplinary exchanges. 'I won't see you,' he said. 'I bring sandwiches in. We never meet people from other departments.' It fell short of the ideal implicit in the word 'university', but turned out to be true. Since the fellowship paid about one-tenth of a salary, long hours of attendance were not expected, and neither was any teaching. I did it because I enjoy the company of bright students, and it allowed me access to facilities like the university library. Also, there was a football match every Sunday morning on The Downs. The dirtiest tackler was Misha Glenny, who has gone on to tackle much dirtier subjects in such books as his excellent *McMafia.*

What I did chiefly was to convene, at my house, a weekly meeting of students who were writing plays. There were five regulars. In the three decades since, Phil Smith has written dozens of plays, directed by another student of that time, Paul Stebbings, and is now an exponent in Exeter of mythogeography. (Don't ask me, google it.) Paul Unwin became director of the Bristol Old Vic, and created *Casualty*. Craig Brown has a national profile as a satirist. We were a lively bunch, and our meetings reiterated what Ghose, Johnson, Stoppard and I had once been for each other, not influences, just climbers on the same rockface, encouraging by example.

Martin White, my colleague in the drama department, was taking a group of students to the Edinburgh Festival to perform two plays. One would be the Elizabethan *Arden of Faversham*. For the other he wanted a new play, and presumed that, as playwright in residence, I would have one to offer him, or could rattle one off. I had nothing to hand but did not want to disappoint him, so had the idea that I might re-adapt the unproduced *Albert's Bridge* screenplay for the stage. With Stoppard's agreement, and some revisions by both of us, it was soon ready. We retained the conceit that half-way through the play the main character, Albert, unable to choose between two possible lives, two wives, splits into two and follows both options, a device repeated twenty years later by the film *Sliding Doors*. It landed the actor playing Albert with a gigantic workload, but Greg Doran, now chief associate director of the RSC, took it on with no word of complaint and performed it admirably. Edinburgh is hard – pizzas at 2 a.m. on the way home from sixteen hours of rehearsal, sleeping six to a room on the floor – but a very enjoyable gig. The grandeur of the city subdued my patriotic piping for Bristol.

The director of the Bristol Old Vic then was Richard Cottrell. He had a pronounced stammer, though one night, when the leading actor rang in at 7.15 to say that he was too ill to perform, Cottrell went on, script in hand, and gave a fine performance with no hint of impediment. On my HTV show I asked him about the difference between directing on stage and on TV. He started: 'In television you need to be aware always of where the ca- ca- ca-' I had no idea what the etiquette was. Should I offer him the word *camera*? Before I had made up my mind he stopped trying to speak, took a packet of cigarettes from his pocket and lit one. All right, I hoped, that will get him through. By now, thirty seconds had passed in silence, which in a live transmission is a lot more than half a minute. Then he started again. 'In television you need to be aware always of where the ca- ca- ca-' 'Camera?' I proposed. 'Camera is,' he agreed.

He was a polished director but had little interest in new plays, and none in work by Bristol writers, which aligns him with most other directors of the BOV. My friend John Downie and I agreed that something had to be done. Downie makes Leonardo da Vinci look like a one-trick pony. At Durham University he starred in the football and cricket teams, he trained as a director with Granada (in the same intake as John Birt), he is a playwright, short story writer, stage director, librettist, artist and composer. He rustles up a tasty stew, and in New Zealand he has created an exotic garden. He retreated to New Zealand in despair at the safe and smug culture of Thatcher's Britain, and has wound up as senior lecturer in film, theatre and media studies at Victoria University.

In Bristol in 1978 we founded the Playwrights Company, which

Writing for peanuts. Buy three packets of KP and you could have a free copy of my *Edward & Mrs Simpson*

With Val Lorraine, outside her house in Clifton

Top: Three-year-old Oliver.
Above: He would grow up to play for English Schools and Young England

I show Oliver the way to do it, at Flax Bourton, in a photo by Roy Swetman

Avon Touring Theatre Company

AVON TOURING THEATRE COMPANY
is Bristol's only professional touring theatre company and performs in youth centres, schools, detention centres, community centres, as well as theatres and arts centres in the region. It aims to present live theatre of local and topical importance to as broad a section of the community as possible. Our fees are negotiable and all we need is a small flat space. If you'd like to know more or book the company please contact Carol Braithwaite and Paul Bassett, Administrators, Avon Touring Theatre Company, McArthur Warehouse, Gas Ferry Road, Bristol BS1 6UN. Telephone: Bristol (0272) 20247.

Avon Touring Theatre Company, 1977. George Brandt is in the middle

With Derek Robinson and Adrian Cairns, Deputy Principal of the Old Vic Theatre School. Photo by Charles Manton

The programme for *God's Wonderful Railway*, at the New Vic Studio, 1985

The doyen. David Foot, voted Cricket Reporter of the Year in his 70s. Photo by Alan Moore

With Imogen, Sophie, Oliver, and Alison, at the launch of my poetry collection, at the Catto Gallery in Hampstead. Photo by Nitchka

With David Wevill and Zulfikar Ghose at Ghose's house in Austin, Texas. Photo by Alessandra Lipucci

Photographs by Graham Burke of the Bristol Old Vic's dockside production of *Up the Feeder Down the 'Mouth* in 2001.
Above: Heather Williams as Mrs Q and Kate McNab as Spot
Below: 'Prince Street'. Foreground from left: Fred Wedlock, Stuart Mcloughlin, Kate McNab, Howard Coggins and Ross Harvey

Fred Wedlock and the Kids

The Feeder Band: John O'Hara, Dave Goodier, Kit Morgan, Rod Salter, Dave Townsend

Portrait of me by Anne Adamson. My children refer to it as the Chairman of the Board

in four years gave public airing to thirty-one new plays – a few fully staged in the New Vic studio, others done in Bath, or as lunchtime shows or rehearsed readings – and six collaboratively written revues, and also provided work for Bristol actors including Amanda Redman, Nicholas Farrell and Alex Jennings, and the director Greg Hersov. Downie was our literary manager, Mark Dornford-May our artistic director, and the general manager was Nigel Cole, nowadays known as the director of such films as *Calendar Girls* and *Made in Dagenham*. We commissioned six new plays. With backing from W.H. Smith we organised an annual playwriting competition for schoolchildren, the winners of which were broadcast on Radio Bristol. From our office by Stokes Croft we ran a script-reading service and workshops, a registry of plays for other companies to consult, and collaborated with Jeremy Mulford's imprint, July Fox, in the publication of some of the work we produced. Downie organised some of us to create a multiple installation at Watershed, called *A History of Airports*.

To pay writers and performers a minimum wage we had to seek funding. A number of companies in Bristol gave us donations, so did local authorities and some private friends, including Stoppard, Martin Lee and Colin Godman. We had Ken Loach on our executive committee, and he accompanied me to a meeting at HTV with Patrick Dromgoole. I knew Dromgoole wanted to give us HTV's support. What I had not reckoned on was how quietly, thrillingly ruthless Loach would be in pushing for quite a lot more than Dromgoole had in mind. We left with HTV's promise to buy a £150 option on every play we put on, which took care of playwrights' fees.

We raised money from a couple of celebrity cricket matches. The first was at Clifton College, between a Playwrights' Invitation XI and one representing Sun Life, a major sponsor of our work. Among those who turned out for us were John Cleese, Terry Jones, Mick Ford, David Hare and Stoppard. Michael Palin and Douglas Adams came to watch. For the crowd, the highlight was when the opposition batsmen were both stout Gloucestershire colts of similar appearance. Tweedledum drove a steepling catch directly above Cleese, on the mid-wicket boundary. As it came down, and down, and Basil Fawlty didn't have to move, just waited under it, two thousand spectators held their breath. His big hands closed safely on it. The ball had been in the air long enough for the batsmen to cross, so that now Tweedledee was on strike. Douglas Henderson must have bowled an identical ball, because up it went again, and up, and down, and down, into Cleese's hands. As Cleese remarked, it is not often you will see so complex a sequence replicated in successive balls.

The *Sunday Times* was at the match, and gave us the entire Atticus gossip page the following week. The reporter of course wanted an interview with Cleese at the end of the match. 'No, I need a shower,' he told him. 'Oh, all right. Come with me. I've never been interviewed in the shower.' I was glad to have booked the College Close for the match, thinking that returning to his alma mater would entice Cleese, who had played for the school 1st XI. He told me he had enjoyed the game, and was glad to have helped us raise money, but he did wish we had not arranged it at a place of which he had unpleasant memories. A week after the match, in which his presence had played a major part in attracting a big crowd, *he* wrote to thank *me*. A proper gent, that Cleese. A few years later, when I was researching the history of Clifton Cricket Club, I discovered from a 1962 scorebook that Cleese and I had batted together before. Our two names were at the top of the 2nd XI batting order, soon after he had left school. He lived in the street next to where I live now.

Stoppard told me that at a dinner in London he had sat next to a merchant banker who had said that his company would like to sponsor a small, aspirant arts venture. Stoppard had told him a little about the Playwrights Company, and the man said he would speak to his board about it, and report back. Soon afterwards I was staying at Stoppard's house. He told me he had just heard again from the man, who wanted to speak to me; Stoppard had told him that, by lucky chance, I was about to arrive, and he had said good, I will ring at eight o'clock tomorrow morning. Stoppard woke me up with a cup of coffee. I was sitting on my bed when he said: 'Perhaps I'd better tell you who is about to call you. It's Prince Michael of Kent.' Then the telephone by the bed rang, and I chatted to the Duchess of Teck's grandson in my underpants.

A sponsorship did indeed result, though by that time I had resigned my chairmanship of the Playwrights. Three years was enough. The sixty or so playwright members of the company had been riven by a dissent over policy. Some agreed with our founding principle, that we should promote the production of the best work we could find, or develop. Others held that every signed-up member had the democratic right to see their work staged, as though it were a club. And another development had sickened me. One of our board of management, a prominent member of the Bristol theatrical community, also sat on the theatre advisory panel at South West Arts.

Word reached us that, with funding cuts on the way, he had advised SWA to end the grant which allowed us to employ a part-time administrator, Liz Keynes, vital to the range of services we were offering.

Mark Dornford-May had moved on from the Playwrights Company to run Solent People's Theatre. He commissioned me to write something for him, and I came up with *Cherry*, a play with songs about a vulnerable young woman. After its run in Southampton it came to Bristol for a few performances in the Hope Centre in Hotwells, which was an enjoyable, community-based venue in a chapel until the trustees decided that God needed it back.

* * *

At the same time as the formation of the Playwrights Company I was invited to direct the Cheltenham Festival of Literature. I never did find out why. Perhaps it was because I appeared on HTV for half an hour every month. The festival in those days was a tiny creature in comparison with the hundreds of events it offers every October now, and it had nothing to do with promotional sessions in a book-signing tent. My task was to think up and arrange a dozen events. Some of them were performance, the rest were argufying. The list of argufiers in the two years I was director included several friends: Stoppard, David Edgar, Geoffrey Reeves, Robert Giddings, Derek Robinson, Terry Jones, Peter Barnes, Brian Aldiss, Eva Figes, Stuart Hall, George Macbeth, Jon Silkin, Clive James, Russell Davies. I instituted the annual Cheltenham Lecture, and to give it invited two men I admired. First, in 1978, was the radical historian Christopher Hill. Over a drink I told him how valuable I had found his work on the Cromwell period for a play I was writing, about James Nayler, the Quaker. He asked to see a draft, and made a number of helpful suggestions. In 1979 the lecturer was Conor Cruise O'Brien.

I also instituted an annual writer in residence. My first was Adrian Mitchell, who interpreted the job as visiting schools and prisons, encountering people on the street, and writing and selling a poetic journal of his week. At the wind-down party I told him he had one last job to do, suggest next year's writer in residence. Without hesitation he answered: 'Allen Ginsberg.'

'Oh yeah?' I smiled.

'Try him,' Mitchell insisted. 'What will it cost you? A stamp.'

I bought a stamp, and Ginsberg came in 1979. I was expecting the beatnik with the beard. Instead, a portly clean-shaven man in a brown three-piece suit led his entourage into Cheltenham Town Hall, and greeted me with a bear-hug. He worked as tirelessly as Mitchell had, and included a four-hour meditation session, with bells and incense and squeezebox and 'sitting practice' in the main hall, which was packed. At the end of the week his pony-tailed friend Peter Orlovsky told me in a husky New England voice: 'Ant'ny, we've had a great week here in Chelt'nam. When I get home to Noo Hampshire, I'm gonna plant a tree in memory of this great week we've had here. What kinda tree would you like me to plant?'

'I don't know, Peter. What kind of tree grows well there?'

'Ant'ny, when I get home to Noo Hampshire I'm gonna plant a walnut tree in memory of the great week we have had here.'

'Right. A walnut tree.'

'What kind of walnut tree would you like me to plant in memory of this great week?'

I shook my head. I did not know there are kinds of walnut tree.

'Ant'ny, when I get home to Noo Hampshire I'm gonna plant a Carpathian walnut tree, in memory of this great week we've had here with you in Chelt'nam.'

I like to think that Carpathian walnuts are still being eaten in New Hampshire every autumn in memory of etc, though both Orlovsky and Ginsberg have moved on to the great meditation session in the sky.

1978 was the bicentenary of Hazlitt's birth. I had heard Michael Foot speak passionately about Hazlitt, and invited him to give a commemorative talk in Cheltenham. He replied that he would very much like to do so, but there was a complication. The date I had proposed was the last day of the annual Labour Party conference. Officially it would finish at noon, but I would appreciate that events might delay Foot's departure from Blackpool. He made a suggestion: would I invite his dear friend James Cameron to Cheltenham? If Foot could not get there, Cameron would do a fine job in his place. If Foot did show up, Cameron would be happy to listen, and join in a discussion afterwards. I wrote to Cameron, explaining the position. The journalist I most admired in my lifetime was indeed ready to come along and sit on the subs' bench, in case.

Foot got there. A quick gin and tonic, and he was into the Playhouse Theatre, speaking without notes, only a few slips of paper in his volume of Hazlitt's essays to mark the quotes. Within twenty seconds of his starting to address the audience in the constituency with the biggest Tory majority in the country, they were purring at him. After exactly sixty minutes he saved me the trouble of explaining why James Cameron was also on the stage with us, by introducing his friend and going with him into a comparison of journalism in Hazlitt's time and ours.

After it, I had booked a table for dinner at the Queen's Hotel. Foot, Cameron, wives and associates, we all went on talking away, Foot most loquacious of all, after a week of talking at a conference and two hours of addressing the Playhouse. I was seated next to him but looking away when I heard a bang beside me on the table. It was Foot's white head, prone on the white tablecloth. His eyes were closed, his glasses fallen off. I looked around in alarm. Cameron said: 'Nothing to worry about. He'll be back with us in a few minutes.' He was right. Foot not only woke up as suddenly as he had fallen asleep, he woke up talking. 'But what you have to take into account is this...'

I too was exhausted by the last day of the festival. I had to be at the Town Hall at noon to introduce Selma James, giving a feminist's view of Jane Austen. I knew nothing about James, other than that she was married to C.L.R. James, author of the best book there is on cricket, *Beyond A Boundary*. Jeremy Mulford, who knew them both, had talked me into booking her for a Sunday lunchtime slot. I slept through the alarm and woke up at 11.50, which gave me ten minutes to dress and run a mile through the streets of Cheltenham, trying to think how to introduce a woman I had never met, and about whom I knew nothing of use. Still, I thought, there will be only a handful of people there. I can bluff it. When I arrived, out of breath, I had to force my way through an audience that had filled the room up, covered the carpet and window-sills and spilled into the corridor, where they could crane to hear through the doorway. I briefly muttered a few introductory blanks, and went to get a cup of coffee. I returned twenty minutes later and, from the corridor, could hear why she had such a following. She was brilliant, culturally dissecting Austen and Jean Rhys.

After directing two festivals I had used up all my ideas. At a meeting with the board of management I thanked them, and asked them to look for a new director. They were taken by surprise, and asked me if I could suggest anyone. I looked at the chairman of the board, the excellent Cheltenham bookseller Alan Hancox. I suspected he had always fancied the job, but had been shy of proposing himself. 'I think you should invite your own chairman,' I told them. They did, and over the following years Hancox oversaw a major growth in the country's oldest festival of literature. He had a sense for literary showmanship that I lack.

I had just had a letter from Eyre Methuen, telling me that, six years on, sales of *Orghast at Persepolis* were down to two hundred a year, and they would be letting it go out of print. I replied that it was a course book in several university drama departments, and was often referred to or quoted in theatre journals. I was wasting my time. They told me that two hundred a year did not 'justify the shelf space for storage'. When Matthew Evans, the managing director of Faber and Faber, came to Cheltenham for some argufying, I ingenuously told him the story. 'I'm amazed,' he said. I began a sentence on the lines of: It's good to know that at least Faber's still understand the value of... and so on, but he interrupted me. 'I think you have misunderstood me. We would have taken the same decision. I am amazed only that, in a letter to the author, they told you it was a question of shelf space. We would never have admitted that.' Let that story be in the stead of a dozen more pages I might bleat about what has happened in mainstream publishing, even before the calamitous overturning of the Net Book Agreement.

13

Henson

AFTER THE WINTER OF DISCONTENT, AND AMID THE FIRST PRICKS OF Thatcher's philistinism, the outlook for writers was grey. What picked me up was an absurd bounce of the pinball. Jim Henson, building on the skills his studio had developed from *Sesame Street* to The Muppets, had moved into feature films. He was shooting *The Dark Crystal* at Elstree, because British animation was both technically expert and cheaper than in the USA. He had required a special language to be invented for the nasty Skekses in the film, rather like Ted Hughes's invention of Orghast, and Alan Garner had done it for him. Henson wanted a novelisation of the film, and had taken it for granted that Garner would be pleased to do that, too, but he declined. He had his own books to write. He suggested they approach Michael Croucher, with whom he had done some work for BBC Bristol. Croucher, in his turn, said he was not a noveliser, but he knew a man who was. Thus I fielded a telephone call from someone who had no idea who I might be but who was now desperately seeking in a foreign land.

I did two books for Henson, *The Dark Crystal* and *Labyrinth*, and thoroughly enjoyed working for him. He was a charming man, but what mattered was that, unlike most people who commission novelisations, he cared about the book as a legitimate child of the movie. He created perfect conditions for my work, paying for me to spend as many days as I needed at Elstree, watching the shooting, getting myself inward to the story, ensuring the detail was right in my descriptive passages. I was supplied not just with the film script but with a stack of research materials, think-papers and production drawings. You owe it to the reader to be true to the script, but I was allowed as much scope as I wanted to expand the narrative, deepen it, comment or digress. When I delivered the first draft, Henson read the manuscript himself, and came back with twenty pages of editorial comment. Once I had taken that on board, he sat me down with him for lunch and a talk through what I had done. On points of disagreement between us his default position was to respect my argument, and only seldom to insist on his. In *The Dark Crystal*, he took out one short scene I'd added. I had got just a bit bored with the Pod People at that point, and livened things up by smashing a basketful of them over a cliff. Henson thought the cruelty out of context, and he was right. Before writing *Labyrinth* I spent a day with Terry Jones, the scriptwriter, at his home in Peckham. He showed me a scene that had been dropped from the movie, for technical reasons. It was beautiful, and I restored it in the book. Henson did not object.

When my final manuscripts had been approved they went to the Henson office in New York for copy-editing – 'translation into American', one of the editors called it. I spent many hours on transatlantic calls with her, working through *The Dark Crystal.* When it came to *Labyrinth*, a few years later, I suggested that it would save money (and be more fun for me) if they flew me to New York for the editing, and they did. I sat with the editor and a word-processor for a fortnight. We spent ninety minutes trying to translate Snakes and Ladders into a game that American kids would know about, and finally gave up: 'They'll just have to figure it out for themselves,' she sighed.

At the weekend I took a People Express flight from Newark to stay a couple of nights with Janet Burroway in Florida. I had thought that kind of thing was what Americans did all the time, but later Burroway told me that I had been the talk of Tallahassee, flying down for a weekend. Luxuriating in her jacuzzi, we discovered, nearly thirty years late, that she too had been in Pamplona in 1959.

Both Henson books came out in half a dozen languages, and still have a cult following on the internet. *The Dark Crystal* was a big hit, especially in Japan. I saw my name on a *New York Times* best-seller list, something that would not have happened without the movie behind it. I have a preference for Jones's Lewis-Carrollesque *Labyrinth.* The film had two human actors in it. The Goblin King was David Bowie. He told Henson it needed songs, and he would write them. Thus I spent an afternoon at Elstree watching Bowie do a complicated dance routine to his own song, on playback. He was required to dance along a twenty-yard stretch, taking the hands of animated puppets as he went. The electronic puppetry was very complicated to do, and as a result it took fifteen takes to get the sequence right. Every time I heard 'Sorry, David, we have to go again' I watched the actor shrug amiably and sit down for a cup of tea with one of the stagehands, not a megastar tantrum in sight. When I got back to Bristol and told my daughters I'd spent the afternoon with David Bowie they screamed *What did he say to you?* I had to disappoint them by admitting that I'd not spoken to him, not wanting to get in his highly professional way. I did dance with the fifteen-year-old Jennifer Connelly at the wrap party in New York. We were never more than nine feet away from her mother, tracking us like a paparazza.

John David, coming to the end of his five years as director of the Bristol Old Vic, told me he had opened a drawer in his desk and found some money he didn't know he had. He decided to use it to pay for a show celebrating 150 years of the Great Western Railway, and would I like to write it? It would be my first work for the BOV, though I had had a play in the New Vic Studio produced by the Playwrights Company, directed by Downie. Entitled *Master of Letters*, it was a jokey thing set in a newspaper letters office, and dedicated to Stoppard, to whom Bristol University had just awarded an Hon. MLitt. The leading actor, though professionally experienced, lost his words every night.

God's Wonderful Railway, in the New Vic, involved historical research, of course, but we also worked from material derived from interviews with people still working on the railway. For *Prostitutes* and *Battle of Britain* I had done all the interviewing myself, but it was the director Debbie Shewell's good idea that some of the railway interviews would be conducted by actors and technicians. It gave them a creative stake in the text. Audiences got on well with the production, which was more than could be said for my relationship with Shewell. We ended up barely on speaking terms. Some directors welcome the writer in the rehearsal room, as long as you know your manners and don't go hiding in corners with the actors to give them whispered notes. But others feel threatened simply by the presence of the writer, no matter how discreet. She would have done better to bar me from rehearsals, but it was a collectively made show, so she settled for undisguised and inexplicable resentment. However, she did a good job with the young actors, Christopher Ashley, Samantha Bond, Jill Brassington, Jonathan Cullen, Tricia Kelly and David Plimmer. John Elvery's design was excellent, and so was the haunting music, by Joanna Macgregor, who has had an outstanding concert career since then. During the run of the show, British Rail, with uncharacteristic punctuality, announced the closure of the Swindon workshop, an icon of the history we were telling.

I was to do two more novelisations. *Wagner* was scripted, brilliantly, by Charles Wood, and his agent was Tim Corrie; between them they decided to ask me to do the book, since I'd got a track record. Handing me his script, Wood advised me: 'I hope you'll take outrageous liberties. I did.' After research, I went far beyond the conventions of novelising, into Wagner's torrent of consciousness. I had been bewitched by the music for twenty years, baptised by Bob Giddings. The film starred Richard Burton in his last major role, Vanessa Redgrave, and uniquely brought together the three knights, Olivier, Gielgud and Richardson. It was produced with a running length of seven hours and forty-six minutes. When the full-length version was shown at the NFT, the following exchange was overheard between two people coming out at the end.

'Well, what do you suppose Wagner would have thought of that?'

'He would have thought it wasn't long enough.'

In Germany and Italy the film was chopped into salami segments and shown as a TV serial. Translations of my book were published in those countries, but in the UK, where the film was commercially invisible, it has never been published in the language in which I wrote it. I believed the book could stand up on its own, independent of film tie-in, and my failure to persuade Corrie's book agent to agree with me reached Valhallan levels of acrimony. However, in spring 2010 I stayed in the Var for a few days with Peter Moore-Robinson and his third wife, Marta. Somehow the sad story came up over dinner. When I had finished telling it, Marta revealed herself as mad for Wagner, and declared: 'I must read it.' I sighed. 'It doesn't exist in English.' Moore-Robinson took out his chequebook. 'Bring it out yourself,' he told me, and paid me a handsome slice of what it was going to cost me.

I had so much enjoyed the techniques I devised for *Wagner* that I went straight into writing a historical novel of my own, about Sebastian Cabot. In 1497 his father John Cabot had sailed the *Matthew* westward from Bristol, intending to open up an Atlantic trade with China and India and the Spice Islands, and instead, to his chagrin, bumped into what we now call the mainland of North America – which, contrary to popular error, had not been discovered by Columbus. Cabot's voyage is the historical origin of our sharing the English language with the USA. Within a few years of his father's death, Sebastian became a great man in Europe, and in Bristol the first Master of the Merchant Venturers, by claiming all the credit for the voyage, and other discoveries besides, such as a waterway from where New York is to where San Francisco is. The height of Thatcherism was an apt moment for a novel about mendacity. It would be the fifth novel I had set in Bristol.

I went to the university library to check a point. I had an old sailor boasting about his exploits among the girls of Cadiz. He was a plain-spoken character, and I thought he should speak of fucking the girls, but I was nervous. The word would draw attention to itself, and allow some scholar to catch me out. Was it the normal usage in the late fifteenth century? I was getting nowhere in my research among the dictionaries when the professor of English, John Burrow, walked past and said: 'Hello, Anthony. What are you working on?' He was a specialist in early English, so I thought my problem had luckily found its solution. He didn't immediately know the dating of the word, but said he would check it in books he had at home. A few days later I opened a letter from him. Under the official university crest and heading, it began: *Dear Anthony*, and then, underlined, the subject heading: *Fuck*. The answer was that he could not find the answer. I chickened out, and used another phrase.

I was satisfied with the support I was getting from Weidenfeld. John Curtis, the editorial director, wrote to me: *I have a good feel about this project altogether.* But something went badly wrong. The first I knew of it was a call from Jon Donovan, at Chapter and Verse Bookshop on Park Street. He had arranged a signing session for me, but the books had not turned up by publication day. Typically, for the best bookseller I ever knew, he drove to London and collected copies of *Sebastian the Navigator* himself. Over the next few weeks there were only perfunctory reviews. When I made enquiries, a deep throat at Weidenfeld told me what had happened. The sales reps had given it the thumbs-down, and in modern publishing their opinion outweighed that of my editor, and even the marketing director's. In effect, the book was never published, only printed. I was facing my mid-list crisis.

The day I delivered the manuscript of *Sebastian*, Weidenfeld had asked me to do another novelisation in a hurry, of *Lady Jane*. I did not want to do it, but I was in a soft trap. The story of Lady Jane Grey happened in 1554, and my Cabot novel finished with the death of Sebastian in 1557. I was steeped in the period. How could I let the firm down by refusing them a few weeks' work? Would that I had known what they would allow to happen to *Sebastian*, a few months later. It was not easy to do a decent job on *Lady Jane*, because of the screenplay. I had to scrape off what I could of the sentimental love story that had been varnished over the poignant true history, probably at Paramount's behest. The actor John Wood later told me that the cast had thought so little of their lines that they altered them ad lib on camera.

People have asked me why I wrote novelisations. The quick answer is that it's a way to earn a living. But there is a more serious one. What their question means is: isn't it beneath a novelist's dignity to write a story that someone else has already constructed? My put-down reply is: was it beneath Shakespeare's dignity to borrow Plutarch's stories, or the narratives of historians, as he did in thirty-four of his thirty-seven plays? He didn't see it as his job to make up new stories, but to tell old ones better. Any writer would be unwise to invite comparison with Shakespeare's words, but one can learn from his working practice.

* * *

To support our children, Alison was now teaching, as her parents did. For about fifteen years she taught French at the Grange School, in Warmley. A few years after the death of John Hill she set up home with Hugh Massey, a lifelong friend of her father. He had known her since she was a girl. Massey did not want to move into our family home, as Hill had done, so they found a flat. Its address was 1, Beaufort Road, the same address as the one where I had lived in 1960, and Alison had first cooked a supper for me. But the Victorian building I'd inhabited had been cleared away to make space for a modern block of flats, built by Tim Organ, the T in JT, the developers. The J was for John Pontin. I knew them both. Our children had been at Durdham Park, a free school set up by Pontin when he could not find any in Bristol that he thought suitable for his own children. The headmistress was a friend of ours, Paddy Stokes, and it was run on the lines of A.S. Neill's Summerhill. Every morning the teachers would announce what subject they were offering that day, and the children made their own choices. If they wanted to spend the day playing football in the big garden, they could. Few did, after the first couple of days. It was never resolved how the pupils would be prepared when they were approaching GCSE age. The school folded before ours had grown that far, and they went off to St John's and then Fairfield and Cotham, academically no worse for their years at Durdham Park, and socially better for it, in my judgment. They all got into universities later on.

Massey came to see me, to ask for my permission for his cohabiting with Alison. He was old-fashioned, and could not believe his luck when I wished them all the best. Alison and I thought we should perhaps tidy up our situation, and talked to a solicitor about getting a divorce, so that she and Massey could marry. The solicitor was a dud, wrongly telling us that one of us would have to stand up in court and heap blame on the other. The only plausible ground would be adultery, and Massey would not countenance that kind of publicity, being a businessman with a reputation to protect. We gave up, and have remained married in law, though neither of us is ever sure which box to tick. At Beaufort Road, Massey would type an instruction on to his telex terminal, and as a result hundreds of men in Morocco and Texas would be set to work on a shipment of baryte. We all spent a Christmas together in Agadir, and another in Cornwall. They lived happily together until Massey's death, a dozen years later.

In May, 1983 I played for Clifton in a twenty-over evening match at Lansdown, an annual friendly event between two clubs who have been meeting since the 1820s. We had no accredited wicketkeeper in our side, so I volunteered to do it, despite having no talent for the job. It is more fun than just fielding. Barney Beddow was a very fast and wild bowler. I stood a long way back to him, but not far enough for one that pitched yards behind the batsman and reached me on the half-volley, knocking two incisors out. If you are going to have your teeth knocked out, Lansdown is the place for it, because you pick them up off the grass and walk across the boundary into the hospital outpatients' department. They lodged them back in for me and told me to see my dentist the next day. It had taken two hours, the light was fading, and I was fed-up because I had driven to Bath to have a bat, and now the match would be over. But it wasn't, quite. We still needed a few runs from two or three overs, and our captain, Guy Eskell, asked me if I fancied batting if a wicket fell. You bet. I put my pads on, a wicket fell, I went in, and my partner and I knocked off the few runs. The Lansdown chaps were very nice to me in the bar afterwards. I had been a bloody sight.

The next day I was at HTV. The ball had cut my lip, and I looked like Elephant Man. I bumped into Bob Simmonds, HTV's publicity officer. He asked what had happened to me, and I told him. 'And you knocked off the winning runs?' he asked. 'That might make a gossip par in the *Bath Chronicle*.'

'Oh come on, Bob, it was only a dozen runs we needed, and anyway, it was a friendly match, no big deal.'

Five days later, the Bath paper did indeed print three paragraphs deep inside the paper, on the grounds that my face was known on the telly. Then my telephone rang: 'That Tony Smiff?'

'Anthony Smith, yes.'

'It's the *Sun* here, Tony. We hear you had a bit of a run-in on the cricket field. Tell me about it, would you?'

I politely outlined the story, and remarked: 'We're in the middle of a significant general election. Have you really got space for a bit of nonsense like this?'

'Ah, it can't all be serious political stuff, can it, Tony? People need a few laughs too, you know. We'll get a photographer round to you this afternoon.'

I shared page 5 of next day's *Sun* with Gary Glitter. I forget what he had done. For my part, I had become *Toothless Tough Guy Tony,* whose *desperate team-mates asked him to snatch them from the jaws of defeat.* The following day, other national tabloids ran their versions. It still wasn't over. At Christmas *The Observer* listed me in their Top Ten Sporting Nutters of the Year. They subsequently published a book of Great Sporting Nutters Of All Time, and I made it into that, too, on the page facing Mary Queen of Scots, who did something at hockey. It was all a hilarious lesson to my children, who knew the prosaic facts behind the story.

Glancing through the *Sunday Times Magazine* I saw a warning about moles that bleed. In the shower I noticed that I had one of those, so thought I had better let my family doctor, Michael Whitfield, take a look. He said, 'Come into the treatment room and I'll take it off. I like a bit of surgery.' I thought no more about it, until he rang me on Saturday morning, to tell me that it had been autopsied, and was a malignant melanoma. 'Nothing to worry about. I've never lost a patient to this yet, and you are not going to be the first, but whatever you have got planned for Monday, forget it. You are booked into Frenchay.'

I replied: 'Mike, this afternoon I am captaining the second eleven in a league match against Midsomer Norton, and they always beat us, and now you're telling me I've got to do it with a life-threatening disease.' For the record, Midsomer Norton beat us easily. On Monday the surgeon removed his pound of flesh, my daughters drove to Frenchay to collect me back, and twenty-seven years on I am still not the first patient that Dr Whitfield lost to what I probably incurred through fooling around with an ultra-violet lamp. The story is not an easy one for me to tell, because its purport is that I owe my life to Rupert Murdoch and, like Mephistopheles, he might come and ask for it back.

When my daughters went off to university, Oliver and I kept

house together. We share sporting interests. We have been at the Cheltenham National Hunt Festival, in the cheap enclosure, every March for the past forty years, bar a couple when one of us was abroad, and have shouted them home at Kempton, Longchamp, Bridgetown, Perth. When, to Oliver's delight, The Dikler won the Cheltenham Gold Cup, I wrote to Fulke Walwyn asking if we might visit the horse in Lambourn, and to some unknown punter and his young son he responded with a cordiality that is characteristic of the National Hunt community.

Once, at a Test match at Lord's, when Oliver's school friend Alistair Smith was with us, I had an arrangement to meet David Inshaw at the lunch interval. In the milling crowd I stupidly allowed impatience to unsettle me while the nine-year-old boys had to wait in a long queue for a pee. I said something irritable to them. Oliver replied, quietly: 'Please don't be angry, Daddy.' More than thirty years later, I am still chastened.

At the age of two he had been watching cricket on TV, sucking his thumb, then announced: 'I'm Alan Knott. Come and bowl at me.' He found something to use as a bat, I tossed a tennis ball for him, and was surprised by two things. First, he stood left-handed, though is right-handed in writing and so on. I have concluded that the minority like him – a celebrated example would be Denis Compton (bowled left, batted right) – who stand the 'wrong' way round have in fact got it right. Their strong hand is on top, in control. Second, he swung straight down the line. I think he was imitating what he had seen the Test batsmen doing. As in poetry, imitation is a very good education. He made his début in adult cricket when he was eight, grew up through junior club and schools teams, to playing county cricket and in under-19 Test matches. I'm happy to take the credit, but deserve almost none of it. All the years in the back garden or side alley would have produced no more than a keen club player were it not for the genetic inheritance from Alison's father. If you want to breed a cricketer, choose a dam from a thoroughbred cricketing sire.

At fifteen he was selected as *Bristol Evening Post* young cricketer of the year. The prize was to take part in a charity match at Badminton, with former Test stars. The day before it he had teeth knocked out in a school match, and the doctor shook his head about playing the next day. All the same, we went to Badminton to watch. Holding our buffet lunch trays, looking for a table, we were called by an Australian voice: 'Hey, Smithy, come over here with us.' It was Bill Alley and his wife.

Twenty years after I'd finished reporting at Taunton, he still remembered me. He had looked after me when, for a newspaper stunt article, I'd batted in the Somerset nets against the county bowlers. He'd asked me if I had a thigh pad on: 'You'll need a thigh pad facing Kenny Palmer.' I'd had to ask what a thigh pad was. He found one and strapped it on me. Now, at Badminton, he called out to someone else: 'Bill, get over here.' I looked up, and saw that Bill Edrich was coming to join us. It was like having lunch with Achilles. With him was a blonde beehive from Pinner, whom he introduced as the lady who in September was to become the sixth Mrs Edrich (though I saw in his obit that it never happened). To Alley, by then a Test umpire, I murmured: 'You ought to go the wedding and call *Over*.'

'We used to have eight in Australia,' he replied.

Because of his cricket, Clifton College generously offered Oliver a sixth-form scholarship. As I had with Harrow, he decided against it, even though he had many cricketing friends at Clifton. His chief reason was that he felt a loyalty to Cotham, where he was head boy. Possibly, also, he declined through principle. Why should the public schools cream off the talent? During his four years at York University, studying linguistics and opening for York C.C., he was signed up as a Gloucestershire player in vacations. It was a better vac job than most. He was in the county side against a Rest of the World XI, who were playing a warm-up match in Bristol before meeting MCC in a bicentenary celebration match. On the last day, he and Mark Alleyne saw it out against Kapil Dev, Courtney Walsh, Maninder Singh, Allen Border *et al.* for two hours, on the way to drawing the match. When Alleyne was out, Oliver was joined by his captain, Bill Athey. He went to meet him, and said: 'Sorry I'm being so slow, skip. I just can't find anything to hit.' 'Aye, Olly,' Athey told him. 'That's why they're playing for t'Rest o' t'World.'

In 1987 he went to Sri Lanka with the England under-19s. I saw him off, and returned home telling myself not to be stupid, I couldn't afford to go, and anyway, fathers might not be welcome. A few days later, I bought a ticket to Colombo. I had read a warning against hotel touts, so arrived with the determination not to be gulled. They were much better organised than I had reckoned. From Colombo I had to take the great train journey through the hills to Kandy, where the second Test match was about to start. Waiting for the train, drinking a fruit juice, I was engaged in conversation by a young Sri Lankan. He soon established that I was going to watch the cricket in Kandy, and asked where I would be staying. I will find somewhere when I arrive, I told him. He said that that might be difficult for me, in a strange city, but he could help. He had an uncle in Kandy, Dr Fernando, who would put me up. He would go and ring him now, ask him to meet me off the train. How kind. Five hours later, at Kandy station, there he was, Dr Fernando, and of course the house he took me to was his guest house. I was cross with myself for having fallen for it. On the other hand, he had met me, driven me from the station, and the price was £1.50 a night, including breakfast. Every morning the cold scrambled eggs were ready served before I sat down, because that is what sahibs ate at breakfast. After that, I could order any of the exotic fruits I had read about, and it would be brought for me.

I needed to let Oliver know I had made the trip. Dr Fernando knew in which hotel the English boys were staying. Everyone knew. Sri Lanka adores cricket 365 days a year. At the hotel I was told the team were at dinner. A message was taken in, and Oliver came out to the lobby, bewildered by who could be asking for him. Back at Dr Fernando's, I could not sleep. On the plane a toothache had started, a sinus infection I guessed, and it got worse throughout the night. I was doubtful about 'Dr' Fernando, but I had nowhere else to seek help in the morning. He told me where I could find a dentist. 'No,' I said, 'it's not a dental problem, it's the sinus. I need a doctor.' 'The problem is in your mouth,' he answered. 'A dentist is what you need.' Very well. Certain that he was touting for his brother-in-law, I went to where he had directed me, above a grocery. The waiting-room was painted in the colours I remembered from childhood visits to the dentist, green below a thick black strip, buff above. Half a dozen patients were waiting around the walls. One of them leaned forward and spat blood into a bucket placed in the centre of the circle. I was the first called in. Sahib's privilege, I feared.

The dentist was a fat, smiling brown man in a suit who spoke beautiful English, reminding me of Malcolm Muggeridge's remark: 'The only true English people left on earth are all Indian.' His equipment, like his waiting room, was perfect 1940s period. He took a look in my mouth and told me I had an abscess. I could choose among three courses of action. He could lance it, but the risk was that I might be back the next day needing to have it lanced again. Second, he could take the tooth out. Yes, I thought, the 1940s solution, any problem in your mouth, knock out a tooth or two. I told him, not untruthfully, that my dentist in Bristol regarded my mouth as though it were a cultivated rock garden, and would be upset if I returned with a gap. The dentist smiled, and said: 'Well, the third option is an antibiotic.' 'Yes,' I agreed at once. That was the word I had been waiting to hear. 'An antibiotic. Can you give me a prescription?' 'Oh,' he chuckled, 'we don't have prescriptions in Sri Lanka. You just go to the chemist's shop and buy one.' He told me what to ask for, and refused any payment. The antibiotic worked in a trice.

The manager of the Young England team was Tim Lamb. He dissipated any fear I had that a Barmy father might be looked at askance. He was starved of grown-up conversation, and regarded my arrival as a treat. In the course of a stand of 213 with Nasser Hussain, Oliver was on 92 when Lamb urged me to leave the ground with him for a visit to the botanical gardens. When I said that I would like to wait a few more minutes, he sat impatiently until I had seen my son complete a century for England, and whisked me away before the crowd had finished clapping.

I travelled around the island in the team bus, to the sound of *Walk of Life*, deeply enjoying the place. It was already the early days of the Sinhala/Tamil civil war; at the close of play each day an overnight guard was mounted on the square, to avert terrorist vandalism. The under-19 players, captained by Michael Atherton, were friendly to me. Oliver had initially shared my nervousness that they might think me a too keen father, to have come all that way, but he told me they reckoned I deserved a pat on the back. So did they. After a long, hot day in the field at Galle (which I saw on television on Boxing Day 2004, devastated by the tsunami), the bus was halted on the way back to the hotel so that all the boys could pay a visit to a home for disabled children. I am moved when I remember Mark Ramprakash walking hand-in-hand with a crippled toddler who gazed up at him with adoration.

Sri Lankan cricket was still striving to break into the Test élite. In consequence, their young cricketers were proud to settle for a draw in every Test Match. I was watching at Galle when, on the far side of the ground, a very long line of young Buddhist monks, carrying umbrellas, came filing in, past the old bat-flitted fort where you can still see the graffiti of seventeenth-century Dutch soldiers. Next to me Perera, the Sri Lanka liaison man with the England party, clucked his tongue. 'They should not be here,' he said, 'They are supposed to forgo all pleasures.' In the next two hours the young Sri Lankan, Chandima Mendis, scored eight singles. Those monks knew what they were doing.

Back in Bristol I went to my doctor to get the abscess site cleared up. He had a look, and told me I should be seeing my dentist. My dentist told me there was only one solution, to take the tooth out. I was humbled, ashamed of all my presumptions in Kandy. The extraction cost me about £30. The Kandy dentist would probably have taken it out for £1, or nothing at all.

14

Rewriting Shakespeare

REEVES WAS TEACHING AT EMORY UNIVERSITY, IN ATLANTA. HE INVITED me there for six weeks to prepare a new text for his production of *Pericles*. The standard text of the play is corrupt, at best two-thirds Shakespeare, probably less. Yet in performance it has a mysterious power. The first time I saw it I'd read it bemusedly, and discussed it with the director and others in order to write the programme for it, and went into the theatre at Stratford expecting nothing much. By the interval I came out unable to speak.

Why it's corrupt, who corrupted it, and to what extent, is a comic detective yarn. In 1607 it had been the hot ticket in London. Editions were rushed into print. But by whom? Not Shakespeare. He never let any other text with his name on it come out as mangled as this one. It was pirated by people out to make a fast groat. The pirates presumably got their text by sitting in the theatre and scribbling down as much as they could. A rudimentary form of shorthand did exist. Maybe they could manage a squint at the prompt book when the stage manager's back was turned. One of the shorthand reporters had exceptionally poor handwriting. The resulting goulash went off to the printers, first to one who then went bust, then to another who had never printed a play before and who was in the middle of moving his premises. At least three compositors were used, one of whom set verse as prose, another set prose as verse, and the third did both. The proof reader had everybody breathing down his neck to get the copies out on to the streets. Then an outbreak of plague closed the theatres, which would have increased demand for the text, prevented any further checking of it, and no doubt took a couple of the compositors to the burial pit.

It wasn't the first time Shakespeare had suffered from pirates, but in other cases – *Hamlet*, for instance – the publication of his own text quickly put the thieves out of business. With *Pericles* that never happened. Alone of the thirty-seven plays we have by him, *Pericles* was omitted from the First Folio that his actor friends Heminges and Condell published after his death, the nearest thing we have to the authorized edition of his plays. That must have been because, like us, they had no decent copy of the text. All we've got is what the pirates printed. Well, nearly all we've got.

The first thing we did by way of trying to excavate the hidden play was to throw out what is irredeemable junk. Then we rearranged, extended, invented, and patched. We had help from scholarly editions of the play, but unlike scholars we were not limited by conscience to what can be proved. We took liberties, some of them large. Our justification was that you cannot reconstruct the hidden play satisfactorily using only the textual materials to hand. It's like trying to rebuild a temple when thieves have made off with half the stones. In the end, you have to trust your experience and imagination and say, well, this is how *I* think it was built. To fill some of the gaps, or stabilize a scene, we patched in lines from thirteen other plays by Shakespeare, plus a line or two from the Sonnets. That was one tactic – patching, or what the music business would call sampling.

A second could be called palaeontology, and is possible only because of the dubious events of 1607. A minor hack playwright called George Wilkins, who might have collaborated in writing the play, had brought out what today we would call a novelisation. Some parts of his prose narrative are simply pinched from earlier tellings of the Pericles legend, the same source books as Shakespeare himself used. But other passages of Wilkins are taken word-for-word from the pirated text of Shakespeare's play, meaning that we are unquestionably dealing here with a man who knew that play well. But what's exciting is this: other parts again of Wilkins are neither in the source books nor in the standard, corrupt text, but, though printed in prose form, are actually iambic pentameters. What scholars surmise is that what we have here is real Shakespeare, lost by the pirates in their rush to the press, but preserved in Wilkins's novelisation. These buried pentameters are known as fossil verse. You carefully extract them from the surrounding clay, clean them up, and neatly replace them where they would belong in Shakespeare's text. Much of this work was done long ago by Geoffrey Bullough, in his seven-volume *Shakespeare's Sources*, and we had no hesitation in using quite lengthy passages of his reconstruction.

After patching and palaeontology, the third P was pastiche, and yes, I did write about six hundred lines of imitation Shakespeare. That sounds so presumptuous that I must offer a defence, of my sanity if not of my verse. And yet, what was it that I did? I presumed to imitate Shakespeare more faithfully than that bunch of groat-grubbing pirates did, with their befuddled compositors. Put like that, I don't mind owning up to it. And my defence rests further on the fact that John Barton, in the first season that I worked at the RSC, did the same thing in amalgamating four of the early History plays into three, under the title *The Wars of the Roses*. To make that work, Barton, too, had to write several hundred lines of pastiche Bard. He is a greatly more learned scholar than I am, but as a practising poet most of my life I don't have to be obsequious in comparing my versifying to his. And there is one more thing. I referred to it earlier. When you come out of a Shakespeare performance, for a few minutes, while the echoes persist, it is easy to improvise conversation in blank verse. It actually seems more natural than speaking in modern English prose. Peter Hall would say that's because the iambic pentameter is the default rhythm of English speech. That phenomenon was something of which I availed myself. Before sitting down to write anything for *Pericles*, I read aloud from Shakespeare – anywhere the collected works fell open would do – just to get the rhythms and the vocabulary sounding inside my head.

Sometimes I had to adapt soggy bits from the standard text into something better, sometimes to come up with completely fresh verse. I went home one night from rehearsal with orders to go in next morning with a soliloquy for Pericles, to cover a costume change. Even harder than writing pastiche Shakespearean verse was imitating his prose. Fortunately, I didn't have a lot of that to do.

John Gower, the narrator of the play, presented particular problems. Gower's part is written archaically, in rhyming tetrameters (four-beat), using Chaucerian words like 'yclept' and 'holy-ales'. It seemed to us pointless to have a narrator who would not be easily understood in Bristol, let alone Atlanta, Georgia, so I translated Gower into Elizabethan English, and good old conversational pentameters, keeping it folksy, to distinguish him from the characters of his story.

I took a break when the rehearsals reached tech week, and rode through the deep South on an eleven-hour train ride to New Orleans. At 3 a.m. on Bourbon Street a boy I knew in Bristol hailed me, and insisted I drink some of the disgusting wine he had clearly been swigging all day. After a couple of days I flew on to Austin, Texas, where Ghose had been teaching creative writing for twenty years. My few days with him and Helena, in their lovely house in the hill country outside town, would soon lead to a change in my life.

When the play opened at Theater Emory, with a mixed professional and student cast, one interviewer after another asked me who did I think I was, rewriting Shakespeare? I developed a weary finger-brush across my brow, and the answer: 'We didn't rewrite Shakespeare. Of course we didn't. You don't. What we did was rewrite those who did rewrite Shakespeare, badly.' Back in England, several professional companies thought about producing it. One project had me down to direct it, and

Stoppard offered to sponsor it, but eventually it was put on in Bristol in 1990 by Sheila Hannon's Show of Strength company.

* * *

Having fallen out with Weidenfeld over *Sebastian*, and with no interest in me or anyone else in Bristol from Paul Unwin's BOV, I felt like a man more written off than writing. I remarked to my son Oliver, the advantage I have when I am up shit creek is that I really know my way around it. My meagre income was mostly from HTV. As well as my monthly arts programme, now produced by Ken Price, I was attending many amdram evenings to adjudicate an annual prize that HTV awarded, and scripting a few documentaries. In the Somerset Levels, to interview a willow grower, I called at his house and was told by his eighty-year-old mother: 'They'm be to the withies.'

My Somersetish was just up to translating that: 'He's at the reed beds.'

While we waited for him, I asked Mrs Fear about her life. Where had she been?

'I went to Bristol once, before the war.'

'What did you do there?'

'I did see a tiger, at the Zoo.'

'And where else have you been?'

'I went to Weston-super-Mare, to see a film at the cinema there.'

'Any other trips?'

'No.'

Through the arts programme I made some good friends, including the singer Steve Tilston, the junk-transformation artist Priscilla Day, and Brian Patten. I had met Laurie Lee years before, in Chelsea, in order to write about him in the arts page. This time we were in Slad, to film an interview with him in his childhood village. Before we started I admired the interior Cotswold stone walls of his house. 'Oh,' he said, 'they're all built like that around here, of course. But in the 1950s, when people had a few pence to spare, they all stuck plaster over their stone walls. And a few years later the fashion was to paper over the plaster. One after another, they all chose the same wallpaper, with a pattern of Cotswold stone on it.'

I interviewed Michael Tippett about a new book of his, and asked him a question about a reference he had made to Beethoven.

'No,' he told me, 'you've got that wrong. I was referring to Mozart.'

'It was Beethoven, I'm sure. I read it last week. You wrote it last year.'

'I'm sorry, but I do know my own mind. You're quite wrong. It was

Mozart.'

I had to eschew a squabble on television with a distinguished composer, but when I got home I checked the book and saw that I had been right. That Tippett was in his eighties probably explains his error, but he had a feline sense of humour, and I wonder if he twitted me just for the fun of it.

When Paul Tortelier was chairman of the Imperial Tobacco 'cello festival, I had to interview him in his hotel at 9am. Famous for his Gallic exuberance, at that hour of the morning he was taciturn, surly even, when we greeted him. The crew set up and the moment the lights were switched on Tortelier came alive, sparkling eyes, lips twitching with wit. You old fraud, I thought, as I began my interview, and then reflected that I was being simple-minded. The man was a great performer. He didn't let you down in public. Why expect him to go on greatly performing when the lights were off? I knew he loved Elgar's 'cello concerto, and thought we should get that mentioned to please an English audience, so I asked him which concertos gave him most pleasure to play. He reeled off 'Bach, Haydn, Dvorak, Saint-Saëns, Shostakovich...'

'Elgar?' I asked hopefully.

He realised his error. He leaned across and gave my thigh a huge slap. 'El-*GAR!*'

Every May our programme concentrated on the Bath Festival. Directing the festival then was Amelia Freedman, who, like Peggy Ashcroft, loves cricket. It came up when I interviewed her, and the next day she rang me to say she was organising a match at Bath C.C. It was Ian Botham's benefit year, and he had agreed to get a team together to meet her Bath Festival Invitation XI. I was to captain her team, she told me, rather than asked me. Who else could we get to play? Stoppard and Downie accepted, and so did the composer David Bedford. Our best player was Sarah Potter, daughter of Dennis, and member of the England Women's team.

I went into the other changing room and invited Botham to come out to the square to toss up. 'No need,' he said. 'We'll bat.' It made sense that the much stronger side should bat first, but I pointed out that there were two thousand people watching, and they would expect the formalities to be observed. 'Fuck 'em,' the beneficiary of their admission fees replied.

Each side was to have two innings of twenty overs. With Martin Crowe, the captain of New Zealand, Botham opened the batting and himself hit around 200 in his twenty overs. My side made a decent total in return, against friendly bowling. Sarah Potter scored seventy. When it was their turn to bat again, we waited to see who would come out. It was Botham again: 'They've come to watch me, haven't they?' At one point, shorn of options, I put myself on to bowl leg-breaks. Botham drove five of my six balls straight into the neighbouring street. Downie still has tears in his eyes when he remembers people running out of their houses to move their cars out of the way.

At the moment the Abbey clock rang six o'clock, Botham was bowling, off a few paces. That was it. The crowd had had their fill. He marked out his full Test run-up. The next ball was remarkable. All the crowd saw was Botham bowl it much faster, and me play a forward defensive shot, as taught by Harry Sharp. What actually happened was more complicated. Seeing him run in at me I had tensed up, and got planted too early on the front foot. The ball swung in, but I could not adjust my foot, and waited for it to hit my pads. Instead, when it pitched it cut away to off, thus finding the middle of my bat. It was the example of a ball that would have got a better batsman out, because he would have adjusted for the swing and nicked it behind.

Stoppard was turning out occasionally for Harold Pinter's Gaieties XI. He sent me a postcard poem:

> There's a breathless hush in Gunnersbury Park,
> Apart from a passing juggernaut.
> Half the team is here for a lark,
> Last man hit wicket (silly bugger), nought.

With Alison elsewhere and our daughters at university, I could supplement my income by taking in lodgers. One was Alfred Fagon, the Jamaican playwright and performer. The timing was unfortunate. His English girl friend had just dumped him. I knew the chap she had gone off with, another playwright, but all Fagon knew was that somebody white had stolen her, and I would do as representative Whitey. He once came into my room without knocking, squatted on the floor and growled: 'It would take me less than two minutes to kill a man like you, Anthony Smith.' I knew he had been an army boxing champion, and that he had done two years for GBH. From my typewriter I answered: 'Don't talk like that, Alfred. You're scaring me.' His response was to emit his deep panto-villain chuckle.

In his unhappiness he fell into the grip of some sectarian belief which required him to take three deep, hot baths a day. We had only an immersion heater. I encountered him on the staircase, with Oliver beside me, and said: 'Alfred, if you insist on taking three baths a day, it means that nobody else can have a bath at all, and we can't even do the washing-up in the evening.'

'I'm a focking better man than you, Anthony Smith, and a focking better writer.'

'That may be the case,' I replied, 'but it's not the point I am making.'

Eventually he disappeared without a word, and I was so relieved that I shrugged at the rent he had not paid. But when I drive through St Paul's and see the statue to him on the green between Ashley Road and Grosvenor Road, I say to myself, yeah, that's what it takes, you go off owing me thirty-five quid and they put up a statue to you. He was found dead on a pavement in South London, and nobody could explain why.

Stoppard rang me. His actor friend John Wood had a daughter, Sibylla, who was reading English at Reading University, but was anxious to switch to Bristol. That kind of thing is normal in German universities, but irregular in England. Was there anyone at the English department in Bristol I could speak to? Well, yes, I knew both the professors, Pat Rogers from my Cambridge days, and John Burrow. Pleading would have been unethical, and besides, I had never met Sibylla. I simply asked Rogers whether the switch would be acceptable in principle. He said they would need to interview the girl. When they did, she was admitted. I happened to have a room free in my house, so that was somewhere for her to live. Her father, like James Belsey years before, completely over-interpreted what I had done. I was Mr Fixit again. My reward soon came. I had to spend a couple of weeks in New York, with Henson's. Wood was there, waiting to be called to Hollywood for a film. The studio had given him a room in the Wyndham Hotel, but now he didn't need it. It was mine, the most luxurious hotel I have stayed in. Before he left for Hollywood, Wood and I had dinner together at Flanagan's. I remarked to him that, although we all spoke the same language, New Yorkers had a way of making me feel more foreign than I did anywhere in Europe. He did an actor's turn. In a voice that carried the restaurant, he boomed, 'Do not be deceived by the language, Anthony. All these people are aliens.' I was under the tablecloth, to avoid every turned head.

There have been many more lodgers over the years, from Iran, the Philippines, South Africa, Hungary, Portugal, Germany, Japan, and a few English ones. Some of them have become good friends of mine.

My friend from *WDP* arts page days, Bob Giddings, was teaching media studies in Bournemouth, at what was then the Dorset Institute. He had an accident, and asked if I could fill in for him for a few months.

I did not want a full-time job, so the arrangement reached was that Downie and I would drive down together for a day each week. During my time there the place changed its name to Bournemouth Polytechnic, and soon it would become Bournemouth University, to feed the national conviction that a university degree, not a technical diploma, was what every further education student merited, even if it was a degree in travel agency, Bournemouth's largest department.

Another source of income was a weekly West Country theatre review for *The Guardian*. David Foot had been doing it with warm wit for twenty-two years, and said he could not face entering a theatre again. With the paper's agreement, he handed over to me. For a couple of years I enjoyed it. What performance in the region I covered was largely left to my judgment, which meant I could give some encouragement to smaller outfits such as Travelling Light, aimed at young audiences, as well as the repertory at the BOV, Bath, Cheltenham, and elsewhere. I tried to continue Foot's tradition of being gentle when fault was to be found, but decided I was overdoing it when Charles Manton reproached me. He had gone to see a show I had mildly praised, and rang me to say it was really not much good, and why had I wasted his evening and money? That reminded me that the reviewer's duty is to the reader, not to the feelings of the performers.

Soon enough, there was an occasion for me to prove that I could gnaw truly bad work. It was a production of *Othello* at the Swan Theatre, Worcester. My companion was a new lodger I had, a wonderfully bright and amusing Greek woman called Eleni Papazoglou, in Bristol doing postgraduate work on Euripides. Nowadays she is a senior lecturer in Thessaloniki, teaching Medea studies. We both sat through the performance with dropped jaws. My intention to write as I did was reinforced when Eleni came back from the ladies' toilet with the news that everyone in there was loudly of like mind to us. My review began: *This is a sorry affair. It looks like wife-swapping in Aldershot.* I heard later that on the day my review came out the theatre was due to welcome a party of patrons. When the director read my piece, she sent people out to the newsagents to buy up and destroy every *Guardian* in Worcester.

* * *

For the last seven years of his life Dad had Parkinson's Disease. He did not know who I was. Unlike Michael Frayn, I was not allowed the blessing of getting closer again to my father towards the end of the day. Hours before he died, aged 88, I saw that he was straining to say something to me, in the whisper of a voice left to him. Gladly thinking that his recognition of me had returned, I put my ear to his lips, and heard what he wanted to tell me: 'Light thickens, and the crow makes wing to the rooky wood.' I had never heard him quote Shakespeare before, and can explain it only by guessing that some corner of his ailing brain still retained verses he had learned by rote at Richmond Grammar School.

After the funeral, I took a holiday. I have, by coincidence, returned several times to the Aegean island of Lesbos, where I started writing my first novel. My 'cousin' Margaret ran yoga courses at Molyvos, on the north coast, and I would hang around the fringe of them, talking, writing, enjoying the restaurant life, and occasionally being persuaded to make a reef-knot of my legs for a few minutes. In a guest house where I stayed, the loo had a window looking across the sea to the coast of Turkey. A rifle was propped against the cistern. When I asked the proprietor about it he told me that he wanted to be ready if he saw the Turks invading.

In a clifftop café hanging high above the wine-dark sea, I was having breakfast. A woman was sitting alone at an adjacent table. The café owner was the only other person there. The air was scented with mimosa. She was pretty. It was ridiculous. I had to say something to her.

'Are you here for the yoga?'

'Yes. It's very good with honey, isn't it?'

We went to the beach, and spent the rest of the holiday together. She was German, a shrink, and fine pianist. Through visiting her in Munich I discovered that great city for myself. She took me to meet her parents, which should have forewarned me. Later she moved to Passau. At a crowded restaurant table there she asked me if we were going to have children together. She had no children yet, I had three. I answered that it was a question I needed to ponder. She rightly took that as a No, and dropped me on the spot. I admired that, a clean break, as abrupt as our beginning had been.

I entered a national poetry competition. I was (am) fed up with the English infatuation with poetry as a romantic response to nature, for which Wordsworth is much to blame. I see almost no poems about public affairs. For those you have look to the Soviet poets, or Neruda, or in Germany Enzensberger. The poem I entered was occasioned by the massacres in the Palestinian refugee camps. The winning poem was a response to nature.

Sabra, Chatila, 1982

We could not know what they would do, he said,
speaking of the Christians in Beirut. Begin
won his vote in the Knesset: there will be
no enquiry. What shall it profit a man
to enquire? Better the corpses be counted
as dead, and buried under the hatching sand.

A politician cannot take the view
revealed to Christian soldiers: history
a black hole, future fused with past,
sucking in the gravity of light,
onward to the infinitely heavy
full stop. What they created in the camps
was eternity, each penis stiff with blood,
and ears shrilling to Pope Urban's trumpets.
God's blessing shall be unto them who know
God's blessing shall be unto them. Begin
said he could not know what they would do.
A Jew cannot divine the will of Jesus.

The Christian soldiers wash their hands. Across
the maps of Palestine, of Israel, what
beast, rougher with feeding, slouches now
to scratch the flowering corpses from the sands
of Kiryat Shemona, Kibbutz Shamir, Maalot?

15

A Brit in Texas

I GOT A CALL FROM GHOSE, IN TEXAS: 'ANTHONY, DO YOU WANT TO COME over here in September and teach creative writing for a semester, maybe two?' He was on the committee for inviting a guest writer to the English department at Austin, and thought he could swing it for me. He told me what I would be paid, and my eyebrows twitched up. But it would be four months, maybe eight, away from Bristol, and I have always been resistant to academic posts, and I was dubious, like most writers, whether creative writing can be taught. I said, 'That's a big question, Zulf. Can I think about it?'

'Don't take long. They've got other candidates being pushed.'

I hung up, and rang back to say Yes ten seconds later. That was how long it had taken me to figure it would get me out of Thatcher's England for a while, and out of overdraft for the first time since getting married, and I like a hot climate. I arranged for Derek Robinson to cover the *Guardian* reviews while I was away. I had to resign from my HTV programme, after presenting some two hundred editions.

Before my first class I sat on a bench in the lovely old quadrangle outside my office, feeling apprehensive. I'd asked for a course curriculum, and been told there was no such thing. It was up to me how I handled it. I decided to use the method of the Chelsea Group, requiring students to read their stories out loud in class, and inviting critical discussion. I had no idea how that would go down in Texas. Also, the moment I opened my mouth they'd be thinking, he's a Brit, what's he doing here? It turned out that both fears were groundless. The Texan kids were immensely rewarding to teach. Unlike students in England, they enjoy arguing with each other in class. One would give an opinion, the next would say, nah, that's a bunch of crap. They are without the *please don't look at me, I don't want to say anything that might sound stupid* reflex that is common in classes here. Often I was no more than a conductor, pointing in turn at raised hands, and fifteen minutes would go by in class argument, and I would be thinking this is not a hard way to earn a good living. It helped that they were all bright; you need top grades at school to get into UT. As for my Brit voice – after my first class I went to my office, and a girl came in to see me. I'd noticed her in the class, a blonde with legs that stretched from her hot pants to Louisiana. She sat down and said nothing, so I followed a line of discussion that had started in class, and still she said nothing, until eventually I said, 'OK, tell me what you think. Are you confused by all that?' She replied: 'Ah just lo-ove the way yuh ta-alk,' which Stoppard points out is staple reportage of how people speak in the American South, but nevertheless it is precisely what she said to me.

My doubts about whether creative writing can be taught were laid to rest. In any class of thirty there would be one who was already writing so well that I could not presume to teach him or her, only talk as writer to writer. Two or three more would be promising, and them I could help in the direction of something publishable. As for the others, I had arrived with the assumption that all of them would be bent on writing the Great American Novel. Not at all. They were modest about their talents, pleased when some phrase or perception in a story was praiseworthy. I used to tell them that this, your ear, is the writer's vital organ, and to remember how provisional all writing is, even when it gets old and we call it literature. It's the best we could do at the time. That's all. It's why I write in pencil. Pencil is provisional. Pencil is the slave at the writer's shoulder whispering in your ear: *Remember, you might not think much of this tomorrow.* Hemingway wrote in pencil, maybe for the same reason.

For those who were majoring in English, writing stories of their own sharpened their sense of how to read. Others were majors in quite other subjects, since all students were required to get 40 per cent of their credits outside their own disciplines, an admirable system. When I asked them why they had chosen creative writing, the usual answer was that they'd figured it would be 'kinda fun', and I hope they were not disappointed. An electrical engineering major turned in a story about naked Jesus clinging to the wall of a Texan prison cell. The English majors, usually vocal in class discussion, were dumbfounded by it. It was not well written, but had a wildness of imagination available to someone who had never studied literature. A giant black chap, on a football scholarship, came to see me about a C- grade I'd given him. Looking at his mighty forearms, I gently but firmly explained the faults in what he had written. In truth, his writing was so poor that I wondered why he had chosen the course. When I tactfully asked him, he told me: 'I'm a business major, and my essays suck. I just want to learn about punctuation and verbs and stuff.' After that, I was delighted to give him what help I could. Students sometimes came to me and said: 'Professor Smith, I just can't come up with a story for my next assignment.' I'd advise them, no problem, tell the story of Cinderella. Look what Angela

Carter did with Little Red Riding Hood, or – my favourite – Puss in Boots. And once or twice the result was a Cinderella like you've never thought of her.

The deal was that each of the students had to write four stories in the fifteen-week semester. Every week my classroom time, with two classes to teach, totalled six hours, I was available for office consultation for three hours, and spent maybe a dozen hours at home with their work, making marginal comments and assigning grades.

Before they started writing, we spent a couple of weeks reading and analysing stories by Hemingway, Flannery O'Connor, Raymond Carver and Angela Carter. One of my faculty colleagues told me: 'I hear you're working with them on Angela Carter. Did you know she was here six years ago, doing your job?' I hadn't known, but later found out that Borges, too, had held the visiting professor post.

Ghose and Helena drove me to see Houston for a day. There are fine things in the city, but it has no centre. It is disorienting. Even if you don't actually visit the centre of a European city, you have a sense that it is there, and where it is. Not in Houston, or many other American cities, Ghose told me. There is a downtown, the office district, and there is a city hall, but the civic layout disregards them. The place just goes on, punctuated by malls, until it ends. I told Ghose: 'When I get home and tell people I was in Texas they will ask me if I went to Houston, and I shall say yes, but I couldn't find it.'

Ghose had got me a small apartment, a short bus ride from the campus. (The buses in Austin were free at that time, let it be noted in green Bristol.) A neighbour in the apartment block was Christopher Middleton, who taught German at UT for many years. Ghose esteems him as the greatest living English poet. He was delightful company, kind, a great reader, generous with his learning. When I told him about Francis Berry's argument that what any poet writes will be pre-shaped by his/her speaking voice, he at once replied: *Beau'y is Troof, Troof Beau'y, that is all yer know on earf an' all yer need to know, Fank you very much*, which put the argument to bed. In the English faculty, a colleague was David Wevill, a friend from the Chelsea Group days, and I soon made more friends there. Maybe an academic post was more genial than I had thought.

Not entirely. I attended a departmental meeting (introduced as 'an English novelist and cricketeer') at which one senior member was vilified by his enemies, and later had a breakdown. I was told that political correctness had been born there, in the UT English department.

It was the time of the first Gulf War, and the ambience was very political. One of my students assured me that Desert Storm was 'payback for Vietnam'. In the student paper there were demands that a statue of Jefferson Davis, the Confederate leader, be torn down. My colleague Jim Magnusson took me to the fortieth birthday party of the *Texas Observer*, a more radical and excellently written monthly than anything I know in England. The people there were an exhilarating shoot-from-the-hip-wisecrack bunch, several of them contributors to the *New Yorker*. The party was addressed by the State Governor, Ann Richards. A Democrat woman running the State Capitol does not match the cliché image we have of Texas, though that image was refurbished shortly afterwards, when she lost the next gubernatorial election to George W. Bush.

Come Thanksgiving Day, my friends were not leaving the Brit on his own. I was driven to a picnic in Bastrop Woods, a mere seventy miles out of town. On the way, the car radio announced the fall of British Premier Margaret Thatcher. The picnic was lovely, sun shining through the leaves, about eighty people there, wonderful food cooked by a Swedish woman, and little kids running around, something you miss in a university environment. There were a couple of brief speeches, and then the cry: 'The Brit, the Brit! Let's have a few words from the Brit!' I thanked them for my treat, and then told them that for the rest of my life I, too, would celebrate Thanksgiving Day on the fourth Thursday of November, but that I would be giving thanks not for the events at Plymouth, Massachusetts in 1621 but for the news I had heard on my way to the picnic, that Margaret Thatcher was no longer Prime Minister of my country. Afterwards, one after another, people came up to me, squeezed my elbow, and murmured a few words of condolence for my loss.

I was starting work on a novel, another historical bio-fiction, after *Wagner* and *Sebastian*. My agent, Gillon Aitken, had suggested the subject of Laclos. Apart from his authorship of *Les Liaisons Dangereuses*, I knew nothing about him, so asked why he made the suggestion. In reply, Aitken smiled mysteriously, and said no more than: 'Just have a look.' UT was the perfect place to start looking, with its wonderful library ('the tenth biggest library in the world, sir'), and the research resource of the Harry Ransom Center, the pre-eminent repository of literary manuscripts. The more I read about Laclos, the more fascinated I became by an attractively unpleasant man, which perhaps was what had lain behind Aitken's Mona Lisa smile; perhaps, though when I later asked him, he said: 'Actually, I knew nothing about Laclos until I read your novel. I just had a hunch.' But I could not find a plot shape, and was close to abandoning the project when, in an obscure little French book of the 1950s, I had read the Laclos essay and was glancing in idle interest through another, on the Marquis de Sade. There I was riveted by a footnote, which mentioned that Sade had been banged up in the Picpus for some months during the period of Robespierre's Terror. Picpus – I had come across that name in reading about Laclos's involvement in the Revolution. It was in south-east Paris, not exactly a prison, rather a political asylum. I checked the two men's dates of residence there, and saw that they overlapped by eight months. It gave me my way in. With four inches of research stacked beside me, I started to write the book.

* * *

Oliver and his friend from Young England matches, Mark Newton, were spending that English winter in Perth, Australia, playing grade cricket to harden themselves up for the coming county season. Rather than fly home for the Christmas break, I went to Australia. My rule-of-thumb geography told me that in Texas I was already half-way there from England; the truth is that Bristol is closer to Perth than Austin, Texas is. On the way, I could spend a week in New Zealand with John Downie. I was by now so engrossed in my novel that I was writing in the Los Angeles departure lounge, on the flight, in an Auckland café...

Here's a relishable irony. Having quit the UK in disgust, Downie, in order to take up New Zealand citizenship, was required to swear a loyal oath to the Queen, an ignominy to which we, her subjects, are not subjected. He asked me if I fancied a game of cricket with the team he had joined. Cricket in December? I couldn't wait. In a country with ten times as many sheep as people, I looked forward to playing on a broad acre. When we got there, I saw seven pitches so squeezed together that, fielding at mid-wicket, I was standing beside cover-point on the adjacent pitch. On a plastic strip I established my southern hemisphere batting average of twenty-eight, which is likely to endure. I had a partnership with a fine, tall batsman who went on to complete a century, and invited us all to his house after the match. He turned out to be one of New Zealand's leading poets, Harry Ricketts, and he has recently published a short book entitled *How to Watch a Cricket Match.*

Landing at Wellington airport I had seen dainty flower borders along the runway, and the cakes in a café Downie took me to were just like those I had eaten in the 1950s; I was thinking, yes, Guildford circa 1952, that's New Zealand. Down at the harbour, the air was so clear I could see pretty well to the South Pole, and I said to myself, a touch of Greece. The hilltops were purple. OK, there's a dash of Scotland in there. And then I realised I could not identify a single fish on the fishmonger's slab, and in the street there were plenty of large, brown, friendly people with broad noses, and slowly I was situating myself in Polynesia. We saw a marvellous exhibition of Maori crafts. When I asked Downie whether the Maori felt treated as contemptuously as the Aborigines had been, across the water, he explained the crucial difference. The latter had been in Australia since the dawn of time, whereas the Maori had themselves arrived as settlers on the island of the long white cloud a mere seven centuries ago.

I had two weeks in Perth with Oliver and Mark, listening to Natalie Merchant sing *Verdi Cries*, celebrating Christmas Day in traditional style, down on the beach with tinnies, eyeing the sheilas, seeing parrots flit through the telegraph wires, walking every day past a yard-long dead brown snake, keeping a wide berth in case it was the Very Clever Australian Brown Snake. At the Waca we saw New South Wales lose their fourth wicket at about 160, and I remarked 'one more wicket now and they are in trouble'. What followed was the Australian record fifth-wicket stand of 464 between the Waugh brothers. Mark Newton also set an Australian record. He was umpiring a midweek match. The side batting second were winning easily, and batsman No.6 announced that he needed to get to the bank, and four of his team mates went with him. Then wickets fell, and at five down there was nobody to come in next, so after two minutes the fielding captain appealed for Timed Out; and again two minutes later, and again, until Newton had given Timed Out five times in ten minutes.

I went seventy miles upstate with Oliver to watch an annual match between the city slickers from Perth and a local side. It was always an unequal match, played to recruit promising country boys. This year it did not go to plan. It started late on account of the tail end of a locust swarm, and the locals won the match, against a city team captained by the Test player Tom Hogan. Afterwards we went to the pub for one for the road. At the long, gloomy main bar, solitary drinkers studied themselves in the mirror behind the barman. We were in one of the private side rooms, with chicken bits laid out on a table. It was time to go when Father Christmas came in with a fresh basket of chicken: 'Dig in, lads.' So we all did, and bought Father Christmas a drink. A young man in a smart suit came in, and shouted at Father Christmas, 'Not this bar. I told you. It was for the bar down the hall.' Father Christmas looked at the emptied chicken basket. At that point a little girl, daughter of one of the Perth cricketers, ran up and tugged eagerly on his red robe: 'Hullo, Father Christmas.' He looked down at her, and growled:

'Not now, dear, I'm in the shit.' When we left, I saw him at the long bar, drinking alone, still in his red robe.

I started my journey back on December 31st, changing planes at Auckland, with a few hours to wait in the city. It was evening, and already there were lights and fireworks for the new year. Flying east, across the international date line, I reached Texas in time for a second new year evening. The next day, I went back to the airport to meet a woman who was joining me for a couple of months. She was another German, and had been teaching in Bristol. With a couple of weeks before the start of the next semester, we flew down to Mexico City for a few days. They have kept Trotsky's house just as it was on the day he was murdered there. On his bathroom shelf is a Colgate shaving stick. I was using Colgate at the time, and felt a male solidarity with him. I murmured 'Keep using the Colgate, Lev Davidovich', and almost heard him reply 'You too, Anton Karlovich'.

We flew on to Oaxaca. I wanted to drink a mescal to Malcolm Lowry. We stayed the first couple of nights in the Hotel Francia, but the linen and floor-cleaning fell short of German standards, so we moved to another hotel, and then another. Something happened to me in Oaxaca which I find as inexplicable as the elevation I had experienced all those years ago on shaking hands with Dr Llewellyn Twentyman. We spent a long, hot afternoon at the pre-Columbian arena of Monte Albán. I did my best to imagine how it would have been when filled with thousands of Zapotecs enjoying the human sacrifices, but I am not sure I got beyond Hollywood images. The next day we went to a little museum in town, the Rufino Tamayo. Two small rooms were crammed full of Zapotec artefacts. They did the trick, and I was not prepared for it, and am still not clear what the trick was. I was sucked into a vortex of time, not exactly imagining myself among the Zapotecs, but eliminating the centuries lapsed between them and me, the passage of time cancelled. Their time and mine were both present time. My friend saw that I was feeling shaky, and took me out of the place, assuming that it was something I had eaten, but it was not. It was, I suppose, akin to a religious experience, weird, powerful, not pleasant, but enriching.

To return to Mexico City I wanted to take a bus-ride, to see the country. I cannot understand why my friend did not tell me she was a bad bus traveller. An hour into the eight-hour trip she was green, and moaning. As Thomas à Kempis remarked, *In omnibus requiem quaesivi et nusquam inveni.* I looked for peace on the bus and found it nowhere. When we made a half-way comfort stop at a shanty in the middle of the desert, she refused to get back on board. I felt for her, but pointed out that once the bus had gone without us, we would be stranded among hot sand and cactus stretching to the horizon. She squatted down in the shade under a roadside table: 'I am not getting back on the bus.'

'The bus is the only way of getting back to Mexico City.'

'You get on it. I won't.'

'I can't leave you here on your own. You'll die.'

'I don't care. I'd rather die than get on the bus.'

An elderly American man who had seen how bad she'd felt came over and talked quietly to her. She got on the bus. I held her tight all the way back. When I asked her what the American had said to persuade her, she wouldn't tell me. Perhaps, simply, she had succumbed to paternalistic authority. I had met her father when he visited Bristol. A handsome, charming man who spoke faultless English, he had regularly beaten her with a leather belt since she was eight years old, and had made her mother's life miserable. She told me all that, but when I asked what her father did for a living, she said only that he'd worked for the German army.

'Doing what?'

'Near the frontier with the East.'

'Ah, he was a spy.'

'I can't tell you.'

Back in Austin she decided she wanted to smarten me up, and took me to the open-air market to buy some second-hand shirts. I let her get on with choosing them, and looked through the book stall, and came across a volume of D.H. Lawrence's letters. I found some that he had written from Mexico, from Oaxaca, from the Hotel Francia. 'Look,' I told her when she came over with four shirts for me, 'Lawrence stayed in the same hotel as we did, over sixty years ago. We might have slept in the same bed.'

'Ja, and in the same sheets.'

She told me, more than once: 'I am very efficient in my sex life, as I am in everything.' When I got it wrong she reached out for the alarm clock and hurled it against the wall, and afterwards I was very careful never to get it wrong again. A couple of times we had dreadful quarrels, caused by my preoccupation with the novel I was writing. Nobody should try living with a practising writer. I started waking up at four in the morning, not my style, and would go to the kitchen for a quick coffee and smoke, and just glance at what I'd written that day, and two hours later would be wrestling with it. A call would come from the bedroom: 'Where are you?'

'I couldn't sleep, so I just did a little work.'

'I want you here beside me.'

'But you were fast asleep.'

'Even when I am sleeping I know if you are not here.'

One night we had a quarrel so fierce that I walked out of the apartment and sat in the car we had rented for a couple of weeks to visit places like the Pedernales Falls, but a January night in Texas can be freezing, and I could not run the engine all night. I went back, tiptoed in, she was still awake, worrying about where I had got to, and we made up, as people do.

For a plot reason, I needed to know what Sade's handwriting was like. On the off-chance that they might have something, I went to the enquiry desk at the Harry Ransom Center. It was not like the British Library when it was in Bloomsbury, where the answer would have been: 'Fill in this form in triplicate, come back at the end of next week, and see if we have found anything.' At the HRC, after ten minutes I was looking at two letters written by Sade, telling his steward back in the Vaucluse to do something about the fences. (His handwriting is tidy, well-formed and aligned.) I had a comparable experience with my computer. I'd lugged my clunky old Amstrad across the Atlantic, but when I switched it on it didn't work. I took it to a computer place. They blinked. 'Amstrad? That's a new one on us.' But instead of turning me away, they said 'Leave it with us, we'll see what we can do', and I had it back the next day, up and running. American can-do.

When the spring semester finished and I came back home to Bristol, I visited my friend a couple of times in Germany, at her home in Trier (Marx's birthplace). She took me to Berlin for a few days, which unforeseeably supplied me with the solution to a problem I had in the structure of my novel. I needed to frame my eighteenth-century narrative with a twentieth-century viewpoint, and post-1989 East Berlin was the perfect stage for that, mirroring the deeply confused hopefulness of Paris post-1795.

She ended our two years together as efficiently as her compatriot had. She was just finishing her degree at Heidelberg, having spent about eight years over it, as they do in Germany, and was now intent on a successful career in business. 'When I am at an important lunch with business clients, how can I have a man sitting beside me who dresses as you do?' There was no answer to that.

* * *

I was not finished with Texas, and glad not to be. I had become friendly with the director of the HRC, Tom Staley, a formidable operator. He arranged to buy my correspondence of thirty years with Burroway, Ghose, Johnson and Stoppard. Before sending him the letters, some seven hundred pages of them, I thought it ethical to ask the permission of my correspondents. Stoppard's answer was:

> What an extraordinary coincidence, I am in the process of selling my own collected correspondence to Staley, including all of yours... And including, of course, all the letters we are now exchanging about selling letters to Staley. And who knows, maybe this letter too will end up in that ultimate self-referential meta-archive. In future, perhaps it will be expedient if we all write to each other by faxing the HRC, who can collect the stuff on the wing.

Staley suggested that when the letters were installed in the archive I might go to Texas to give a talk about them. When I mentioned this to Christopher Levenson, who had been lecturing in Ottawa for thirty years, his wife Oonagh rang me in secret and insisted on paying for me to travel via Canada, since my trip would coincide with Levenson's sixtieth birthday, and a surprise visit from me would be a present for him. I wondered if I should arrive with a ribbon tied in a bow over my head. Ottawa was in its harshest winter of the century, and was colder than I knew the earth could be – waterfalls frozen in mid-air, hot dog stalls on the river, an exhibition of ice sculptures which had lasted three months, and *we don't smoke in this house so you wouldn't mind, would you, smoking outside* in minus 23 degrees centigrade? But in Texas I swam in Ghose's garden pool.

As the title for my talk about the friendships recorded in the archived letters, I borrowed James Joyce's phrase prescribing the conditions under which writers can get their work done: *Silence, Exile, and Cunning.* 'B.S. Johnson is dead – that is Silence. Zulfikar Ghose is exiled from his native Pakistan, and from his adopted Britain, and has been living for over twenty years here in Texas. And Cunning is Tom Stoppard, as those who know his plays will agree.'

While I was in Austin I was invited to return in the fall for another teaching semester. I did that, got good grades from my students (yes, they grade us as we grade them), and might have done more but for a *putsch* within the committee that invites visiting professors. The post is intensely competitive, attracting hundreds of applications from all over the USA, and an English male was no longer welcome. Ghose had twice saved my bacon in Texas hogtrading, but now he was outvoted. I will not record the committee arguments he described to me. Those who spend their professional lives exploring the moral values of literature may not be conspicuously moral in their own actions. How different from the professional theatre. And from classy journalism, I was about to discover.

During that semester I made a good friend in one of my graduate students, Cody Garrett. We shot pool and played poker and talked about Hemingway and took girls out for a drive in his 'old green dog'. He comes from a working-class background, much like mine and Johnson's, and is making a career in political journalism. He introduced me to a group of Mexicans in Austin, political refugees from an agrarian rebellion in Chiapas. When I told them I was a sometime *Guardian* journalist, they urged me to go with them to Chiapas, where they could get me through the military cordons and take me to their Zapatista leader, Subcomandante Marcos. It sounded like the kind of mission Graham Greene would have relished. I contacted *The Guardian* to offer them the story. They said don't worry, our man in California will keep an eye on it for us. He was no more than 2,500 miles away from the action, after all.

Worse was to come. Back home, *The Guardian* dumped all its fifteen regional theatre reviewers, but did not have the guts to admit it to us. They simply ignored all our proposals of shows to cover, waiting for the message to sink in, as a coward would end an affair. Some of the money they were saving was soon spent by the arts editor on flying himself to Venice to review an opera. Then he was dumped, to the obits desk. Theatre companies were assured that coverage would continue, from London, which in practice has meant only the big companies and productions. I would soon have had to resign the reviewing job in any case, because I was becoming too involved in Bristol theatre myself to remain critically detached; but I was shocked by the shabbiness of the affair. *The Guardian* would have deplored it in another organisation. It had forgotten where it came from, the place where fifty million of us enjoy not living in London – and forgotten, too, its own breast-beating about the plight of regional theatres.

Alison, after Hugh's death, had moved to France, and lived there for some years with friends of ours who had set up a theatre centre to accommodate touring groups, teach theatre practice and do a few shows of their own from a travelling wagon. I, too, was pining for France, and thought I saw a way to set myself up there. Gillon Aitken wanted to buy a place where he could take his family in the summer. I was to have an abode in the grounds, live there out of season and bark at intruders. He sent me house hunting for him in the Hérault, and after a few weeks I returned with details of several propositions. He had declared himself delighted with my Laclos novel, now, at Ghose's suggestion, entitled *The Dangerous Memoir of Citizen Sade*, and decided that it should go to Faber and Faber.

Everything collapsed. Aitken's agency was being roughly shaken about by partnership changes, and he had problems in his marriage. The house in France was off the agenda. Faber's thought my novel 'often brilliant' but could not see a profit in it. I was tempted to write to the fiction editor, Robert McCrum, and remind him how much profit his firm had made from my introduction of Stoppard to them, and incidentally to mention that I'd chatted to him when he was but a little tiny boy and his father my senior tutor. But one does not write such letters. Aitken was not used to rejection, and tried only one more publisher. Then Faber's took on a new fiction editor, back my often brilliant novel went to them, and it was again declined. Aitken, a proud Etonian, was by now personally affronted, and wanted nothing more to do with the book. I eventually brought it out in 2000 with my friend Jeremy Mulford, whose small firm, Loxwood Stoneleigh, could do little or nothing to promote sales, but at least gave it a physical existence in the cold world.

As one door closes, another one slams in your face. It was time to get a new pinball in play. *Boy, mix me another metaphor!*, to quote S. J. Perelman.

16

Up the Feeder

CLIFTON CRICKET CLUB, ITINERANT SINCE 1819, HAD MERGED WITH Flax Bourton C.C. The gorgeous ground at Flax was soon the home of the regional league champions for several seasons, and the club was at one time assessed in *The Cricketer* magazine ratings as the strongest in the country. Saeed Anwar played a season for us, just before he became captain of Pakistan, and we had others with Test experience. I was a 3rd XI player by then, but did once bat with Saeed in a midweek friendly. He got nine, I got 22. And still I haven't been selected for England. Where's the justice? We had had international stars at the club before that, acquiring experience of English conditions. Barry Richards played a season for Clifton in 1964. Not surprisingly, he topped our 1st XI averages. It happened that that year I was top of the 2nd XI averages, allowing me ever since to say, yeah, that year it was Baz and me. None of the stars was ever paid. The club was not well off.

In 1995 Oliver was club captain. He had talked about the life of a professional cricketer with Mike Brearley, who is a friend of my friend Ted Braun, with Michael Atherton, his captain in Sri Lanka, and with some of the Gloucestershire players, in particular Paul ('Human') Romaines, and decided that he did not want it. Instead he played cricket for enjoyment, and was building a career in market research. That year our 1st XI reached the final of the national club knock-out competition, at Lord's. Our opponents were Chorley, who had won the trophy the previous year. Four of our team had come up through our junior section, which I had managed for close on twenty years. Our players and committee members were accommodated in the Hilton the night before the match, and we attended a dinner addressed (rather well, to my surprise) by Fred Trueman. Several thousand people were in the ground the next day. Geoffrey Reeves, an MCC member, remarked to me that Middlesex would be glad to attract that many. Oliver won the toss for changing rooms, so of course chose the home one, which England use. He also won the toss on the pitch, and put Chorley in, because research had shown that they preferred to chase a target. We supporters were strolling through the Long Room as though it were our club house. It wasn't quite the cathedral of cricket, however. The Chorley crowd, about two thousand of them in coachloads, were packed in front of the Tavern doing their football chants. First over of the day John Meadows (who is slightly portly, though a county badminton player) goes to fetch it from the boundary in front of them, and to a man they stand up, jabbing two thousand forefingers at him, and chant: 'You fat bastard, you fat bastard, you ate all the pies.' We had them controlled, looking like something over 200 in their 45 overs, but a left-handed wicketkeeper went berserk at the end, smashed sixes over the short boundary on the Tavern side, and our team were chasing 239. At 158-1, in good time, we looked like winning, but then Oliver was bowled round his legs (that slope at Lord's) for 90. Meadows kept it going, but was lbw for 73, and we fell 12 runs short.

I was working on a screenplay for Natural Nylon, a company formed by the young shooting stars in the London film world at that time – Sadie Frost, Jude Law, Ewan McGregor, Johnny-Lee Miller, Sean Pertwee, Rufus Sewell, collectively known as the Primrose Hill Mob. Their intention was to set up and control their own work. Stoppard had rung me with an invitation to write *The Hellfire Club* for them. He never told me so, but they must have asked him first. You would, wouldn't you? For whatever reason, probably lack of time, he had persuaded them that I was their man, but he would be there as script consultant. And so he was, while I got through three drafts, until the project sank, and the company soon followed it down. From an afternoon I spent with Law and the producer, Damon Bryant, I knew that they really were attached to their independent aspirations, but the stars had become so much in demand from other producers that they had no time to care for their own baby.

I switched back to theatre work. In 1996 Bristol staged the Festival of the Sea, commemorating five hundred years (well, 499) since John Cabot's voyage in the *Matthew.* With my interest in the Cabots, I asked Andy Hay, director of the Bristol Old Vic, whether there would be any theatre input to the festival. What a good idea, he said, and what a pity the city council had not already thought of engaging their own resident theatre company in the big event. We went to talk to the striped-shirt banker in charge of the festival. At our enquiry about theatre he shrugged, and murmured something about a fit-up group putting on a nautical entertainment. Hay persisted. Was there not scope for a full-blown musical show? Ah, the striped shirt said, music, oh yes, we do plan to have some music. What music? We'd have to ask his wife, he said. That was her bag. 'She is very fond of music.' Walking back up

Prince Street, Hay was so frustrated that he punched a brick wall. Then he said: 'We'll do it ourselves.'

He commissioned me to do a play about Bristol docks, in the researched documentary vein of *God's Wonderful Railway*. It would take account of the thousand-year history, but would focus on the industrial experience of dockers still living. Like a Bristolian Studs Terkel, I listened to about fifty old dockers and their wives and a few seamen, and wound up with a hundred close-typed pages of material, about five times as much as an evening on stage would need. The job, then, was selection and shaping. People might think it an easy way to write a play, to base it on documentary material. It is not. Often I longed for the licence just to write a scene out of my head. Some linking parts were like that, but most of the scenes had to respect the human experience of the source. Even some of the songs arose from the research. An old seaman said to me: *Prince Street, look at it now, what have you got?* Those words opened the closing number. Hay drove me through nine drafts on the first production of *Up the Feeder, Down the 'Mouth*, in the Theatre Royal, and four more on the 2001 revival, not to mention on-the-wing tweaks in the course of rehearsals.

We heard that Fred Wedlock had got wind of the show, and was keen to be in it. Hay liked the idea, but was cautious. The gifts of a stand-up entertainer and singer would not necessarily convert into the skills of an actor in a company. Hay was cunning. He asked Wedlock if he would be kind enough to join him and me for a read-through of the script, and comment on its language and authenticity from his experience of growing up in a Bristol docks pub. Wedlock did make useful remarks about the script, but the true purpose of the event was to audition him informally. Hay said: 'Thank you very much, Fred. Incidentally, we have started to think about casting the show. Would you be at all interested?' In the first week of rehearsal, Wedlock's inexperience did show. He was performing like a one-man entertainer, and when Hay stopped it and asked him to go at it differently, the expression on Wedlock's face was saying: 'This is what I *do*. If it's not what you need, what am I doing here?' But behind that affable Bristolian manner was a sharp brain that had done an English degree and continued to think deeply, and soon he learned to be part of a large ensemble. He ended the show by reading the letter in which Dolly Gray, our principal character, bade farewell to forty-two years of working on the docks. Wedlock and Gray were to die within weeks of each other, in 2010.

In the Theatre Royal in 1997 we had a professional cast of eleven, plus five musicians and thirty-four extras as dockers and chorus. The extras had their own director, Mike Shepherd of Kneehigh. Over the three-week run we filled about 70 per cent capacity, with full houses in the last week. There were up to six curtain calls, and enthusiastic reviews. Every night elderly dockers were in tears. Many in the audience had seldom or never been to a theatre. They shouted out in recognition, ignoring the shushing. It was recognition of the way of life they had known when there were still working ships in the heart of Bristol. Liverpool dockers on strike came down, and told us they recognised every docking dodge and slang phrase.

Hay commissioned me to do another play about the docks, written this time, not documentary. I had a strong story, which I had come across when listening to an eighty-year-old docker in poor health. After a few reminiscences he mentioned that his father before him had also worked on the docks, and then he broke down, shoulders heaving. I assumed that he was still grieving for his father's death, but I was wrong. When he spoke again, he told me that his father had been the victim of a wicked injustice, over 'the *Montreal City* business'. He had papers in his loft to prove it. I asked if I could see them, and he said he would fetch them down when he felt stronger, and ring me. I never heard from him again, and his telephone line did not answer.

I was intrigued. I asked Dolly Gray about the *Montreal City*. 'Oh, we were out for five weeks over that,' he said, 'and no strike pay. The union wouldn't recognise it.' I asked what the issue had been. 'These Canadian seamen were sacked while they were in Bristol port, and asked for our support.' Why were they sacked? 'I can't tell you. We never did know. It was just that working men had been treated badly, and we felt we had to support them.'

Research in back issues of the local papers came up with nothing. Then I took a line of enquiry through Levenson in Ottawa, who asked a trades union contact he had, who gave me the title of a book that would explain it all. The only copy of the book in the country was in the British Library. I read it there in an afternoon, and had on my hands an astonishing story from the late 1940s, which led from Bristol dockers to Brandoesque Mafia murders on the American waterfront, and the McCarthy hearings. As far as I know, the story has never been told in this country. The play is still waiting for a production.

Hay started to work on it with me, then changed his mind. He said: 'First, I want to revive *Up the Feeder*, but this time we'll do it on the docks itself.' The revival was to be staged on Prince's Wharf in 2001, with the enthusiastic collaboration of the Industrial Museum. It would be a much larger show, with a very big real ship docking, and cranes and a shunting engine and a van performing. We needed to introduce new material. John O'Hara, the musical director, called me in to hear a canon he had written: 'I've always wanted to write a canon.'

I liked it, and told him I'd often complained that it was the writer who had to do the stone-breaking work, finding the form and the rhythms, making things easy for the composer. I would enjoy doing it this way round. I began to feel less easy, however, when we agreed it had to fit into a sequence where our cast of extras were unloading bananas from the ship. I was not brimming over with witty lines about unloading bananas. At home, I had more trouble writing those words to fit O'Hara's canon than any other song I've done. I never got them quite right, and would have a fresh go if there were another revival.

Throughout rehearsals and the run I was on crutches, having broken my ankle when delivering, on a wet pitch, the most literal leg-break in the history of cricket. The BRI did a brilliant job, on what they told me were four snapped bones, one of which had 'migrated'. Since I had recently suffered a broken arm, playing cricket of course, they wanted to be sure that I was not developing osteoporosis. They did a bone scan, and as a result I now have it written down, on NHS-headed paper, that I am *essentially normal.* I carry it in my wallet to rebuke doubters.

The revival booked out its entire run before the opening night. The Theatre Royal production had primed demand, and local television news got interested. Sarah Smith, the BOV general manager, told me it was just as well we sold every seat, because staging the show had cost so much that 70 per cent, good going normally, would have left the company on its uppers. To this day people tell me how much they enjoyed it, or how cheesed-off they were at not getting in.

Every night, watching the show, I felt like Saint Sebastian, pierced by all the little things that were not quite right. Stephen Sondheim once watched a show of his in rehearsal and at the end said: 'Perfect. Now make it better.' It's always like that for the writer. You miss the bigger picture. But the reviews were warm. *The Observer*, in its 2001 annual review of British theatre, called it the single most magical moment of the year. The first I knew of this remark was, typically, when Stoppard rang me from the house he had in France. It was the second time I had made an *Observer* Top Ten of the year. The first had been for having my teeth knocked out by a cricket ball. The most withering comment on the show was just outside L Shed, where the audience entered. The pavement had been dug up, so there was a big sign to redirect people, with an arrow pointing towards the theatre entrance. What the sign said was: *Pedestrian Diversion.* Surely it's a bit better than that, I thought.

The production manager, Derek Simpson, got the credit he deserved. Sadly, Hay did not. Having conceived the show and set it up, he had resigned from the BOV before rehearsals began, and the production was directed by Heather Williams and Gareth Machin. After ten years as artistic director, Hay felt crushed by the bureaucracy of dealing with the Arts Council, and tepid support from the city council. He wanted an easier life, in television.

People from the National Theatre came to see the show but it was too site-specific (and, I suspect, too Bristol-specific) for them to consider a transfer, even though, I pointed out, they have got a river outside their place. So many people had been turned away at the box office that the BOV were debating whether they should put it on again in 2002, but decided that that might turn it into an annual rite, and it would be better to wait a year or two. [Editor's note: the playscript of the 2001 BOV production was reprinted by Redcliffe Press and launched, with song and extracts from the play, at the Industrial Museum, by then M Shed, in 2012.]

I was content with that, eager to move on to the *Montreal City* play, and others I was working on. I had supposed that such reviews, and selling 20,000 tickets, and standing ovations every night, would open doors. Not only has *Up the Feeder* never been put on again, but I have not earned another penny from the BOV. You're only as good as the last thing you wrote, but sometimes you're not even that good. A hiatus occurred when a new regime took over in 2003. Soon the company's future was, according to the *Evening Post*, 'hanging by a thread.'The new vice-chairman of the board was Giles Clarke, better known as the ECB man who sold Test cricket to Sky the day after The Downs were covered with kids swinging bats and saying 'I'm Kevin Pietersen', and later granted the fraudster Allen Stanford helicopter-landing rights at Lord's. Early on I wrote to Stoppard:

> You said, let you know how it goes with the new directors at the BOV. Not well, is the answer so far. I met Reade last week. He did ask me to let him see what I've got up my sleeve (cascade of dramatic writing pours out, yr old joke), so I have sent him two finished plays, but have decided to keep the new, half-written one (Redcliffe, 14th-century hermit, quantum theory) to myself for now. It is too precious to me to hawk around promiscuously. But he remarked, as though on the weather, that he doubted if they would be doing new stuff, but wd stick

> to classics. 'Of course,' he volunteered, 'if a new script from Stoppard landed on our desk...' I said nothing, not even 'Fat chance'. I wondered if he knew that I know you, and there was a subtext: play your cards right... I can't believe that. They know little about this city they have come to. When I mentioned Bristol Bridge, he said: 'Which bridge is that?' That one, I said, pointing out of his window. Next thing, they sack the MD, John O'Hara; the head of design; and the chap who was acting director for 18 months before they came has resigned. I had to speak at a big meeting of the theatre club on Saturday to thank the three of them, and to warn people about what is happening. That will have given me form in the new chaps' files. I have never known such depression in King Street. No one smiles.

Soon afterwards, I wrote to him again:

> That was a kind thought, to let me know about the *Observer* piece on the BOV. Unfortunately, it turns out to be a shabby piece of journalism, unworthy of the paper. She has swallowed their PR whole, without asking about five questions that would have given it all some context. She travesties what has hitherto been going on in King Street... I don't disagree with the view that mundane work was done there, but if the paper had sent someone who knew their stuff, or asked outside the new directorate, they would have allowed that five or six shows in the past ten years have been exceptional. A striking and brave *Marat/Sade*, an unexpectedly fascinating *Xmas Carol* of all things, the première of *Little Voice*, a rock-concert show (just about a play) that traversed the auditorium, an admirable *Streetcar,* incomparable pantos every winter, and others, modestly disregarding a decent production of *The Real Thing* and my own Studs Terkelesque record-breaker (successive shows, as it happened). If Andy Hay had been granted a million a year, not less than half that, he might have come up with much more; and, crucially, under him it 'connected with its area', as an approving caption to the article quotes the Leeds director, instead of what it

> looks as though we are about to receive, a little bit of Notting Hill that Bristol can call its own. The villain of the piece is the manipulative Arts Council, who were influential in appointing the new directors and then more than doubled the grant, as though saying, We know best what Bristol needs. The *Obs* harpie shrieks about new productions of Wedekind etc, omitting to point out that they will be youth theatre performances – all very well, but 'a National Theatre for the South West'? Come on. I would be delighted if the new régime can deliver what it talks, and more so if they include me in the equation. But they will do themselves and everyone else no favours if they proceed in disregard of what has happened hitherto, and the culture in which their theatre is situated. So far, they have pissed off swathes of people, including, I'm told, three of the governing board, who have resigned. New brooms sweeping clean will do that, natch, but they'd have been better advised not to sweep so clean that Andy Hay is calling it 'a scorched earth policy'.

The BOV is in better shape, now, but it remains to be seen whether, after the restoration, it will have any interest in plays concerned, as mine are, with Bristol's cultural roots, the sources of its humour, its points of stress, its voice. *Our current project is to be explicit in our desire to tackle the now,* they wrote to me. The End of History, then. No back stories.

17

For Larks

ALISON HAD SPENT HER YEARS IN FRANCE LOOKING AFTER A LARGE vegetable garden, which included many herbs. She came back home to do a correspondence degree in herbal medicine, and got a First. The family talked about giving her a pointy hat and a broomstick as a graduation present. We might have thrown in a cat as well, except that she is ailourophobic. That had not prevented her from bravely accommodating cats for our children, when they were little. The longest-lived of them, named Minack, I had buried in the back garden. When Alison set up a practice she had a wing built in the garden for the purpose. Since it entailed digging up the cat's grave, we named it the Minack Wing. She was the kind of cat who would have thought that a memorial building was the least we could do for her, after seventeen years. As Robertson Davies observed: *Authors like cats because they are such quiet, loveable, wise creatures, and cats like authors for the same reasons.*

All our children were now living in north London, near each other. Imogen has two daughters and a son, Sophie followed with two boys, and Oliver with three girls. Until his family life precluded it, Oliver played a few seasons for Brondesbury C.C. I watched them at The Oval in 1997, winning the London clubs' knock-out tournament.

Clifton Flax Bourton, like other clubs throughout the country, was declining through lack of players. Of the team that played at Lord's, within two years only three remained. The others had left Bristol to follow their professions. I went on playing for a while, but had missed a season with my broken ankle, and now did not know half the players. At my level, cricket is social or it is nothing. Also I had started to drop catches, not all of them, but too many. And I do not like the league matches we play all the time now, or the witless aggressiveness on the field. More seriously, I had a falling-out with the club committee over their exclusion of my friend Maurice Perl. Rightly or wrongly, Perl sniffed anti-semitism. Together with Ivan Brown, who had left South Africa because of apartheid, I asked the committee for an explanation. They refused to give one. That pretty well ended my club cricket career, after more than fifty years, though I did guest in a match when I was seventy-three, and might do again, on a sunny day.

I had a play about cricket on HTV, filmed on Clifton College Close by Bill Butt's independent company, Atlas Adventures. *Breathless Hush* was about thirteen-year-old Arthur Collins in 1899, setting the world record of 628 not out in a school house match, but really it was about the impact of the Great War on the British imperial class, represented by Henry Newbolt (Paul McGann), whose 'Breathess Hush' poem *Vitaï Lampada* had been inspired by a match at Clifton, and about how the empire did for Collins, who died at Ypres in 1914.

My producer at HTV, Derek Clark, had retired but continued to come up with documentary ideas for them, which he set up as an independent. We did one on Allen Lane, born in Cotham. Richard Hoggart talked about how Lane had head-hunted him as editorial director of Penguin, but he had chosen to stick to university work. He called Lane and John Reith the two most important cultural producers of the twentieth century, yet there was no memorial to Lane in his native city, bar a small plaque on an extension he had opened at his old school, Bristol Grammar. There is now a plaque on his birthplace, 11 Cotham Vale.

The once busy studios now stripped out by Carlton, the new owners, my last work in HTV's final agony was a three-part documentary, *Up In Smoke*, on the heyday of the Wills company before its absorption into Imperial Tobacco. I interviewed a couple of dozen old workers, who described the excellent working conditions they had enjoyed, and the civic philanthropy of the Wills family. I was hoping to recycle the material as a stage play, but that didn't work. No one would say a bad word about the firm. No villain, no drama.

1999 was the fiftieth anniversary of the Cheltenham Festival of Literature. All the former directors were invited to come up with a few ideas for events, and to host them. My daughter Imogen called us the ex-directory. At my invitation, Peter Hall gave a wonderful, unscripted talk about speaking Shakespeare's verse. When I invited questions from the audience, the first was: 'When can we read the book?' With my working interest in music-theatre, I also set up an event about writing words to be sung. On the discussion panel I hosted were Michael Berkeley, Tim Rice and Marina Warner. Any reader who has noticed that I have a fondness for cricket will understand that I was delighted when Warner mentioned to me that she is the grand-daughter of Plum Warner. Come the evening, I was reeling with 'flu, but it was my event and I had to go through with it, feverish. Rice gave us his opinion that any song by Abba is more valuable than the collected works of Benjamin Britten. I don't know if he knew that Berkeley, son of Lennox Berkeley, is Britten's godson, or chose Britten at random.

The Writers' Room, the green room for performers, is a place for encountering people you know or recognizing people you don't, sometimes in bizarre juxtapositions. I was in there talking to Hoggart, whom I had travelled to Cheltenham to see for the first time in a while. The festival director Sarah Smyth brought in Robin Cook, and asked me to give him my seat, so that he could talk to Hoggart. I admired Cook politically, and also because he was a racing tipster, so as I reluctantly stood up I said: 'Welcome to Cheltenham's second-best festival.' It took a moment: 'Second-best... ah!'

Another time, I was in there on my own when Smyth brought in a white-haired gent and mumbled, 'Anthony, do you know [inaudible]?' and left him with me. We talked a bit, he in an American accent, but it was a while before he said something that clued me. It was Joseph Heller. Two pretty girls in short skirts sat down near us, and Heller swivelled ninety degrees in his seat to see them. Good for you, I thought, and thought it again a few months later, when I read his obituary.

I once attended a panel event at which I knew all the speakers: Libby Houston, whom I had driven there from Bristol, Malcolm Bradbury, Raymond Williams and David Hare. Afterwards, in the lobby, I said hello to each in turn, amid the throng of autograph seekers. The last one I got to was Hare. After an hour of intellectual debate, I figured he might prefer a chat on the lighter side, so asked him if he had played any cricket that year. His face lit up: 'Yes. When I was directing *The Bay at Nice,* the National had a match against Sadler's Wells, and I carefully arranged my rehearsal schedule so that I could play in it. My bowling figures were five overs, two maidens, five runs and three wickets. [Note to Editor of *Wisden*: my memory of what Hare told me may not be exact.] The Sadler's Wells lot tried to spoil it for me. They said: "Well, you weren't bowling against our best batsmen. There was a dress run for *Rigoletto* this afternoon, and it took both our openers out." But I didn't care what they said. Three wickets in five overs!'

With Stoppard's agreement I reworked the stage script of *Albert's Bridge* as a school-of-Sondheim music-theatre piece, with the composer David Lyon. We had a try-out production at Shaftesbury Community Theatre. The band was a section of the Bournemouth Symphony Orchestra, the performers amateur. Stoppard professed himself pleased with the show, but he and Lyon and I all knew that we had more work to do, which we have been doing.

When Val Lorraine was dying, Stoppard came to Bristol to see her. We went together into her room, and she was pleased to see us. After we left her we had a cigarette, and then Stoppard said he wanted to go back in to see her again for a few minutes. While I waited, I thought regretfully about the last stage work she had done, as the title part in *The Witch of Edmonton*, which I had directed. A week into rehearsals, it had become obvious that she was not going to remember all her words. I was hoping to get through somehow, but the management told me I would have to stand her down and get someone else in quickly. I had to break it to her. She was not surprised. After a lifetime in the profession, she knew it was the right decision. Stoppard came out from her room breathing more easily. What she had really needed was those few minutes with him, the boy in whom she had believed forty years earlier.

* * *

My old leg-spinner in the Sunday 2nd XI, Richard Lee, was president of the Canynges Society, who raise money for the upkeep of St Mary Redcliffe Church. He had persuaded me that there was a play to be written about the district of Redcliffe, but it had taken me some years to find it. Eventually, mooching around the place yet again (an hour before 9/11 happened), I began to experience what is not here, not any more: a mild version of my vortex in Oaxaca, and perhaps a belated answer to John Berger's question: *What has time meant to you in your life?* I wanted to tackle what Nathaniel Hawthorne called *the attempt to connect a bygone time with the very present that is flitting away from us*. Lee gave me so much support that I nominated him for one of the awards that the Writers' Guild give for the encouragement of new theatre writing, and went with him to the presentation lunch.

The Redcliffe Hermit was the most experimental play I have written. I tried to meld a number of preoccupations I had, all my bees in one bonnet. There was the history of the place. In the Middle Ages, Redcliffe was the residence of great shipping merchants, chiefly the Canynges family. William and Joan Canynges feature in the play, in a bad temper, both of them. The outline of the stories about them I found in an old book of Bristol romances, possibly made up by that mischievous Redcliffe boy, Chatterton. It was a prosperous and busy place, and a medieval bookie might have laid you odds that in days to come the conurbation north and south of the river would be known as Redcliffe, with a suburb called Bristol. History did not go that way.

The hermit was a real one. We know his name, John Sparkes, and that he was installed in his cave in 1346 by Lord Berkeley. The cave is still there, across the road from St Mary's. I imagined his religious devotion alchemising itself into a loathing of the upper class, and so into fundamentalist socialism, drawing on the Book of Revelation. But how could I use him as the telescope through which to view the centuries until 1941, when a bomb on Redcliffe Hill on Good Friday blew a section of tramrail into the churchyard of St Mary's, where the authorities have splendidly left it, embedded at an angle in the grass? As George Bernard Shaw remarked, plot has always been the curse of serious drama.

The answer came to me from my amateur interest in quantum mechanics. I consulted a physicist friend, Bálazs Gyorffy. He invited me to a conference at the university to celebrate the hundredth birthday of Paul Dirac, who won the Nobel Prize in 1933 for his discovery of anti-matter. Dirac was born in Bristol, and educated at what is now Cotham Grammar School, which also, astonishingly, produced Higgs of the Higgs boson. The conference, attended by 250 international physicists and two playwrights – Gyorffy's wife Carole Boyer and me – was more entertaining than many evenings in the theatre. We were treated to a quote from the taciturn Dirac. When he heard that Oppenheimer was writing poetry, he told him: 'Robert, in science, one tries to tell people, in such a way as to be understood by everyone, something that no one ever knew before. But in poetry it's the exact opposite.' Ouch. When someone is lost in memory, or rapt in devotion like a hermit, they say: time stands still. That phrase can be taken seriously in quantum theory. Dirac liked to take long walks, so I had him walk from his home in Horfield, and in the twentieth century, to argue about time and faith with my fourteenth-century hermit in Redcliffe. In the theatre, as witness pantomime, you may offer the audience an outrageous conceit so long as you stay consistent to its proposition. I hoped what I was writing was a comedy. At any rate, it was fun to do.

Every head of department had quit the BOV. Taking time off from the BBC, Hay formed us all into a new company, a kind of

BOV government-in-exile, called Head Heart + 2 Fingers. We raised some funding, with generous help from Louis Sherwood, Mike Bothamley, Arup, and the city council, and in 2005 produced the play independently. Hay, with Elwyn Johnson as co-director, drove me through ten drafts this time. He had decided to embody the play's games with quantum theory by staging it in three areas simultaneously (the Uncertainty Principle, get it?), all under the one big roof of L Shed, and inviting the audience to promenade around between:

1. where the actors were, though behind a screening wall in which there were slots through which you chose your angle of vision;
2. a separate enclosure, black-draped-off, in which some screens monitored the stage action but others displayed film shot around Redcliffe;
3. another black-draped-off enclosure, low-lit, in which you could watch the musicians play John O'Hara's excellent Reichian/ Glassian, through-composed, underscored music, and hear the play as on a radio.

I had known all this months in advance, and kept questioning it, but had to settle for it, not only because Hay had done a wonderful job, just as audacious, the last time we had worked together, on the docks play, but also because in the end the director is the boss.

Commercially, we came in just ahead of the game, hampered by a lack of the marketing that a big permanent company has. None of the national papers, who had so praised the same team's *Up the Feeder*, could be bothered to come down and review this one. In London such a spatial experiment would have been thoroughly discussed. It was a controversial production; it divided the audience every night for sixteen nights. In Elizabethan terms, we were both clapper-clawed and pippin-pelted. A minority of the audience, perhaps 15 to 20 per cent, thought it was just wonderful ('Funny, poignant and astonishing' – *Bristol Evening Post*). Maybe 25 per cent found it enragingly impossible to take in. My playwright friend David Henry Wilson told me: 'I feel really angry with Andy Hay for what he has done.' The rest came out dazed and confused. Time after time I heard someone say: 'I really think I need to see it again.' An emphasis on 'need' – not that it was so great that it promised two evenings of enjoyment, but that it was so demanding that they felt frustrated in their expectation of just taking in a play.

Stoppard remarked that it was a difficult play, and I thought, uh-oh, if he thinks it's difficult... It reminded me of the last line of Butch Cassidy: *For a moment there I thought we were in trouble.* What Hay did was extraordinary, flattering even, in its outrageous presentation of (some of) the play's themes. But it did me no favours in a first production of the play. All in all, *pig-headed but brave,* as Colin Godman reported to the Arts Council. It would be rewarding to see the play done again in a more conventional staging. So far, just a few scenes from it have had a revival, directed by David Collins in St Mary Redcliffe, to help Richard Lee raise funds for the Canynges Society.

A little two-hander of mine, *Chess,* was one of an evening of several short plays produced in 2007 at the decaying Roman Catholic Pro-Cathedral in Bristol, before its conversion. The leaking roof and rotting stage boards were less of a hazard than my having to direct the play, since there were no funds to pay anyone better. It was redeemed by the courage of my actors, Kirsty Cox and Jonathan Nibbs. I am intrigued by the game of chess, but have never made the time to play it seriously since the games with Stoppard half a century ago. Bridge has always been my indoor game, played irreverently with old and congenial friends, a university philosopher, a businessman, a scholarly trade union secretary, but I have not worked out how to reconcile the conventions of five-card-majors and Roman key card Blackwood with the conventions of the theatre.

The following year, the composer David Lyon and I presented *Doctor Love* at the Tobacco Factory. I had adapted the libretto from Molière's *L'Amour Médecin.* I was asked if I had taken liberties; the answer was yes, liberties and egalities and fraternities. I put Molière himself on stage, complaining about the indignities of theatrical life, and introduced Louis XIV into the action. I'd like to think the greatest of French writers would not have disapproved of what I did with his piece, which he had knocked off in five days. With thirty-one people on stage, including six musicians from the Emerald Ensemble and the music director Christopher Northam, we had to find an experienced stage director, and the answer was Vicki Klein. Music-theatre requires actors who can sing, in this case quite a demanding score, Sondheimish-Brittenish. The lead part, Molière/Scandrell, was particularly taxing for David Collins, but I kept him calm by hacking around Ashton Court pitch-and-putt with him a few times.

It was my responsibility because this time I had to act as producer. We had some funding from generous friends, but even with nearly full houses most nights, which we achieved, Lyon and I knew we would be out of pocket, and could not afford to pay anyone else to do the producing. My competence in the job was summed up late one wet night when, leaving rehearsal, I put my thick file of papers – bills, accounts, cheques, notes, contacts – on the car roof while I unlocked the door, forgot about it, drove home, at 2.30 a.m. looked for the file, remembered, drove back to Southville, and spent fifteen minutes gathering papers scattered by the rain and wind in all the front gardens along Clift House Road. When the show was over, I told someone that I had learned a tremendous amount about producing, but I could sum it all up in two words: never again.

Why do it, when you know you will lose money? Well, Cameron Mackintosh just might drop in and love it, but the real reason is simply the joy of making. 'We do it for larks,' Ezra Pound told James Joyce. Working with John O'Hara on the songs in *Up the Feeder* and *The Redcliffe Hermit*, and with Lyon on *Albert's Bridge* and *Doctor Love*, I had at last discovered what I want to do when I grow up.

At the Tobacco Factory I spotted a man I knew, Chris Davies, come in with his wife to see the show. He had been a docks copper, and a source of merry stories for *Up the Feeder*, so I went over and kidded around with him. As he left to go into the auditorium he asked me: 'Do you know what I'm doing now?' I had no idea. He gave me his card. It said: *Lord Mayor of Bristol.* Among our backers was Jay Tidmarsh, the Lord Lieutenant of Bristol, whom I had known since I'd arrived in Bristol in 1960. At a jaw-jaw meeting at the Watershed I had been approached by Helen Holland, Labour leader of the city council. I didn't know her, but I did know she had been influential in getting council backing for *Up the Feeder*, so I was pleased, and taken by surprise, when she informed me that we are very distantly related, by marriage. As for my old friend Richard Lee, he had become High Sheriff. All my life a non-prefect, a quiet bolshie where high office and honours are concerned, by dint of living here long enough I found myself good friends with the dignitaries of Bristol.

18

What We Are Looking For

THE QUESTION IS: HOW TO GET THE WRITING DONE? THE ITALIAN playwright Alfieri ordered his servants to chain him to his desk. Simon Raven was locked in a room until he had finished the scripts of *Edward and Mrs Simpson.* Hemingway started each morning at 5 a.m. by sharpening twenty-two pencils, and then wrote for two hours standing up at a lectern before going out to give the marlin a hard time. Stoppard was once observed by his wife wandering around the garden when she knew he was right on the deadline for delivering a play to Trevor Nunn, and when she asked him why he wasn't at his desk he said: 'I'm just looking for my tennis shoes.'

'You don't play tennis.'

'No, but someone might ring me up and suggest a game, and I wouldn't know where...' and he broke off in laughter at his own absurdity.

No, the question is: why are we *scared?* Scared of starting the day's work? It is supposed to be enjoyable. It is enjoyable afterwards, and during, just not at the moment when you were intending to start. Is it like stage fright? You never quite know where the writing comes from, especially the good stuff, and so you can never be assured that it will come this time. Writers tend to be superstitious. B. S. Johnson made a point of starting to write a new book on January 1st. You can construct a narrative arc and plug in inciting incidents, and there are plenty of expensive seminars that pretend to teach you how to do that, and you can make thousands of character notes and file them in neat little drawers with a card index. But that's not writing. At best it's preparation for writing, for those who prefer to work that way. Writing is getting the words right. And all the questions that phrase begs can be answered only by someone who could explain how the imagination works. That is where the true making takes place, the voice heard in your head. The nearest I have heard anyone get to explaining it is the artist Paul Klee, who said what he did was to let his pencil take a walk. Iris Murdoch said she'd start by letting the characters talk to each other, and something like that is pretty much my experience, too. It's a wasteful process. You fill up waste-paper baskets.

In Texas I told the kids the story about Newton's bridge. It is probably not true, but that is beside the point. Behind Queens' College at Cambridge there is a little wooden bridge over the Cam. A folk tale grew up that it was built by Isaac Newton. It has no nuts and bolts to hold it together, only a cantilever design that the Fellows at High Table one evening, around 1900, agreed they could not understand. They resolved that next morning the engineers among them would deconstruct the bridge, keeping a careful diagram of how each part fitted, and chalking numbers on the parts as they put them aside. At the end of it they were dumbfounded by Newton's cunning, two centuries ahead of what they knew. Then, consulting the diagram, they put it together again, and it fell into the stream. Now it is held up by nuts and bolts. Try examining how your creative intuition works, I finished, and that is what happens, it will fall into the water.

The pleasant jolt of being abroad has several times jump-started me on a new project, as it did my first novel in Mytilene. I have written when seated under my cousin Christopher Smith's pomegranate tree in the hills of Ibiza, where I have stayed several times. I have mentioned that I wrote some of the early chapters of the Laclos/Sade novel on aeroplanes and in airports, and the rest in Mexico and Texas. In Budapest, where I stay with Hungarian friends, the café life is vivacious, and perfect for sparking thoughts. I remember translating and libretto-ising an entire scene of *Doctor Love* on the train to London. With my dear friend and former lodger Eleni I have stayed in Thessaloniki, and started work on the libretto of *Albert's Bridge* at her family's seaside place at Chalkidiki. Another time she invited me to a friend's wedding on a mountaintop, where the little Greek priest did winking theatrical asides in English about what he was up to in the service, for the benefit of the bridegroom's American family, and later the entire wedding party was transported in coaches for a week on the slopes of Mount Pelion, mythically piled on Ossa, and I wrote two poems there, and in my notebook added to jottings that might come in handy one day. One place to which Eleni and her husband Victor Arditti took me and I wrote nothing was Epidaurus. Awe forbade, and anyway, we were there to see Arditti's production of Sophocles's *Women of Trachis*.

Parts of this book were written in a house overlooking the valley of the Dordogne, thanks to my friends Mike and Agnes and Hannah Segal. Right outside the window is a twelfth-century church, which the lifting mist magically discloses on an autumn morning. I am writing these words now in the Var, at Peter Moore-Robinson's house, after a long morning walk with him and his labrador Sumi. He has just handed me the heartbroken letters I wrote to Miriam when I was in Cannes in 1965, thinking her an intercessor. I shall continue when I get to Richard Hawkins's house next week, in the Vaucluse.

At home, the ceiling above my desk has a broad brown stain, because that is where nearly a score of books, about the same number of plays, and uncountable scripts and articles have been worked on. When I stopped smoking some years ago, for the obvious reasons, my fear was that I'd never get another word written. That turned out to be a superstition.

In daily life, I have routines. My daughters entertain dinner parties with stories of what their father eats every lunchtime: a handful of pumpkin seeds (tasty, and said to ward off prostate cancer), five hazelnuts (it used to be fourteen, but have you seen the price of hazelnuts?), a couple of brazils, a couple of dried unsulphured apricots (delicious, and bursting with antioxidants), a dried fig, three prunes, a bowl of muesli with cranberry juice, a banana, grapes (in an attempt to give up smoking I once took the grape cure, eating nothing but grapes for two weeks – it should have been three but I was desperate for something savoury, and Oliver broke me by toasting himself a cheese muffin). I enjoy that every day, so that I don't have to think what to eat when there are more interesting things to think about. When I get out of bed there are eight things to be done, including yoghourt with fresh lime juice and honey, twenty back-stretches as advised by my osteo friend Jon Thompson, and the breathing routine that Andrei Serban taught me in Iran (in to a count of seven, hold it in for four, out to seven, hold out for four, repeat cycle twice more). There are twelve sub-routines within washing, and another six-beat cycle before going to sleep, but I'll do you a favour and skip them.

Brecht had two identical black suits and never wore anything else, to save himself the chore of deciding what to wear today. That's why I have my routines. Or maybe it is what Pushkin said: *Habit is a substitute for happiness.*

* * *

I remain grateful to Ghose for fighting for my appointment in Texas, which got me out of debt. He has published twenty books of fiction, poetry and criticism. His reputation in his native country, Pakistan, is high, yet his literary roots remain in England. Many years of teaching the craft of fiction have distilled in him an intolerance of any writing short of what he considers the greatest, an intolerance which includes his own work: *Each finished book is a failure and only fills me with an anxiety to complete one more before I die.*

I see him when he is passing through London, and I visited him in Texas again in 2005, when I was invited to give another talk to the British studies group at the Harry Ransom Center. In the course of that visit the HRC's director, Tom Staley, expressed interest in buying my entire archive, since they already had the correspondence between Ghose, Johnson, Burroway, Stoppard and me. Before going ahead with the sale, I spoke to Jamie Andrews, the head of modern literary manuscripts at the British Library, whom I know from his Bristol University connection. I wondered if it was unpatriotic to be shipping it all to Texas. His advice was professional, not rivalrous: given that the correspondence was already at the HRC, plus the entire archive of Ghose and some of Stoppard's, it would be a service to researchers to keep everything in the same place.

Lou Gasparro of Avon Bookshops packed and dispatched it all for me, in seventeen boxes. Some of it, particularly all the rewrites that Andy Hay had put me through, were in irredeemable disorder. It reminded me of the dry comment Euripides makes about Pentheus's body scattered by the Bacchantes: it would not be easy to put him together again. I consulted Joan Sibley, the head of archiving at the HRC. She was familiar with the problem, and advised me to 'respect the Principle of Original Order', which meant that I should leave everything as I found it. Some researcher one day might be able to formulate a quasi-geological theory by examining the order in which I had laid down the disorder. I wrote back to thank her, and remarked: *If you have ever received the archive of a theatre production in tidy order, I hope you regarded it with grave suspicion. The best I have been able to do is to distinguish, more or less, the 1997 chaos from the 2001 chaos.*

When he sold his archive to an American university, Robert Graves remarked that he earned more from his waste paper basket than he did from the book. It is not without poignancy. It reminded me of watching your children leave home. You wonder what strangers will make of them. Tell me, did I include that one-sentence postcard that my school friend Paul Lock, with fifty-year foresight, sent me: *I thought you might need some short messages to break up the layout of your collected correspondence?*

Stoppard once admitted to me that he was 'avid for other people's correspondence'. I am aware that people collect memorabilia for the same reason as I once train-spotted, and that some would pay good money for a Kleenex in which Picasso had authenticatedly blown his nose. But we cannot second-guess what might be of interest, even useful, to posterity. The current state of the literary stock exchange offers only hints as to how it will stand a generation or two from now. History is littered with writers greatly admired in their time whose readers would be astonished at the neglect in which they now languish. Not as common is the reverse case, writers considered to be in the first rank who were widely ignored in their writing lifetime. Gerard Manley Hopkins would be one example, recognised by Robert Bridges, but scarcely read and certainly not canonised until he was championed by Dr Leavis. Usually some coterie following has preserved the texts, and one is bound to wonder what texts haven't been preserved, what fine writers were never discovered. It must be the same in other fields. Prejudiced valuations, tinsel excitements, fashion, warp judgment in any subject where objective proof is not available – philosophy, music, the beauty of women, single malt whisky. Even in fields where performance is statistically verifiable, quantum mechanics, say, or cricket, we see the market valuations fluctuate. Would Aristotle make it into the Physicists XI at Lord's today?

The British studies group in Texas used to publish an annual volume of the talks they had hosted. I was invited to the 2006 book launch at the Reform Club. In the entrance lobby I was intercepted by a female jobsworth: 'Sorry sir, denim is not permitted in the club.' I was wearing a blue cotton shirt, much finer in texture than any pair of jeans. I pointed out that it would be barely visible if I buttoned my jacket. 'Sorry, sir, that's the rule.' I mentioned that I had come a hundred miles from Bristol, to spend maybe an hour in her damned club. I might have added that I had had the wit to wear a suit and tie, which I do about twice a year. Seeing that I was spoiling for a scrap, she summoned the manager, who took one look and waved me in. I can accept that they will have rules barring jeans, but it is weird when one type of cloth is deemed offensive to members' sensibilities.

The room for the launch was already crushed tight. I saw the Texan host, Roger Louis, in the middle of the scrum, and squeezed through to him. 'Anthony,' he said, nodding at the large man in a brown suit he had been talking to: 'Do you know John Davis, the Warden of All Souls?' He left us, to get to the dais and introduce the speakers, and I was crammed navel-on-navel against Davis. He beamed at me, I at him, and I waited for him to start up some conversation, figuring that a man in so distinguished an academic position must be adept at small talk. But he said nothing, just beamed amiably, so I blurted out the only thought that the mention of All Souls College had brought to mind, the story of John Betjeman and Henry James's underwear. When I finished the story Davis was dabbing his eyes with a handkerchief, but not in laughter. 'I'm sorry,' I said, 'are you all right?' 'You weren't to know,' he replied, 'but when I was a young man I was so terribly in love with John Betjeman's daughter.'

I wore my suit again the following week when Lucia Donovan asked me to read a poem at the funeral of her husband Jon, late of Chapter and Verse bookshop, alas. The poem she had chosen was Kipling's *Tommy*, a favourite of Jon's. I was well into the reading when a terrier came trotting up the aisle between the mourners, its claws clicking the tiles. People were frowning at its intrusion, but it had timed its entrance perfectly to allow me to address it:

> We aren't no thin red 'eroes, nor we aren't no blackguards too,
> But single men in barricks, most remarkable – like you.

* * *

Boorman has lived in Eire for many years. He invited Alison and me to his seventy-fifth birthday party at his daughter's house in Chelsea, along with other old friends from Bristol, including Stoppard and Nichols, and in 2010 we were together at the Watershed, where Andrew Kelly had booked him to talk about his career. A week later there was a showing of all the *Newcomers* episodes, plus *Deadly Serious Smith*. At Kelly's request, I introduced the latter session, and fielded questions at the end. After sitting there for nearly five hours, I said, the only question you can have is: can we go home now? But the archival interest of the films was potent. Helen Holland, a patriot for Bristol, told me she would have contentedly watched another five hours.

Nichols moved to Greenwich, then Shropshire, where he spent years growling with John Osborne into their pints, and writing plays about why he will never write another play for the ungrateful British theatre. He is in Oxford now. Charles Wood, who enjoys making up malicious stories, told me that Nichols was walking along Greenwich High Street on a windy day and a sheet of newspaper was whirled down in front of him. Nichols withdrew his foot sharply, guessing the subject of the encomium he was about to touch. 'Stoppard!' he hissed. The story tells us as much about Wood as it does about Nichols. In his BBC television series *Don't Forget to Write*, in which George Cole acted out at length the premise of this book, how writing gets done, Wood entertainingly dramatised the whole Stoppard-Nichols-Wood amused-rivalry nexus, as well as gratuitously biting many other hands that had fed him. He lives in Oxfordshire now.

Derek Balmer remains in Bristol. He made a good living as a photographer, but is back to full-time painting. In 2010 he had a sell-out exhibition at the Catto Gallery in Hampstead, where my daughter Imogen is one of the two partners, assisted by her sister Sophie and sister-in-law Kate. [In 2012 Redcliffe Press publish Derek's memoir *A Singular Vision*.] For ten years Balmer was president of the Royal West of England Academy, where Stoppard's accountant brother, Peter, was his honorary treasurer. Balmer is one of a group of RWA artists who meet for a monthly lunch together, although, being artists, they get it organised twice a year at best. The others include David Inshaw, Alf Stockham, Robert Hurdle, George Tute, Neil Murison, and John Huggins. And me: I am invited along as the pet poet, rather as Apollinaire used to enjoy running around with the Cubists. I was responsible, twenty years ago, for instigating another monthly lunch meeting, in a pub, this one a loose assembly of friends who write, paint, act, or think about it, most of them already mentioned in earlier pages.

Burroway's home now is in Wisconsin, with the film scholar Peter Ruppert. Like mine, and for similar reasons, her interest in writing for the stage has drawn at least level with her novelistic impulse. When I read through her wonderfully warm and writerly letters before packing them off to Texas I found that they traced the contours of a life with more than its share of tragedy. In the furtive Fifties, she noted:

> ...women of my generation blamed Doris Day for a falsely happy picture of the monogamous family, perfect love lasting ever after. But in one film after another the message we got was serial monogamy.

When the *New Yorker* brought out Janet Malcolm's long psychological take on Sylvia Plath, Burroway told me I had to read it. Leaving the house in search of a copy, I found an envelope propped against my front door. It was from Stoppard, and contained a copy of the *New Yorker.*

On his achievement as a playwright I need not dwell here. The body of his work I find admirable and, it's curious to say, underrated. I most admire *Travesties* and *Arcadia*. The latter I am sure will still be regularly performed a hundred years from now, if plays are still done. Reviewers talk about his 'darkening vision'. I don't think so. He has blown away the verbal froth, that's all, revealing more clearly the love of glinting ironies that has been there always.

> The water in a vessel is sparkling;
> the water in the sea is dark.
> The small truth has words that are clear;
> the great truth has great silences.
> – Tagore, *Stray Birds*

The most common complaint you hear is that Stoppard is too clever by half. On a first hearing I never felt I have taken in everything there is in any new play of his. I would, once, have had to say the same of any play by Shakespeare. But I will have taken in enough, and been sufficiently amused by the wit and glitter of the thing, not to mind going to see the play again, or even better sitting down and reading it at my own pace. If Stoppard acknowledges that demand he makes, for more work than just one hearing, is it unreasonable? It is unfashionable, sure, in the age of the sound bite.

Another complaint used to be that he wrote about nothing that matters. When are you going to address a social question of the day, he was asked, and to my shame I was one of those who asked him. Shame, because the question got to him. He decided enough of frivolity, and wrote a preachy play, *Night and Day*, about the freedom of the press, newspapers being the only social formation in which he thought himself versed. I watched it with a heavy heart, blaming myself for having harangued a dancer that he must learn to march. The truth is, look what an extraordinary breadth of subject he has covered in his career. Moral philosophy and relativism, the metaphors of quantum mechanics, soviet double-think, chaos theory, the growth of radical thought in nineteenth-century Russia, married love... I could go on. This is not the oeuvre of a man who writes about nothing that matters, but of one who is committed to the international work of PEN. When other writers forbade the production of their work in apartheid South Africa, he allowed his plays to be done there, and gave the royalties to Amnesty. On *the evil of apartheid,* he wrote to me, *the antis in the UK reach a point of action by a correctly rational process, but then act emotionally.*

Behind the effervescence, his play *Travesties* is about the saving remnant, in Matthew Arnold's phrase, those who carry on a tradition while living in occupied territory. It is a defence of the artist, the maker, under pressure. He is not the only one disappointed by what is called dumbing down. Sloppiness in speech, and so in thought. Advertising that infantilises our desires. When Arthur Miller died, The *Independent* gave it the entire front page, with the headline *DEATH OF A PLAYWRIGHT.* The *Sun* had one paragraph inside the paper, headed *MONROE'S EX DIES.* It is not as simple as serious versus populist. Everywhere, celebrity is the rattle of empty shells in a bag. It creates a parallel world that the media prefer to one (the real one) that they can't manipulate or even understand. It is fifty years since Daniel Boorstin wrote that *a celebrity is a person who is well known for being well known,* and about 160 years since Hans Andersen's little boy observed that the emperor had no clothes on. The opposite of dumbing down would be wising up, but anyone arguing for critical discrimination must expect to be written off as an elitist. *Judgmental* has become a dirty word. In a consumerist society, we argue about fashion. Or issues, the orphans of political debate, which are subject to fashion.

Like Ghose, Stoppard has always evinced a patriotic love of Britain, the country that adopted him at the age of eight. It led some to see him as a Tory nationalist, forgetting Orwell's distinction between patriotism and nationalism. (The difference, Orwell said, is that the patriot loves his country, the nationalist hates other people's countries.) Stoppard has no political barcode on him, to be easily swiped. He knew he'd arouse prejudice when he accepted an invitation to dinner at 10 Downing Street with Mrs Thatcher. He didn't give a damn. He was interested to see what it would be like. He was invited to dinner at Windsor Castle. So, for that matter, was Ted Hughes, who afterwards told me that he had fallen in love with the Queen, and I've always supposed that that was why he accepted his ludicrous appointment as Poet Laureate. When I asked Stoppard if he had fallen in love at Windsor Castle, he said: 'Oh yes, I went heads-over-heels for the silverware.'

When he didn't have to be somewhere else, for a while he lived in southern France, in the small town where the Marquis de Sade's château is, a ruin. The tourist trade is growing, and Stoppard wrote to me to complain that the place is *becoming too busy, Sadists thronging by my door. Pierre Cardin has bought the château: Sadists in smart blazers next, all too much.*

In 2009 he rang me to say a small press had invited him to choose a few poems which they would publish as a pamphlet representing his editorial taste. He said he would like the poems to be mine, and asked me to send him some. I sent him fifteen, of which he chose eleven, and I could see the reasons for his choice. Then he said: 'The earliest of these poems is dated 1959. It would be nice to have one dated 2009. Have you got one in you?' It is an odd thing to be asked. Poems find you, not you them. I looked through a thick file of things I had started and abandoned, and came across a fragment, just a line and a half, which began to sprout in my mind. I worked it through to seventeen lines and sent it to him. He rang me to say thanks, and he was glad to have provoked it, and he would add it to the pamphlet.

'I've got just one or two quibbles,' he said, and went on to quibble with six details. I accepted five of them at once, dug my heels in over the sixth. It is a better poem thanks to his quibbling. When I put the 'phone down I thought, 'the world knows what talent he has in writing plays, but this, to read a new poem and spot flaws, is supposed to be a job for a specialist, yet he can do that, too'. Tony Astbury of the Greville Press launched the pamphlet at my daughter's gallery in Hampstead, with readings by Stoppard and me. The centrepiece is the poem which was published three times in the 1960s, *Structures of Cancer,* and it has since been picked up for yet another appearance in a Carcanet anthology.

Every two or three years, Stoppard throws a wonderful garden party. The faces would be a gossip columnist's dream, since it is an occasion for him to reassure friends and working associates that he has not forgotten them, but his hospitality embraces families as extended as mine. Watching my grandchildren's faces as they watched Punch and Judy, I was deeply grateful for our lifelong friendship. Michael Billington, the *Guardian*'s theatre critic, told me that he seldom goes to any theatrical party, 'but this one – just look around. This one you have to come to'.

All his writing life Stoppard has felt so lucky to be doing what he most enjoys that he is sure that one day some functionary will come up behind him, tap him on the shoulder and tell him sorry, it was all a clerical error, you will have to find yourself a proper job from now on. Alan Plater expressed the same fear, so did Anthony Hopkins. Years ago Stoppard charged me, in the event of my surviving him, to see to it that his tombstone reads: *Here lies Tom Stoppard. He had it coming.*

When I look through my folder of correspondence with him, I find comic sketches of what was going on in our lives, first drafts, copies of significant letters to other people, news of projects, books, radio, TV, stage, always about five on the go, critiques of what I have just sent him, thanks for critiques I don't remember having sent, and, in the early days, arrangements to repay loans I forget having made or having been in a position to make. Many games of correspondence chess were started, none finished. Once he sent a postcard with four opening moves, two for Alison and two for me. *At four games per p.c. it's quite economical,* he wrote.

And now and then, he hints at the thrill of having found what he is always looking for, the radioactive particle. As it is for a physicist, when a writer finds something beautiful, he knows that truth is present. It is what we are all looking for. After that, delivering it is the hard work. But then, Rome wasn't built in a day, and anyway, it all fell down again.

Index